W9-COG-386

STARTING
ON A
SHOESTRING

Building a Business Without a Bankroll

FOURTH EDITION

Arnold S. Goldstein

John Wiley & Sons, Inc.

To my wife, Marlene,
for the encouragement she gave me to write this book
and her tireless efforts in helping me to create it.

Copyright © 1984, 1991, 1995, and 2002 by Arnold Goldstein and Edward Myers. All
rights reserved.

Published by John Wiley & Sons, Inc., Hoboken, New Jersey.
Published simultaneously in Canada.

No part of this publication may be reproduced, stored in a retrieval system, or
transmitted in any form or by any means, electronic, mechanical, photocopying,
recording, scanning, or otherwise, except as permitted under Section 107 or 108 of the
1976 United States Copyright Act, without either the prior written permission of the
Publisher, or authorization through payment of the appropriate per-copy fee to the
Copyright Clearance Center, Inc., 222 Rosewood Drive, Danvers, MA 01923,
(978) 750-8400, fax (978) 750-4470, or on the web at www.copyright.com. Requests to
the Publisher for permission should be addressed to the Permissions Department,
John Wiley & Sons, Inc., 111 River Street, Hoboken, NJ 07030, (201) 748-6011,
fax (201) 748-6008, e-mail: permcoordinator@wiley.com.

Limit of Liability/Disclaimer of Warranty: While the publisher and author have used
their best efforts in preparing this book, they make no representations or warranties
with respect to the accuracy or completeness of the contents of this book and
specifically disclaim any implied warranties of merchantability or fitness for a
particular purpose. No warranty may be created or extended by sales representatives or
written sales materials. The advice and strategies contained herein may not be suitable
for your situation. The publisher is not engaged in rendering professional services, and
you should consult a professional where appropriate. Neither the publisher nor author
shall be liable for any loss of profit or any other commercial damages, including but not
limited to special, incidental, consequential, or other damages.

For general information on our other products and services please contact our
Customer Care Department within the U.S. at (800) 762-2974, outside the United States
at (317) 572-3993 or fax (317) 572-4002.

Wiley also publishes its books in a variety of electronic formats. Some content that
appears in print may not be available in electronic books.

Library of Congress Cataloging-in-Publication Data:
Goldstein, Arnold S.
    Starting on a shoestring : building a business without a bankroll /
Arnold Goldstein.—4th ed.
      p. cm
    Includes index.
    ISBN 0-471-23288-2 (paper)
    1. New business enterprises—Management.   I. Title.
HD62.5.G65 2002
658.1'141—dc21

                                2002022590

Printed in the United States of America.

10 9 8 7 6 5 4 3 2 1

PREFACE

The signs of quiet desperation are still everywhere. Corporate serfs and bored housewives, blocked executives and ambitious dropouts, real people, unhappy people from every walk of life, continue to be joined by the common goal of owning their own businesses. They also continue to share a common problem: They have too little cash to make it happen.

Not much has changed about this scenario since 1984, when the first edition of *Starting on a Shoestring* appeared in bookstores. Tens of thousands of frustrated entrepreneurs still seek their piece of the American dream. But many others have learned from *Starting on a Shoestring* that it is indeed possible—even in today's complex world—to buck the odds, defy the rules, and bootstrap ventures into profitable enterprises.

This fourth edition of *Shoestring* has been written to help thousands more achieve their entrepreneurial dreams now that we have entered the 21st century—a world of different rules and opportunities. New chapters have been added on writing a winning business plan, successful marketing on a shoestring budget, using the Small Business Administrative, finding venture capital sources, and using the World Wide Web.

But, as in my earlier *Shoestrings*, you'll receive the tested strategies that cash-shy, ambitious people need to know if their aspirations to own their own businesses are to come true. No, you'll find no inspirational pep talks about building castles in the air or how to magically go from rags to riches. Motivational books have their purpose, but this book is designed to be instructional. You face the mundane problems of the real business world and need concrete advice, in place of cash, to start, grow, and survive in the twilight world of creativity.

Every start-up has its own blueprint for success. As we proceed through the book I'll ask you to set aside your opinions and misconceptions about what it takes to achieve a successful start. You'll see how to test your business idea to see if it's right for you. Capital? Of course you'll need some—you'll learn what the best sources are and how to approach them.

As you claw your way to success you'll face numerous day-to-day problems. I'll guide you over these operational bumps with proven solutions, and I'll give this advice to you in easy-to-understand, everyday language by avoiding textbook theory or technical jargon. When you put this book down, you'll have new insights and information that any business person can use and relate to effectively.

Starting on a Shoestring is a game plan—a strategy. But strategy is only one dimension. Your thought process, willingness, and desire to see the business through inevitable challenges make up another dimension. Success won't come with a wave of the wand. Every story in this book shows how a business was born. But the people involved with these projects couldn't have succeeded without plenty of hard work, sleepless nights, and commitment to financial victory.

Professional confidentiality requires me to change the names of many individuals and businesses in the cases presented here. However, every one is true. As I have learned from their successes, so will you.

CONTENTS

1

YOU MAKE YOUR
OWN MIRACLES

What is it really like to take an idea and fashion it into a successful business? Are the new entrepreneurs like the success stories crowding the pages of the money-making opportunity books with their happy tales of the John Js and Sally Ss waxing rich overnight, or is there something more to it? Do the inspiring words match the realities?

Let's separate the wheat from the chaff. Real people create businesses, not words from the pens of creative writers. And these very real people have interesting stories to tell. Meet and talk to these people and you begin to share their experiences, their triumphs, and their tragedies in trying to put together a business—and make it work.

In writing this book I have talked to hundreds of people who have journeyed through the entrepreneurial process, with an abundance of enthusiasm if not an abundance of cash. Like snowflakes, they were joined by this common thread while weaving a story with their own unique pattern. They were found in retail shops, small manufacturing plants, service businesses, and in hundreds of very different enterprises ranging from a deep-sea treasure salvage firm to a manufacturer of telescopic lenses. Seduced by the attractions of a new and better life, they come from every background, age group, and educational or work-life level. Some seem to have made it and many others didn't, but for most the final scorecard still isn't in as they struggle one day at a time.

I remember how it was with my own first "shoestring" venture. Monday, October 1, 1973.

Zero hour minus one minute.

It was my big day. With bright purple letters the proud banner flurried over the near-empty parking lot announcing the grand opening of Discount City. Beneath cavorted two clowns anchoring dozens of colorful balloons for the crowds to come.

Thirty seconds to launch.

A shrill noise broke the air as three kids hired from the local high school band trumpeted "Dixie." Quite unusual, I thought, considering we were in Massachusetts, but then again, Discount City was an unusual store.

Zero minus ten seconds.

My eyes scanned the mountains of merchandise jam-packed on a wide array of used fixtures painted a nauseating green to hide their disparate origins. "Who could resist?" I mused. To my left were the $3.98 garbage cans and to my right, the crates of six-fingered back scratchers direct from Taiwan at the incredible 49-cent price. Wherever I looked there were bargains galore, hustled and conned on credit from every corner of the map.

Outside the cacophony of noise changed to the lively tempo of "Alexander's Ragtime Band." Everything was set. All was ready. It was the moment of truth.

Four . . . three . . . two. . . one . . . blast off!

The doors swung open to welcome swollen crowds. All that appeared was a little old lady in tennis shoes swinging an over-sized pocketbook. Out she quickly marched with a deftly shop-lifted $6.98 can opener safely tucked in her now heavier pocketbook. It was a start. Discount City was christened; the Discount City with $120,000 in unpaid-for merchandise heaped on $20,000 in fully mortgaged fixtures sitting on retail space with three months' deferred rent. It was the Discount City which came to life owing everybody for everything. But it was also the Discount City built on a financial house of cards that somehow made the grade and mushroomed in three years to 12 more stores ringing up a profitable $6 million in sales. Best of all, it was the Discount City started on a shoestring with only $2600 of my own cash.

It's never easy. You wonder how it can ever happen when so many people say it shouldn't and predict it can't. Sydney, my Valium-popping accountant, would label me the "lunatic with the big dream and the small bank balance." It hardly inspires confidence. And while you're in the trenches trying to turn a dream into reality, your family thinks you've lost your marbles and you find your friends scanning the auction pages anticipating your bankruptcy. They may send you flowers when you open, and with them their well wishes. Still, they never quite believe.

But that's the thrill of it all. You want a business of your own so you go for it. You connive, beg, borrow, hustle, and manipulate to get it together and keep it together. You work your butt to the bone to make it happen. In the process you thumb your nose at a world of nonbelievers, skeptics, pessimists, and conventionalists with their words of wisdom on why you can't or why you shouldn't. No, it's never easy, but when you're through and have the business off and running, you stand tall and pat yourself on the back. You did it and did it on a shoestring. In short, you made your own miracles. It's quite an experience.

Flushed by my Discount City days, I journeyed into nine more shoestring start-ups. By then I had the money to invest, but I was spoiled. I didn't want to invest. My philosophy was simple and it never changed. Any idiot with a bushel basket of money can land himself a business, but also it doesn't take a genius to do it without cash. Chutzpah is a powerful substitute. Tight with cash but heavy on chutzpah, I wound up my entrepreneurial spirits, took a few working partners in tow, and opened two drugstores, a health food store, two greeting card and gift shops, a furniture manufacturing plant, and even a direct-mail firm for import items. Total personal investment? Less than $10,000. Were they all successful? Nope. Most came under the broad heading of "winner," but a couple were blunders and would have been the same blunders even if heavily bankrolled. The education was had and the lesson learned as these and so many other businesses capitalized with little more than heart, hope, and hard work have taught me. You can start on a shoestring and succeed.

ARE YOU THE ONE IN THE CROWD?

No longer is my office a dank corner of my first store, spartanly equipped with a war surplus file cabinet and discarded door bolted to two orange crates. Today I'm in a high-rise office building. Directly across the road from my building—in easy view of my office—is a large tire plant employing thousands of people. At precisely 8:45 each morning they stream through the front door to punch a clock. The executives, salespeople, clerical staff, and factory workers—like bees abandoning a hive—all stumble out the same door at precisely 5:00 each afternoon.

How many are happy at their work? How many would rather be at the helm of their own business? You never know the answer. Some probably never even thought of their own business, quite content to punch a clock, pick up a paycheck, and head home to drink a few beers before the television. Others harbored the idea but are slaves to the illusive security of employment, afraid of the gamble, the inherent risks of running their own show. Still others, the timid and the tired, lack the self-confidence while they mistakenly believe management is magic. Whatever their reasons, these same people wouldn't venture out on their own under the best of circumstances. And they shouldn't even try.

No, we don't know who they are, but in that endless stream of people marching in to work every morning there are the few who want their own business and have what it takes to run it successfully. There's only one thing holding them back—money. They have yet to develop the shoestring mentality.

Now let's turn the spotlight on you. With this book in your hands you're planning, or perhaps just thinking about, starting your own business. You too are wondering about where the money will come from. Now I know nothing about the type of business you have in mind, but it doesn't matter. Shoestring startups are pretty much alike for all businesses. I have no conception of how large or successful it will become. That's for you to decide and achieve. My job is to show you how to put together your business and get it started without digging deeply into your own pockets. In the next several hours you'll see how. Your job is to take the ideas and turn them into action. But I know as well as anyone that it's easier said than done. Standing between you and success may be a lot of fuzzy thoughts and nonsense ideas of what it takes. That's what this chapter is all about. If you're the one in the crowd, it's time to develop your own shoestring mentality.

Let's get to work on it. And the only way to start is by knocking out a few dangerous myths.

MYTH #1: YOU NEED MONEY TO MAKE MONEY

People say it and people believe it. That explains why there are so many poor people. I agree that the rich get richer, but that doesn't preclude a bit of success for the rest of us poor souls.

It's easier selling vacuum cleaners door-to-door than selling people on the idea that they too can get started on a money-making venture without using their own money. Robert Allen, best-selling author of *Nothing Down* (Simon & Schuster, 1990), had just this problem when he tried to convince his readers that they could buy real estate with little or no money of their own. Allen was no fool. People could read, but would people believe? Not according to Allen. The skeptics were everywhere. So Allen threw out an interesting proposition. "Put me in any city," siad Allen, "give me $100 for living expenses, and in 72 hours I'll return owning several properties without using a dime of my own money." The *Los Angeles Times* took the bait, handed Allen $100 and shipped him to San Francisco to turn his boast into proof. A few days later the triumphant Allen returned, clutching a few deeds to some choice Frisco properties.

Oftentimes I'm tempted to match Allen's challenge by boasting that you can land me in any city or town and within one month I'll have a good, solid, healthy business started and running without spending a dime of my own. But who needs another business?

Now what's the message? It's not boasting, and it's not about either real estate or starting a business. It's about money. While you may need money to make money—it doesn't have to be *your* money. Better yet, it *won't* be your money.

Shoesting entrepreneurs understand it. So did Henry Ford.

Henry was fond of saying that he might be flat broke but he'd never be poor. Armed with nothing more than a good idea, old optimist Henry would soon have all the money he'd need pouring into the venture from everyone else's pockets. You may not be Henry Ford, but his philosophy will work equally well for you. If you have that solid business idea, you'll find the money to make you money.

MYTH #2: A HEALTHY INVESTMENT MAKES A HEALTHY BUSINESS

Accountants always advise it, professors teach it, bankers love it, while the gullible swallow it. What nonsense!

Bob Kuzara knows how to punch holes in this fallacy. Bob started his successful North Pine Furniture with $80,000 in borrowed funds and today grosses $2 million annually, distributing his natural pinewood chairs, tables, and bookcases through local furniture stores and his own packed showroom. So as a shoe-stringer extraordinaire, Bob frequently joins me to address business start-up groups.

Not long ago a young lady attentively listening to Bob's pitch at a start-up seminar jumped up and said, "If I don't invest a substantial amount of cash from my own funds, my business will collapse from excessive debt before it even has the chance to get off the ground. How can you dare suggest I do it on a shoestring?"

Bob had a ready answer. "First," he said, "whether your business makes it or not has little to do with your own investment. The secret is to structure the debt so it fits the payment capabilities of the business. You can safely start any type of business with 100% leverage once you know how to program the debt. I agree. There's no such thing as the undercapitalized business, only the poorly planned business."

Bob overlooked the most important reason why a healthy investment does *not* necessarily make a healthy business. In fact, it usually creates a sick business. Owners throw more money into the business than it needs. It spoils them. They don't start out "lean and mean," and that leads to foolish expenditures. I'm reminded of a young MIT grad who started an electronics assembly firm with his wealthy father's generous $150,000 investment. A healthy business? Hardly. Six months later the Bankruptcy Trustee auctioned off its swanky furniture, a $38,000 Mercedes, and $20,000 of computer equipment. A healthy start would have been the father throwing his son $5000 to rent a garage and sit behind his own orange crate desk. If the business was destined to make it, it would make it building from the bottom rather than destroying it from the top. And the only way to build from the bottom is to lock up your checkbook so you do have to pinch pennies. And when you're borrowed to the hilt you'll have few pennies to pinch. It's therapeutic.

MYTH #3: DEBT IS BAD

Not by my book. I love debt. No, not when it comes to personal finances, but when you're talking in terms of business. And you can't really shake yourself clear of the first two myths unless you're willing to start in over your head and walk a financial tightrope until a business is eventually on its feet.

Most people are terrorized by the thought. They've been programmed to think of debt as a curse since they were old enough to understand the word. You may have the same problem. It's time to change your perspective.

Several years ago a young man retained me to help him start a marina on Cape Cod. His grandfather left him some choice waterfront property so it was only a matter of construction. The demand was fabulous and boaters hearing of his plans were already lined up. Within a month we had the lowest construction bid— $250,000. "How much money do you have, Jack?" I asked. "About $10,000 to $15,000," he replied. No problem, I figured. With the valuable land owned outright we'd have no problem finding a $240,000 construction loan from a local bank. And the numbers worked beautifully. Projected income would exceed expenses and mortgage payments by about $50,000. Jack would have a perpetual annuity and would hardly have to work for it. Do you think he did it? You know the answer. His mental block to signing a

$240,000 note blocked his success. Eventually Jack leased the land to a "go-getter" who did build the marina and is now the owner—mortgaged to the hilt—who's making the big money.

Sure, debt can be scary. A cash-poor start-up puts you in the twilight world of constant bank overdrafts, overdue bills, sleepless nights, and robbing Peter to pay Paul. It comes with the territory. But you do it because it's the only way you *can*.

Look at it the way I do. On the tenth of each month I sit down and write out some pretty hefty mortgage payments and payments to suppliers. As I write each check I'm actually creating wealth. It's a simple philosophy. What I owe today I'll own tomorrow.

Think about it. How many wealthy people do you know who didn't start out up to their eyebrows in debt? It's the American way. For most of us it's the *only* way.

MYTH #4: STARTING ON A SHOESTRING IS STARTING SMALL

Not always. Remember my first Discount City? It opened its doors with over $200,000 in assets working for me. It was a shoestring deal because I had so little of my own money into it. That's the only definition of a shoestring start-up.

They say that Monsanto Chemical started with only a $5000 investors pool. It didn't start out as the industrial mammoth it is today, but it didn't begin in someone's basement, either. It started at the logical size that could get it off and running as a viable company.

Plenty of shoestring start-ups are nothing more than cottage industries with industrious entrepreneurs moonlighting at a kitchen table or tinkering in the basement. For some it's the best place to start. Small can be beautiful, as the saying goes. In a year or two many of these same businesses will have graduated to full-time, full-scale ventures. Others will begin operations with considerable assets behind their launch. As I write this book I'm consulting to a husband-wife team who developed and patented a "zip-lock" rainhat. It's an interesting device to provide a rainhat that folds to the size of your thumb. You'll find them hard at work in a spare bedroom, slaving away behind two used sewing machines. All they needed was $1200 to start, and when it comes time to grow they'll find plenty of backing.

Ever hear of Boston-Bio/Tech? You will. At least I think you will as soon as we can find the final $200,000 to complete a $1,300,000 capitalization package. Behind it are two bright Harvard Ph.D.s holding some interesting genetic engineering patents.

Right now they're busy cloning frogs but they evidently assured plenty of investors they'll soon be cloning money once their capital intensive laboratory is complete. And it'll take every penny of the $1,300,000 to put it together—scrimp and save as they may. What are our bright Harvard boys investing? Only an assignment to the company of their patent rights. Here's a case where large is logical, while showing shoestring start-ups come in all sizes and shapes.

Later in this book you'll see how to shape your start-up to just the right size. And it may be healthier looking than you think.

MYTH #5: MY BUSINESS CAN'T BE STARTED ON A SHOESTRING

Sure it can. It'll work for any type of business. Now that's a bold statement, considering I have no idea of the business you have in mind. But I make the statement because I have seen it work in just about any business, and the few that haven't crossed my path are no different. Service businesses are a snap. They usually require so little start-up capital that it hardly pays to read a book about it. Retail shops? They account for about 70 percent of the shoestring start-ups. And they're the most fun because you can bootstrap them in so many interesting ways. Whether it's a bookstore or a bagel bakery, if you can't shoestring it your creativity is on the blink.

How about starting your own manufacturing plant? From aircraft components to zipper factories, thousands have started on a shoestring, although it's always a bit more of a challenge when you consider how capital intensive and risky they can be. Scan the list of Fortune-500 companies. Trace their histories. Check their pedigree. Whether it's Apple or Zenith—most started with less capital than you can probably raise right now.

MYTH #6: ONLY WHEELER-DEALERS NEED APPLY

This is the biggest myth of all. Experience and watching hundreds of ordinary people bootstrap their way into business have taught me otherwise. Wage earners who don't know the difference between a profit and loss statement and balance sheet have done it. Housewives who have never signed a check have done it. I've even witnessed a group of high school kids do it.

Northeastern University did a bit of research to find out just who shoestring entrepreneurs are likely to be. They discovered the best bets were people who were never in business before, had no business education, and were cash shy. In plain language, they didn't know any better and couldn't do any better. It once again shows that what you don't know can't hurt you. To solidify the case, the least likely people to start a thinly capitalized business were MBAs, or people with extensive business experience. You'll find them hiding behind a desk at General Motors, believing businesses are really started "by the book." They've been reading the wrong books.

Now most people starting out in business don't consider themselves entrepreneurs any more than they perceive themselves as "wheeler-dealers." I point that out because I sometimes use the word in this book. It may throw you off track, as it does conjure the image of a dashing promoter overseeing a vast conglomerate that he started three weeks earlier and will probably bankrupt three weeks later. But that's not you, either. All you want is your own little shop to open with short money. Wheeler-dealers need not apply.

WHAT IT TAKES

Starting a business with little or no cash of your own is more than a technique, a mathematical formula, a way of business, or even an objective. It's a state of mind.

After you finish this book you'll know the techniques and the strategies, but to turn it from theory to practice requires a unique individual. It's not everyone's cup of tea.

Precisely what does it take to go for it and succeed? I offer no long shopping list of personal attributes or managerial skills. It doesn't work. Too many times we have seen the village moron end up owning the largest and most successful business in town while the smartest kid on the block ends up his bookkeeper. So put away all the books prodding your managerial IQ. It's only filler and doesn't mean a thing. You never know if you have what it takes until you actually do it.

Neither does it matter why you want to do it. Most people don't really know why they want their own business. Their mind plays nasty tricks on them. Ask them why and they'll say money, when it's really the challenge. Or they'll say the challenge when they can't bring themselves to admit it's only to break away from an overbearing boss. It may be an ego trip or a combination of a hundred reasons. What difference does it make? If you want it—or only think you want it—then do it. Either you'll swim like a fish in water or decide it's not for you. But at least you'll have it out of your system and stop wondering about it the rest of your life.

I will tell you this. Whatever any reasonably capitalized business takes to succeed, it will take more to succeed in a shoestring start-up. There's no such thing as a free lunch. In one way or another you pay the price for going it on a hope and a prayer. And the two absolutely essential ingredients you must provide are:

1. Double determination.
2. Ten times the work.

"Bull," you say. "You can't scare me." Well, that's good. It shows guts. And you'll need plenty of that also to succeed. Earlier in this chapter I called it chutzpah, a precise word with an imprecise Anglo-Saxon equivalent made up of equal parts of aggressiveness, courage, daring, and plain moxie. I've yet to see a shoestring business succeed without it.

DOUBLE YOUR DETERMINATION

You never quite know what the word *determination* means until you try to build something from nothing. You can't do it with half-hearted attempts. That's one reason why so many bootstrap deals do succeed—once the doors open. An enormous determination brought it that far and that same determination usually carries it over the survival stage. It's a far cry from the owner who mortgages his home, then invests all that cash into the business on a whim. That's not determination. It's only a mortgaged house. When you knock on a hundred doors, tell a hundred stories, and with sweat on your brow try still another door—then you know what determination is. It turns the soft metal of ambition into the tempered steel of resolve.

I opened this chapter telling you about the first day in the life of Discount City. Words are easy to write, but it wasn't quite so simple. The mountains of inventory didn't just appear at the loading platform. Without cash and without credit it was a mighty tough sell. We had to bang on the doors of 980 prospective suppliers before we could find 38 who would gamble on us and ship on lenient credit terms the business could handle. We had to listen to 300 suppliers laugh us out of their offices before the first order was accepted.

It's enough to send you back to the time clock. It was the same for everything the business needed. Fixtures? We scoured 27 auctions before we landed an assortment of gondolas, showcases, and counters we could buy dirt cheap and on credit. Location? It was the hardest part. We needed both a high-traffic location and a landlord who'd wait two to three months for his first check. Mission impossible. Finally, after two months, we found a strip shopping center whose landlord would talke a chance on us in return for a higher rent in the later months. Heck, we couldn't even afford the $900 for an electric deposit. Using a borrowed portable generator we had the lights to operate for several weeks until we could cover the $900. It may sound like war stories, but that's how it happens in the real world when you don't have money behind you.

Others have their own stories. Don Pendergast is an interesting example. Don designed a new style boat anchor offering the twin advantages of lighter weight and greater holding power than conventional anchors. Boating firms and enthusiasts endorsed the anchor, but it wasn't enough to help Don raise the $200,000 he'd need to start production. For almost four years he banged on doors. He contacted over 200 venture capital firms and 60 banks. Still no money. But Don never threw in the sponge. Early in 1983 his determination paid dividends. An investor from Spokane heard about the anchor, investigated, and decided to capitalize the start-up for a 50 percent interest. Think about it. Over four years between dream and reality.

I came across plenty of people with business ideas and limited or no capital. It's interesting to test their determination. Many will make a few feeble attempts to raise a few dollars from a bank or relatives, and when they come up empty they walk away from the idea. It's a blessing in disguise. If they can't walk the extra mile to get it going they don't have the determination to work it through the trouble spots and make it succeed.

THE ONE-TENTH PRINCIPLE

I borrowed the term "One-Tenth Financing Principle" from Jerome Goldstein (no relative) because he aptly sums up what I'm now about to say. You can start a business with one-tenth the capital normally required (or even no cash at all), but in return you must work ten times as hard to make it succeed.

Any business—even the heavily capitalized firm—takes plenty of commitment and elbow grease to make it. That's common knowledge. The shoestring start-up needs more. Lots more. It all comes down to doing things for yourself instead of using precious capital to have other people do it for you. You find yourself working around the clock, and typically, your family by your side. Every penny saved is a penny less you need to start. Before you know it you're a genuine workaholic.

Peggy Lebow is. She admits to working 16-to 18-hour days to make her artificial flower distributorship hum. "It's all economics," says Peggy. "I spend evenings making the flowers instead of buying them ready-made at double the price. During the day, I'm out selling rather than paying commissions or salary to someone else." She's not alone.

Hard as you may work, it's all to your advantage. Control is one. Nothing escapes your eye because you are involved in every phase of the operation. You measure costs, control waste, and don't hesitate to knock three hours from a stockboy's schedule if you can. Costly mistakes are few and far between because you realize you can't afford mistakes. As you grow you do it with extreme caution because you remember where you came from.

While studying for my MBA I burned the midnight oil with two brothers. One went on and is now a regional manager for Coca-Cola. The other scraped together a few dollars and started a wholesale bakery firm. "You know," he said, "I work morning, noon, and night and my brother, the Coca-Cola executive, never understands why. And he'll never understand it until he's in his own business—a business he enjoys. Then and only then will he realize that it only looks like work."

THE TIME IS ALWAYS RIGHT

Behind my desk is a framed self-portrait of an elderly gentleman named Harold, poised with a palette in one hand and a paint brush in the other. Neither the artistry nor a deep personal relationship with the artist compelled me to buy the painting. It was his smile. It carried an important message, and I wanted that smile to be my continued warning that hopes can grow old.

I met Harold while visiting my grandfather in a nursing home. As a patient he'd spend his day painting and smiling. Striking up a conversation with him, he confided the reason for his ever-present smile. "You know," he said, "when I was a young art student just out of high school, I wanted to open an art gallery. My father wanted me to be a dentist instead. Well, I spent six years getting through NYU Dental School, hating every minute of it and wishing I owned my own art gallery instead. I wanted a career in art, not pulling teeth. But life plays nasty tricks. First came the Depression, so I drilled teeth to make a living. Then came the war, and the Navy needed dentists. When I got back I had a wife and two kids to support, so I pushed aside my dreams of an art gallery and resumed my dental practice. When I hit 50 I figured it was time. My kids were on their own and I had money in the bank. My wife called it mid-life crisis and my kids thought I was insane to give up a lucrative dental practice to open an art gallery. So for the next 20 years I continued to push aside the idea of my own gallery and drilled more damned teeth. Well now I'm 73 years old and too ill to start an art gallery so I paint instead. You wonder what happens to all the years and all your dreams." I never wanted to forget those words.

People always have reasons for pushing their ambitions into the future. Excuses come easy. If you really want your own business you'll face only one real enemy—procrastination. You can read this or any other book 56 times and memorize every word, but what good does it do if you don't put it into practice?

The procrastinator always has a reason. How many times have you heard someone say "the time isn't right," "the economy is bad," "money is too tight," or "I want to make certain there'll be no war in the Mideast." The list is endless. Year in and out the procrastinator reasons while someone else makes the money.

One thing is certain, my friend. Nobody is going to knock on your door, lead you by the hand, and do it for you. Nobody is going to give you the push to get started today. Why should they?

So let's face facts. Some of you will never start your own business. Your dreams are nothing more than fantasies. You'll hope for it, think about it, and fabricate ten more reasons why you can't do it. And you shouldn't. Whatever you want from your business, your business will need more from you.

Then again, you may be one of the few who are ready. Perhaps you've been in business before and know what it's all about. Maybe it's your first time and you have kicked aside all your fears and doubts and are anxious to tackle it. Welcome to the club. Someday you'll look back at your own grand opening—your first day at the helm of your own business. And when you do, you'll also stand tall and give yourself a hefty pat on the back. You'll deserve it. You made your own miracles.

2

CHECKING OUT
YOUR WINNING IDEA

You can imagine the pained expression on the faces of Gary Dahl's astounded bowling buddies when he announced his plans to package ordinary sandstones in cage-like cartons and market them as everyone's favorite pet—"The Pet Rock." Who in his or her right mind would want a rock for a pet? It can't curl up on you lap, beg for a treat, or fetch a newspaper. In fact, it can do none of the heartwarming things we've come to expect from the more animated variety of household additions. About all it can do is slumber in its clever striped box with the $4.98 price tag and hope people would learn to love it. And they did. For a while, "Rocky" ranked third as a household pet, after Fido and Tabby. As one proud master asked, "Why can't you love a pet rock? Did you ever see a rock bite?"

Marketing experts scratched their heads in predictable disbelief, while psychologists threw up their hands in mock surrender. Saner people laughed, while the rest of the world bought. It was the story of one more idea—and one more instant millionaire.

So who wants to be a millionaire? Not Beverly Zintgraff, who at 32 is still scraping together a few dollars to open a lingerie shop in Cleveland's swank Shaker Heights suburb. "I'll be happy if I can someday take out enough money from the business to have a home without a leaky roof, a mortgage that doesn't pinch, a Buick in the driveway, and a few bucks for my kids' college."

You'll also find Ken Engour on the slow track to success. "I'm not looking for a quantum leap to a fast fortune. What I do want is a sideline business to augment my salary as a flight engineer. And that sideline business is a newsletter to corporate pilots." Listen to the stories. It's the stuff the American dream is made of. Ordinary people in ordinary businesses, however, do make very unusual stories. But it makes you wonder. How many are selecting their right business? Are you?

THE ONE MOST IMPORTANT DECISION

This year maybe half a million Americans will start their own businesses. Burt Nicholas, a career consultant, estimates that 60 to 70 percent will select the wrong business for them. That's why so many people do fail. There may be nothing wrong with the business idea itself, or their own management capabilities, but still the owner and the business may not fit together. And when that happens the venture never works out. The first ingredient for success is the perfect match between the entrepreneur and the enterprise.

I enjoy talking to entrepreneurs planning their first venture. It's interesting to probe their thoughts and discover how they came to choose their intended business. One young man recently told me he looked at various opportunities over a two-year span. He considered everything from a restaurant to a franchised real estate office, finally settling on opening an automobile tire and accessory shop. "So why did you pick that business?" I asked. "Easy," he replied. *Entrepreneur Magazine* predicted auto-related businesses will be the best money-makers in the years ahead." Maybe so. But will it be *his* best money-maker?

It's an easy trap to fall into. Some are blinded by what they see as the best way to make money. Others mistakenly look for prestige or glamour. Many others simply go into the easiest entry business. And with less thought behind it than in selecting a new car, they somehow think it will work for them. Too often it doesn't.

Doesn't everyone want to run a restaurant? Kirk Begogian thinks so. Kirk manages a Boston brokerage firm specializing in restaurant sales, and he'll tell you that the money motive can be a killer—and everyone thinks the biggest, fastest, and easiest money can be made in the food business. "Not so," Kirk adds. "The restaurant business is the world's toughest business, and for every millionaire it produces there are 100 bankruptcies. Still, they line up knowing nothing about the business except the delusion it's their pot of gold."

"Whenever we sell a business brokerage franchise," reports one unnamed executive of a franchise brokerage system, "we do sell opportunity, but we're also selling prestige and glamour. Seventy percent of our franchisees have no business trying to sell a business. Mechanics, assembly line workers, route delivery people, and other blue-collar types are always dreaming of the day they can trade dirty work jeans or a soiled apron for a three-piece suit and a chance to sit behind a desk. Most of them don't belong behind a desk. They belong in dirty work clothes or a soiled apron doing what they do best. But they will shell out $30,000 for a chance to grab what they see as prestige."

"We can put people into a franchised food store for as little as $4000 down," claims a supermarket executive who started a successful program for licensing convenience stores. "So as you'd expect we have a waiting list of hundreds of willing food store operators. If you cull the list you'd find out that 90 percent are interested only because we do give them the opportunity to get into business with so little cash. How many are on the list because they really want to operate a convenience store? Damn few. That's why we have such a high turnover of franchisees."

You can't fault many of these people who opened in haste and repented in leisure with little to show for it but boarded up store fronts, going-out-of-business sales, and broken dreams. Choosing the right business is one of the most important decisions of your life, and before I show you how to start on a shoestring I want to help you check out what you intend to start. Let's make it a winner.

NARROW THE RANGE

Start-up entrepreneurs can be divided into two categories. First are those with a reasonably precise idea of what their business will be. They know the type of business, its size, marketing approach, and general location. They have a fixed mind-set. They can close their eyes and visualize it—make it come alive. Some do even better and have it all reduced to a comprehensive business plan nailed down to its smallest detail. Well, that's good. It's a starting point and the essential starting point for this chapter and the chapters to come. If you're such an entrepreneur, you have your own mind made up. That doesn't mean that what you have in mind is a right or logical choice, but it *is* the starting point. We have something to test. We can kick its tires and see if it'll stand up. When we're through you may decide to go ahead with it, reshape it, or abandon it altogether. Keep an open mind.

The "shoppers" are the second category. Their mind is far from made up. In a maze of indecision they wander through a wide selection, hoping to narrow the range to the one best choice. If you're a shopper, make a list of businesses you're most interested in. Rank them so you too have your starting point. Let's see how your list looks when we complete the chapter.

CREATING THE PERFECT MATCH

When is there a perfect match between entrepreneur and enterprise? I recommend a four-part test:

1. Can you *enjoy* the business?
2. Can you *manage* the business?
3. Can you *earn* from the business?
4. Can you *afford* the business?

Doesn't it make sense? These four points answer the question of what you can bring to the business, and in return, what the business can do for you. As with any relationship, you and the business must mesh together to create a workable bond, and it only happens when you score on all key points. Consider them one by one.

THE PSYCHIC REWARDS

For Gary Gygax, forming his own company, TRS Hobbies, Lake Geneva, Wisconsin, was like a return to his childhood. "The real motivation is that I like games," he reports. "I've been playing chess and Parcheesi for longer than I can remember, so I made a business out of my hobby." You probably know Gary through his now popular "Dungeons & Dragons" games. Gary, I bet, is a man who whistles while he works, and that always means a man in the right business.

Most people think money is the number one priority in selecting a business. Put it on the bottom of your list. The psychic rewards—enjoyment—head the list. When you enjoy your business, the success and money are bound to follow, but it never quite works in reverse. And if you happen to make serious money in a business you don't enjoy, I'll guarantee you'd make twice the money in a business—any business—that does get your adrenaline flowing.

So what business would you enjoy? No quick answer is needed. It may be the line of work you have experience in, but in a real sense you're never sure what will provide the greatest pleasure because you are limited by your own experiences. The unknown may be even better.

Starting your own business may be breaking away from your working past. For many, it signals not only the transition from employee to entrepreneur but from "what they have been" to "what they really should be." And for many, it's like being reborn. But for many others, breaking from the past for the challenge of a totally new career path is too much to tackle and there are always the few with their blinders on who never really think about it.

One of my brightest associates in our law firm had this problem. Peter would sit behind his desk poring over legal briefs but was always thinking about marketing an adult game he was developing. He'd walk into my office and talk games while I wanted to talk law. Finally I asked him why he didn't quit the practice of law and go into the full-time business of promoting his game. It wasn't money or security. Peter, lucky enough to be born to the right parents, had more money than any senior partner in our firm. It was his own self-image. "My folks would have a heart attack if they found out their son the lawyer was selling toys." So Peter's not selling games. And as an unhappy lawyer he's not living much of a life either.

Peter's story isn't unique. People everywhere are so busy making a living they think they can't switch gears to have a more enjoyable career. Not long ago we were asked to handle the legal work for a 42-year-old gas station attendant about to open his own service station. So you talk and you learn. What I learned was this chap was a photography buff. Pumping gas was his life. It wasn't easy to convince him to give up his idea for a gas station and go for a photo shop instead. With 25 to 30 productive years ahead of him, why waste it on a business he didn't enjoy? Today you'll find him operating not one but three camera shops and loving every minute of it. You only live once.

I've been in many businesses. Some I thought I'd enjoy and learned to dislike, while others I enjoy more than I thought I could. That brings us to the other side of the coin. Sometimes the grass only looks greener.

One misadventure of mine was a movie theater. I was a movie fanatic since I can remember and can tell you who won the Academy Awards in 1956. So when I had a few chips to spare and another adventure to conquer, it was only logical a movie theater would catch my eye. That's when I learned you don't know a business until you're in it, work it, and live it. While I thought I'd be partying with movie stars, I discovered it was a headache business, hassling film distributors, chasing rowdy kids, and working weekends. It cost me $30,000 to find out that you have to look before you leap.

Look *before* you leap. Important advice. Since my bygone days as a movie mogul I fight like a madman with clients going into a business they don't know, just as I'll push to get a client involved to test an untried business. Then, and only then, do you know whether the business will give you a psychic reward or a royal headache.

This may be your best opportunity to experiment and try your hand in several situations of interest to you. Why jump into uncharted waters? When Taylor Lynch decided to leave his job as a dispatcher for a freight-forwarding firm his target was to open a travel agency. As Taylor admits, he knew nothing about the travel business. While keeping his daytime job he learned fast, working in a local office evenings and Saturdays. It still interested him, but he had his doubts. Taylor never realized how difficult it was to satisfy the vacationing public. "I didn't think I had the patience to handle it," says Taylor. "Not after a lady phoned me from the Bahamas screaming that her plane was late for take-off. When you're in the travel business, everything's your fault." But that's what it's all about. When you're on the outside looking in, any business can look good. You have to crawl inside to feel the pulse, see the problems, detect the difficulties, and see if it's for you. Try it on the installment plan.

Every aspect of a business can add or detract from its enjoyability. The type of business—and nature of the work—is only one factor to be considered. "But even a slight modification from what the entrepreneur is comfortable with can throw him off balance and make him a fish out of water," says career counselor Burt Nicholas. "Some people are totally inflexible. For example, a manager of a high-class steak house reasons he can enjoy operating any type restaurant. But throw him into a different type restaurant with a different clientele and you may as well put him into another business. On the other extreme are entrepreneurs who can happily adapt to a wide range of opportunities within or beyond a given field. The entrepreneur has to discover this about himself."

The structure of the firm is one more dimension to consider. Frequently people will hunt for a franchise for management support because it offers a financially attractive opportunity, and never consider the control they have to surrender. A franchise can make a free-wheeling entrepreneur's life miserable or it can be a bonus to a less secure type happy to exchange decision making for firm guidance. The same can be said for partners.

Don't overlook business hours or travel demands. Frequently the opportunity for travel is an attraction because it is a novelty. The novelty wears off as so many people discover, and spending half your life away from family can quickly destroy enthusiasm.

When you're in the right business, there is a thrill to it all. You see the business born. You nurse it through the survival stage. You navigate it to its apex. And when you're through you'll probably sell out, if only so you can start again and enjoy it again. It sure beats going to work.

Will you enjoy your business?

MEASURE YOUR MANAGEMENT MENTALITY

What management mentality will your start-up need? Plenty. And it will need considerably more than the venture that started with a healthy investment, because when you start on a shoestring you don't have any margin for error. And as the Bankruptcy Courts can tell you, entrepreneurs don't always use the right yardstick when they do measure their management mentality.

Elliot Galahow, a small business consultant, says, "It's not so much a matter of *what* the entrepreneur can manage as much as *when* he or she is ready to manage the start-up they have in mind." So it's timing and prior experience rather than capability that's usually the decisive factor. "And while you're learning you can be nickeled and dimed to death with 100 small but nevertheless fatal mistkes," adds Bill Portnoy, who confesses to making enough slip-ups in his embryonic Philadelphia restaurant to teach a course in "mis-management" at the Harvard Business School.

Just as a business can look like *fun* to operate, it can also look *easy* to operate. Illusion on the first point means only less fun. Illusion on the second means failure. And few businesses are as easy to operate as it may appear. But still the naive optimists beat their drums: "What do you have to know about running a pinball arcade, shoe store, or coffee shop?" I don't know. I never operated one. But why don't you ask someone who has? Take your notebook along and be prepared for a long and hard education. Every business has its tricks.

It amazes me how many people have never worked in a business, know nothing about it, and with a refreshing mixture of chutzpah, enthusiasm, and sheer optimism throw their life's savings into the venture. What's more amazing is that some people actually make it. They're the fast learners. The slow learners are wise to make their mistakes with an employer's money, so they'll make a few less with their own.

Experience alone does not magically transform itself into management ability. Years of experience coupled with narrow responsibility still deprive the enterprise of the broad skills necessary to master the operation.

One characteristic of a shoestring start-up is the ability of the entrepreneur to parlay his managerial strength into financing. Creditors have their own perception of your management ability, and when you're collateral shy, it becomes the major selling point. One wholesaler comments, "We helped a young fellow get started in his own liquor store with a lenient credit line. We had confidence in him because he managed a large liquor store for one of our accounts and did a hell of a job building the business. In fact, we knew him better than we did his boss. It's a different story with someone off the street who wants to try his hand in the liquor business."

So the message is clear. If you don't have the experience in the type business you have in mind, then don't try to open it just yet. Defer it until you can obtain valuable "hands-on" experience as an employee. You may have to moonlight to pick up the experience or sacrifice some income for a few months, but it will be a much smaller loss than what you will sustain by operating a business you know nothing about. There are some other steps to consider:

1.   A franchise is one. A major selling point of most franchises is that they will train you and then provide the close supervision to keep the business on track. It works well in the

fast food fields, but I question whether it's enough background in more complex fields such as business brokerage. Watch the economics. If you're essentially buying the "training," you're over-spending. The reason to pick up a franchise is that you want the name and system a good franchise can offer.

2. Partners are another possibility. I have seen many cases where a partner provided the experience and management "know-how." A partnership can also be ideal for a larger business requiring either a broader span of management or a division of responsibility. It also has its downside, as you'll see in Chapter 7.

Don't be what I call a "minimum-wage manager." What's a "minimum-wage manager"? Anyone who knows so little about a business that all he or she is worth is the minimum wage. Few can take an idea and make it a winning idea.

LIVING WITHOUT A LIVING

"Tighten your belt and don't expect to eat for a few years," comments Pat Mone who is still waiting for enough money from her struggling bookstore to finance her first legitimate meal in as long as she can remember.

Nobody can predict with a straight face how wealthy your business will make you 10 or 15 years from now. That's up to you and the business. It's the first year, or second or third, that counts. That's when the mismatch between what you need from the business to live and what the business can afford to give you takes its toll. And the answer can only be found with a realistic look at the business itself.

The mismatching process continues. Entrepreneurs, for example, will leave a $100,000-a-year position and start a bootstrap business that can only generate $50,000 a year for the first year or two. For some people it's not a problem. For the guy who *needs* $50,000 to support a wife and three kids it's a $50,000 problem. Common sense? Maybe. Usually, however, it's a wildly optimistic type who either overestimates his earnings potential from the business or somehow thinks he can live on less.

It's endemic with all shoestring start-ups. You pay a price for starting poor, and the price is staying poor for some time to come. But what entrepreneurs don't realize is that some businesses will keep you poorer longer than others. An example: When Phyllis and Barry McLean decided to leave their respective jobs as teacher and commercial artist to start their art gallery, they knew they would immediately sacrifice $83,000 in combined income. "We had several options," explains Phyllis. "One of us could have remained with our job until the business was large enough to need us both, but we wanted to start with myself handling retail sales while Barry went after corporate sales. But even with the two of us pitching sales we knew our art gallery was a business with a very slow take-off. So to create a larger cash flow—and base to draw a salary—we altered our plans and made it a combination art gallery and greeting card and gift shop. It required very little additional capital to triple our sales but now the numbers begin to make sense."

Take off your rose-colored glasses when assessing the short-term income potential of your business. What you need is a cash flow statement that shows how much you can safely draw from the business. And with your rose-colored glasses beside you, look at it with a jaundiced eye. Whenever I project income I deliberately underestimate projected income by 20 percent while overestimating expenses by 10 percent. It usually takes you closer to reality.

Here's another mistake to avoid. Don't think you can defy the odds. Even shrewd management isn't magic. Three years ago I was taking two young partners through an exercise of projecting their cash flow and take-home income from a planned tool rental shop. Admittedly, a cash flow statement is at best a guesstimate of what a business actually will do, but even under the best of circumstances the business couldn't afford more than $10,000 a year for each of its two partners. That's not how they saw it. Working backwards they conveniently pumped up the projected sales to give them the bottom line they were looking for. It's an idiot's game.

Frequently a partnership produces a greater strain on earnings. While a single-owner business can juggle personal finances to subsidize what a business can pay, it's rare that two partners can perform the same juggling act. So with one partner willing to bite the bullet and take home less, the other needs more. It's not only poor partnership planning but poor business planning. The solution is usualy a larger business.

Don't concern yourself with the income potential a few years into the future. The business at maturity may be too small or unprofitable to provide the income you want. In itself it's not the criterion for defining your business. You can always expand, sell-out, or trade-up. What you want now is a threshold business. Something to get you started.

Ron Chisholm, who started many bootstrap companies and most notably a four-store music and stereo chain, says it's all a matter of "staying power." "When you recognize how little a business can afford you can plan for it—deal with it. I went for broke in my first record shop and instead of opening a small 1000-sq.-ft. store, I gambled all the way on a 3000-ft. operation. With a larger store I'd have a larger cash flow and that always translates into more cash to take home. Why die on the installment plan?"

There are a hundred ways to shape a business—or shape a situation—to make ends meet so you have staying power. Thousands of successful start-ups had their owners moonlighting to keep their income flowing so the cash could remain in their business. Others live on cash reserves. Still others, the retired or bored housewives, may not need present income. The same is true if you have an income independent of the business. But when you can't shape the situation, you do have to shape the business to give you the income you do need.

CAN YOU AFFORD IT?

I'll have considerably more to say about this in the next chapter, but capital is the *least* important factor in selecting a business or in defining start-up size. Perhaps that one point is the central theme of this entire book. You can start just about any type of business, regardless of how much capital you personally have, once you know how to put together what you do want with everyone else's money.

A case in point: Overlooking Cape Cod's Buzzards Bay you'll find several very successful restaurants. But the largest and most successful was started with absolutely none of the owner's cash. Several years after it opened I came to be friendly with the owner, and he confided, "I came to the Cape from New York not only penniless but $300,000 in debt from an aborted business deal. I was ready to go bankrupt, but decided to wheel and deal just once more. Either I'd bail myself out or go bankrupt with a few more creditors. So I decided a restaurant would be my logical choice. Now, of course, I couldn't afford to open even the smallest restaurant, so why not go for the largest? It's my way of making the illogical logical. Within six months I put together a syndicated partnership. The 20 investors each contributed $40,000 for a total of $800,000, while I retained 50 percent ownership as the mastermind. But I looked ahead and gave myself the option to buy out my partners for $1,200,000 payable over five years. Within a year of the opening I exercised the option and just finished paying down my ex-partners. Now it's worth $2.5 million and it's all mine. You don't start a business on what you can afford—you start the business with what others *let* you afford."

It was an interesting story and I never forgot it. Neither should you.

What do these four points really come down to? Self-assessment. Admittedly it's never easy to be objective when you're asking the tough questions about yourself. But when you do know your own goals and needs, strengths and limitations, you have one part of the matching process. And only then can you define your perfect match.

THOUSANDS OF SUCCESSFUL NEW VENTURES

The small business movement is on the march. The number of start-ups has grown to about 950,000 new ventures yearly. Why the groundswell of entrepreneurial activity? New consumer trends and recent technology, coupled with the fact that more people than ever before want to be their own boss, create the momentum. And while large corporations can't or won't respond to the needs, it leaves vast pockets of opportunity for the small venture.

I simply don't understand people who want to start their own business but complain the opportunities don't exist. They're wrong—dead wrong. Not only do more opportunities exist today than ever before, but even newer opportunities are on the horizon for tomorrow.

Consider all the new businesses surrounding you. A nearby shopping mall tells part of the story. Almost half the tenants are operating businesses unheard of only ten years ago. Specialized shops—a designer jean store, a video shop, a store devoted only to jogging shoes, to name a few—are peppered throughout the mall. Turn to the yellow pages, 40 percent of the listings are businesses in embryonic industries bypassing the imagination of yesterday's entrepreneur. Did you know that more than 50 percent of all service businesses offer services that only recently came into demand? The computer revolution alone created its own tidal wave of opportunities. I can point out 30 publishing firms, for example, riding on the coattails of a public clamoring for computer information. Not one of these firms was around in 1975.

If the future presents its opportunities, the past makes its own contributions. Traditional businesses are being reshaped into brand-new opportunities as people discover new ways—better ways—to do business and grab their healthy share of a market from traditionalists who won't change.

You can't find one industry that won't go through a radical restyling in the next several years. Society is on too fast a track for anyone to stand still. And as always, the change will be pioneered by enterprising individuals who can see opportunities while others see none.

So your winning idea is more than an inward look at your own talents, interests, and motivations. You want to find a market niche for a viable, successful venture. And thousands of opportunities await you.

Where can you find ideas for a moneymaking opportunity?

Entrepreneur magazine is one of the best sources I have found. *Entrepreneur* is on the cutting edge of all that is new and promising in the small business field. Each month they feature several new and unique businesses that can be easily opened in other areas.

HOW OTHERS FOUND SUCCESS

How do people find success? What formula do entrepreneurs use to discover opportunity and their perfect business? There is no one answer, but a wide range of approaches. For some it came after months of active, deliberate searching and sifting, while for others the transition from personal interest to business took place so gradually that they were surprised to discover themselves actually in business. And not a small number will tell you that "something snapped—an idea was born."

Let's meet some of these people as they tell their stories.

A visit to the dentist to cure a cantankerous molar was the launching point for Gary Klein, a shipper for a New York firm. "While waiting for the novocaine to put me out of my misery, I studied the deplorable condition of my dentist's aquarium. It was a natural observation for me," says Gary, "because I'm an aquarium buff and have a few fish tanks of my own. My dentist clearly didn't have the time or inclination to keep his fish happy, so I offered to—for $25 a month. Within three months he referred me to several other professionals with their own problem aquariums. By moonlighting I could handle about 50 calls a month, and at $25 an office visit (less than what my dentist charges), I was soon making more money by moonlighting than from my regular job. Before jumping into the business full time, I advertised for new accounts in local professional magazines, and surprisingly, obtained a slew of new customers. Now I have two panel trucks on the road, and a full-time assistant helping me handle 300 accounts a month in the New York boroughs. It's still a small business—grossing about $100,000 a year—but the net profit is fantastic because I'm only selling a service. Within the next year or two I plan to triple the number of "office calls" and perhaps open a retail aquarium shop. For me it all started with a toothache."

Ask Bob Crisafi if he expected to own his own business. "No way," voices Bob. So how was it that one month later Bob was the stereo king of Cambridge's Harvard Square? "I owned a small block of stores near Harvard, and one of my tenants was a highly successful stereo shop pushing hi-fis to the college crowd. And I knew just how successful they were because their rent was based on sales, and that gave me a look at their books. One blustery winter evening the store had a fire, destroying most of the inventory. Although the partners in the business collected insurance, they decided not to reopen and instead parted company. Well, that gave me an empty store. I lined up another tenant in a hurry, but when it came time to sign the lease my hand froze. I kept getting flashbacks to the income statement from the stereo shop and simply said, what the hell—I'm going into the stereo business. I didn't agonize over the decision. I just knew what I had there and the idea wouldn't let go. Since I knew nothing about the business I hired a top-notch manager away from Tech Hi-Fi and never regretted the decision."

A warehouse loaded with imported neck pendants was the starting point for Dave Scribner's Royal-Wear Jewelry, a mail-order firm nicely chugging along. Dave explains how the company came to be: "My father was a commercial auctioneer. Very often he'd bid in himself for the merchandise and re-sell it later at a profit. Evidently a large jewelry firm in Providence folded, and my dad purchased $60,000 worth of jade and gold neck pendants for about $10,000. He planned to sell the merchandise to a few department stores when he unexpectedly died. At the time I was just graduating from Brown University and had the task of liquidating my dad's estate—including the warehouse loaded with jewelry. So I toyed around with several methods to unload the merchandise and finally settled on a mail-order campaign. I gave the neck wear the 'Royal-Wear' name and had a Boston freelance ad man work me up several ads for *Cosmopolitan* magazine and *Ladies Home Journal*. We tested the ad in one or two journals and found they pulled orders. It's a great feeling to look in your mailbox and see it stuffed with 200 to 300 envelopes—each with a $15.95 check. Within two months the inventory was gone and we had a $20,000 profit. It was then I decided I thoroughly enjoyed mail-order promoting and wanted it as my career. Borrowing my share of the inheritance, I scouted out new direct-mail items—from digital watches to a unique collapsible hunting knife. Of course, I had to change the name of the firm to 'Royal Sales' because I was no longer just in the jewelry line. Growth has been deliberately slow. Mail order is a tough business, and you need the instinctive touch for gauging the market. Now that I've been in the business several years, I'm developing the touch and expect the company to reach the $1 million mark within two years. It's interesting. I was forced into the business by circumstance, and I always wondered what I'd be doing today if I wasn't left a warehouse full of jewelry."

For Martha and Joe Beaumont, everything about their decision was slow, painstaking, and deliberate. "We knew we wanted our business to be a family affair," says Joseph, a burly ex-marine with a service pension. "We had no particular skills, but we knew that the business would in some way be connected to food, beause both Martha and I enjoy cooking. Opening a small restaurant or even a coffee shop looked like our logical choice until we took a trip to New York and spotted a crowded gourmet shop selling delicacies from around the world. We immediately liked the idea because it was not only the food business—but one with an exciting twist. Best of all, our neck of the woods in southeastern Massachusetts didn't have a comparable business. Rather than rush into it we spent a full year talking to suppliers, reading specialty food journals, and checking out similar businesses on the east coast. And the more we learned the more we were convinced it was our *right* business." Today, the Continental Gourmet has 12 employees and sales of nearly $2 million—but you'll still find Martha and Joe behind the counter explaining to yet another amateur gourmet the secret pleasures of their 27 blends of imported coffee.

You won't read about these people in the *Wall Street Journal*. But each in his or her own way found the path to success. Gary Klein perhaps says it best when he philosophizes, "Somewhere in the zigzag of life, you snare your enthusiasm on an idea. that's when you've found your opportunity."

GIVE YOUR IDEA THE ACID TEST

Do you have the *right* business idea? Don't look for the answer in this book. If I had the foolproof crystal ball I'd be too busy sipping piña coladas in the Bahamas to tell you. And nobody else (except for the few quacks who pretend to have all the right answers) can tell you either. That too is part of the fascination of business. It bears its similarities to the Las Vegas slot machines.

Ask Gary Dahl, "Mr. Pet Rock," how many people believed that not all his rocks were to be found in cardboard cages. Ask Henry Ford about the 400 MBAs with 198,000 pages of "market research" who *proved* every American wanted an Edsel in the driveway.

So, my friend, being an entrepreneur is being a gambler. But there are ways to stack the odds in your favor. Put your idea to the test.

Test One. *The Test of Time.* Stay with the idea at least several months before you take the plunge and commit to the venture. If the idea fades before then, it doesn't necessarily mean it was a bad idea, only an idea that you didn't believe in strongly enough to make work.

Test Two. *Measure the Market.* Identify, isolate, and rate the potential users. Plenty of ideas collapse, not because the market isn't there, but because it's too small or poorly defined to turn into a money-maker. This advice extends to even traditional retail stores who may enter under-populated or overly competitive areas. Are the customers there to support your business?

Test Three. *Test the Pulling Power.* You may see a huge demand out there for your winning idea, but the way to turn demand into dollars is to convert your demand to *demand pull*. In other words, come up with the selling point. Nobody sells a product or service. We all sell a "benefit." How will customers benefit from what you have to sell?

Test Four. *Test Your Reach.* Even with a well-defined market and an approach with pulling power, you need the means to reach your market. Many start-up firms stumble on this one, underestimating what it takes in advertising or promotion costs to capture the interest of a sufficiently large percentage of users to make the venture worthwhile.

Test Five. *Pretest the Idea.* This is a particularly important point in product marketing. Always pretest the idea. Try it out on a small scale with select advertising, or try to line up your customers before you commit yourself to the business. Gary Klein pretested the demand for his aquarium service business before he ventured into it on a full-time basis, and so do the largest corporations. Always test the gamble first with a few disposable dollars.

Test Six. *Game-Plan the Entire Venture.* Acid test the basic assumptions on which your business will be built. Market potential is only one of many assumptions. Check the others: Can you obtain the product? Can you buy—and sell—at the right price? Do you know your costs? Will the numbers work? Every business is a long chain of integrated factors, never stronger than the one weak link.

Test Seven. *Test Your Knowledge.* This is the key to it all. Businesses fail because the entrepreneur at the helm didn't know enough about the business to psyche out and correct the weaknesses or exploit the potential strengths. It's all in the homework. And while you never come up with foolproof conclusions there's no excuse for overlooking the obvious. So become a sponge, soaking up as much information as you can about the business, because eventually you'll need it all.

KEY POINTS TO REMEMBER

1. Your success—or failure—will depend more on selecting the *right* business than on any other decision. It's your most important decision.
2. Don't chase elusive reasons in deciding upon a venture. Money, prestige, and easy entry are never strong reasons.
3. Develop the mind-set of what your business will be. Visualize it in as much detail as possible so you can evaluate it.
4. Match the business to yourself before you match it to the market. Remember, you want a business you can enjoy, manage, and earn from.
5. Don't limit your sights by what you *think* you can afford.
6. There are more opportunities today than ever before. Boot-strap pioneers are invading traditional fields and pathfinding new industries.
7. There's no one right way to come across your perfect opportunity. In the zigzag of life, you too will snare your enthusiasm on a winning idea.
8. Put your idea to the seven-point test. It can improve your odds, but never expect foolproof results.

3

SHOESTRING ECONOMICS

Shoestring economics? Don't look for it in the catalogs of the Harvard or Stanford Business Schools. Yet this year many thousands of bootstrap entrepreneurs will enroll and sweat through the course on the self-study plan. Their laboratories are the countless shoestring enterprises started with high hopes and low cash. The exams come fast and furious, testing skills on how to make a cash-shy business come together and stay together. Tuition? The willingness to dig in and do whatever's needed to survive. Four out of five drop out. The graduates never receive a sheepskin but do win a successful business. The class motto: "Who needs cash?"

Building a shoestring enterprise demands mastery over numerous problems ignored by the well-capitalized entrepreneur. Essentially they can be boiled to one—an acute shortage of capital to follow conventional economic rules. You plan differently and operate with different priorities. Survival is the ability to always compensate for lack of cash.

The economic theme is the same during each of the four stages of the venture's development: the planning stage, the start-up stage, the survival stage, and the growth stage.

During the planning stage, the entrepreneur conceives and roughly shapes the idea for the venture. He may do preliminary research on a fixed idea or seek out opportunities. It's at this stage that most shoestring ventures become "still births," as the entrepreneur concludes either that the idea is in itself unworkable, or the capital needs are too excessive. For every business that is started, many more are put on hold or dropped because the entrepreneur didn't analyze how the business could come together using the right economic perspective.

At the start-up stage, the organization begins to take form. During this period the entrepreneur begins to assemble financing, assets, locations, and personnel. It may be a methodical approach, or the venture may simply stumble together as a predestined event. In either case, the later success of the enterprise is chiefly dependent on whether the organization is formed on a financial foundation that will get it through the early years.

The survival stage can be roughly measured as that period between commencing operations until the business is both profitable and operating with a surplus cash flow. For most firms this represents at least the first two or three years. During the survival stage the focus is on the operational decisions to build sales and cash flow to stay ahead of the cash demands. It's during this period that most failures occur because either the entrepreneur couldn't achieve this objective or the financial commitments made during the start-up stage were too burdensome to begin with.

The growth stage may, in reality, be more an expression of stabilized operations rather than actual growth. The majority of small ventures do not expand much beyond their original size and scope and for them "growth" is only the "light at the end of the tunnel" when they can declare themselves free of a constant cash crisis. It's at this point that the shoestring start-up begins to converge with the economics of the well-capitalized firm. Still, 20 percent of the small start-ups will considerably expand. Here the economic decisions are on both the timing and the growth strategy.

Each stage presents its own economic pitfalls. That's what this chapter is about. Although you can't anticipate all the booby traps, most are predictable and confront every type venture. So let's put you through a primer course on what I see as the fourteen essential economic lessons to be learned by every shoestring entrepreneur.

FOURTEEN ESSENTIAL LESSONS FOR EVERY SHOESTRING ENTREPRENEUR

Lesson #1: Set Realistic Goals

Pinpointing the right size and scope for the start-up is the essence of a successful blueprint. While every business can begin within a broad range, you eventually reach the extremes when the planned venture is too large or too small.

Those who go beyond the reality zone are entrepreneurs who either try to match their venture to their dreams or try to match the venture to their pocketbook.

The ambitiously large and grandiose blueprint brings about self-defeat during the planning stage, since the entrepreneur can seldom reconcile the financing needed with the financing available. Rather than lower his or her sights from the desirable to the attainable, the idea is on perpetual hold. These are the dreamers.

The danger is not necessarily in thinking big, but in refusing to think smaller by carving a fall-back position that is attainable. I have seen many shoestring entrepreneurs put together six- and seven-figure start-ups, but for every one who can there are ten other entrepreneurs who plan on the same scale only to run into stonewalls. Reality for them is the ability to redesign the venture on a smaller scale. There's an old adage that advises: "You never know what you can afford until you try." It was tailor-made for the shoestring entrepreneur.

Thinking too small is an appreciably greater danger than thinking too big. While the stubborn dreamer simply doesn't start, the overly cautious entrepreneur finds it easy to start— only to fail. From my viewpoint, the majority of shoestring ventures do fail because they began on too small and unrealistic a scale. The venture simply didn't have enough momentum to get off the ground. It's not necessarily true with service and sideline businesses that can flourish from microscopic beginnings, but it certainly is so with retail ventures dependent upon internally generated profits for survival and growth.

The anemic start-up is almost always the creation of the entrepreneur whose plans are based on his pocketbook rather than the profit potential of the venture. What he thinks he can afford overrides the question of what makes sense. So with a few dollars he whips together a few assets and expects it to turn miracles. That's not planning a business but planning a disaster.

When is your venture the right size?

1.   When it's *small* enough to be financed.
2.   When it's *large* enough to give you a healthy start.

Stay within this range and you have the correct yardstick.

Lesson #2: Nail Down Start-Up Costs

The actual start-up is always the end point of converging costs with financing. While you may have an approximation of what the business will be, you can't seek financing until you have nailed down the cost components of the start-up.

Don't proceed with vague ideas of what the costs will be. Even a small venture can demand $100,000 or more to be properly capitalized. Conversely, many entrepreneurs overestimate start-up costs because they didn't make the effort to seek lower-cost alternatives.

The first step is the preparation of a detailed and itemized schedule of all the beginning assets required. For example, when I plan a retail operation, I divide inventory down into product lines, and can estimate within 5 percent what the actual beginning inventory will be. It's the same with fixtures and equipment, listing even items as small as office supplies.

The Small Business Administration (SBA) has prepared this excellent start-up costs worksheet (Figure 3.1). It lists several start-up costs frequently overlooked.

The shoestring objective at this point is twofold. First, you want to go through the detailed list of what you *think* you need and reduce it to what you *actually* need. There can be a substantial difference. The main characteristic of the shoestring venture is that it always begins on a Spartan note, confining assets to the bare essentials.

WORKSHEET NO. 1			
ESTIMATED MONTHLY EXPENSES			
Item	Your estimate of monthly expenses based on sales of $_____ per year	Your estimate of how much cash you need to start your business (See column 3.)	What to put in column 2 (These figures are typical for one kind of business. You will have to decide how many months to allow for in your business.)
Salary of owner-manager	Column 1 $	Column 2 $	Column 3 2 times column 1
All other salaries and wages			3 times column 1
Rent			3 times column 1
Advertising			3 times column 1
Delivery expense			3 times column 1
Supplies			3 times column 1
Telephone			3 times column 1
Other utilities			3 times column 1
Insurance			Payment required by insurance company
Taxes, including Social Security			4 times column 1
Interest			3 times column 1
Maintenance			3 times column 1
Legal and other professional fees			3 times column 1
Miscellaneous			3 times column 1
STARTING COSTS YOU ONLY HAVE TO PAY ONCE			Leave column 2 blank
Fixtures and equipment			Fit in worksheet 2 and put the total here
Decorating and remodeling			Talk it over with a contractor
Installation of fixtures and equipment			Talk to suppliers from who you buy these
Starting inventory			Suppliers will probably help you estimate this
Deposits with public utilities			Find out from utilities companies
Legal and other professional fees			Lawyer, accountant, and so on
Licenses and permits			Find out from city offices what you have to have
Advertising and promotion for opening			Estimate what you'll use
Accounts receivable			What you need to buy more stock until credit customers pay
Cash			For unexpected expenses or losses, special purchases, etc.
Other			Make a separate list and enter total
TOTAL ESTIMATED CASH YOU NEED TO START WITH		$	Add up all the numbers in column 2

Figure 3.1. SBA Start-Up Costs Worksheet

The second objective is to find ways to reduce each item cost to the absolute minimum. This is particularly so with fixtures, equipment, and leasehold improvements where there can be enormous price spreads. In Chapters 10 and 11, I show you specific ways to slash start-up costs on these items, but for the moment the strategy is to shop alternatives and price until you know what each item will stand you.

"Knowing your costs is the key to financial planning," advises Steve Carmoy, whose first business was an ice cream shop in a resort town. "My original estimates were that it would take $30,000 to equip the shop and another $12,000 to install plumbing, electrical, and leasehold improvements. Another $8000 was budgeted for signs and furniture. The $50,000 price tag came from talking to one fixture supplier, but it's only when I began to shop around that I found ways to cut costs to about $12,000. Used equipment was located for $7000 and the particular store I had in mind offered the plumbing and electrical service with very little additional cost. It's a different ball game when you're trying to put together a $12,000 deal compared to a $50,000 proposition."

Legwork is also the science of uncovering unanticipated costs. One dismal story involved a small manufacturer who scraped together the assets to produce an organic fertilizer, only to shut down when town officials required installation of a $150,000 waste converter to avoid pollution. Hidden start-up costs are an ever-present problem with manufacturing and technically oriented start-ups who face a host of regulatory requirements. For this reason I always suggest bringing in someone who knows the technical problems that may escape the entrepreneur unexperienced in the industry.

The same can be said of marketing costs. All too often an entrepreneur will accurately predict product demand while overlooking the capital really needed to push the product through the channels of distribution.

Lenders and investors may detect a business plan hurriedly rushed together without adequate homework and research. Typically it is a case of not uncovering all the costs or not putting a realistic price tag on them.

The well-capitalized firm can cope with a few unanticipated expenditures. Not so with the shoestring enterprise with a taut financial tightrope. Guesswork doesn't count. Know your costs.

Lesson #3: Put the Money Where it Counts

When you do have limited cash and borrowing power, the objective is to deploy them where they will do the most good. An over-expenditure in one area is likely to result in a forced underexpenditure in another.

Balancing investment between "fixed assets" (furniture, fixtures, and equipment) and "working assets" (inventory and working capital) requires special consideration with the shoestring enterprise. The successful start-ups throw as much money as possible into the working assets and as little as possible into fixed assets.

There are two reasons for this strategy. First, it's the working assets that create the lifeblood for the shoestring venture—sales and cash flow. The second reason is that the carrying costs on expensive fixtures are a fixed cost the struggling shoestring venture can well do without.

I have seen many start-ups, particularly in the retail trades, with the fanciest fixtures in town and reciprocally the least amount of inventory in town. The lesson is that customers buy inventory not fixtures. My philosophy has always been that I'd rather see twice the inventory on used fixtures instead of half the inventory on spanking-new fixtures.

Upgrading the physical plant can always come later when the business is on a more solid plane, but during the start-up stage your money should be in the assets that will work the hardest for you.

Lesson #4: Financing Is the Sum of its Parts

Financing a business is a misnomer. You never finance a business. What you do finance are the individual assets needed for the business. The sum of the parts always produces more financing dollars than could be achieved by financing the whole.

Consider financing much as you would a giant jigsaw puzzle—one small manageable piece at a time. The strategy allows you to exploit each asset for its maximum borrowing power.

And you'll be amazed to see how much of the venture is financed once the pieces come together.

The conventional financing path on a $100,000 venture is to borrow perhaps $50,000 to $60,000 from an institutional lender and add the difference from investment capital.

The shoestring strategy can't follow the conventional niceties. Leverage is putting together every financing block possible to build a total pyramid with few of your own dollars.

This has been the key to my own shoestring ventures. Using the schedule of assets needed for the start-up. I'll go down the list item by item asking, "What's the best way to finance this asset with the fewest upfront dollars?" Merchandise is a matter of wrangling trade credit from suppliers, as I discuss in Chapter 12. Fixtures and equipment go through the same exercise. For example, on a cash register I'll not only negotiate price, but negotiate to buy it on terms, lease, or financed through a finance company. However I do it, it typically means that I'm spending few or no upfront dollars.

As you go through this book, you'll see the various ways to exploit the credit potential of the assets needed in your business. Once you're fully familiar with all the sources of money that can take the place of your own cash, you may find that the available financing blocks come remarkably close to 100 percent of total start-up costs. Experience will not only let you design a 100 percent financed pyramid, but in many cases you'll have sources of financing actually competing for a place in the financial pyramid.

Only *after* you have exploited sources of credit offered by the respective assets should you consider institutional financing. For example, you may line up credit for 90 percent of the start-up costs through a potpourri of trade credit, leasing, or equipment financing, and be shy the 10 percent to complete the package and for working capital. Now you can reasonably borrow for these purposes and probably can borrow enough to create a healthy cash reserve.

That's one advantage of using bank financing as the capstone of your financial pyramid. Once you've amassed the assets with supplier credit, you can use bank financing for working capital. And that's when the sum of its parts can exceed the whole.

Lesson #5: Building the Best Financial Pyramid

Achieving 100% financing—or as close to it as you can reasonably come—is only one part of the strategy. You need a strong financial pyramid, and every building block has its own characteristics—its own advantages and disadvantages.

The trade-offs must be considered both from the point of view of the business and yourself. The ideal financing block will:

1. Provide the longest payback period.
2. Carry the lowest interest rates.
3. Require little or no collateral.
4. Demand no personal liability.

No one source of financing will display all these characteristics. Bank loans may give you an adequate payback period, but the downside is your personal liability and tying up the business assets as collateral. Supplier financing ordinarily won't involve personal liability but may require a speedy payback. Partnership funds will satisfy all these points but require you to give up a piece of the action.

Considering these conflicting characteristics, the objective is to shape each so that it both makes sense to the business and yourself. For example, I'm risk-conscious, so I won't take on more bank financing than I think the collateral can safely cover. My next objective is to select financing with the longest payback. For the shoestring venture, reducing cash flow demands is considerably more important than a slightly higher interest rate or whether the debt is secured. Supplier financing is conventionally short-term, but properly negotiated it may be an excellent source of long-term financing. But at what point is short-term debt still so excessive that you're forced to retrench either to more long-term bank financing or partnership funds with their own inherent disadvantages?

It's always a matter of profiling your interests with the business. Understand your priorities before you seek financing.

Lesson #6: Navigate by the Numbers

Cash flow controls every decision in the shoestring process. Cash flow is the name of the game and the only way to navigate during every stage of the start-up.

Don't be your own navigator. Preparing a legitimate cash flow projection takes both objectivity and competence. It's the role for your accountant. Your role is to make planning and operational decisions based on what fits within the cash flow framework.

A start-up without a carefully planned cash flow statement is a ship without a rudder and a compass. You neither know nor can control where you're heading. It explains why so many small ventures do fail. It's not a matter of being undercapitalized, but of failing to properly plan the undercapitalized operation.

While in broad terms the cash flow statement measures projected income against the outgo of cash (operating expenses and the paydown of debt), its initial function is to test the viability of the financial pyramid. Only the cash flow statement can tell you whether you're top-heavy on short-term debt, necessitating a switch to more long-term financing. You live by the numbers.

"Mastering the shoestring start-up is really a matter of mastering cash flow under the worst of circumstances," says David Dube, a management and financial consultant to small firms. "It's a twilight world of constantly trying to get money in so you stay ahead of what you're forced to pay out. When you achieve that constant objective—you survive. When you fail—you sink. It's all in knowing how to go about it."

I agree. A cash flow orientation takes the place of even a bottom line orientation during the start-up and survival stages. It's only when you're in the growth and stable periods that decisions can be made to enhance profits instead of cash flow. Entrepreneurs sometimes stumble over this one. They'll start a venture and every decision is directed to profits. Yet the decision that's right for the bottom line may be counterproductive from a cash flow viewpoint. The two don't always coincide. Only when the business becomes strangled does the entrepreneur become forced to focus on cash flow. By then, however, it may be too late.

That's the overview. Shoestring economics is the ability to master your own cash flow game. The next several lessons can show you how.

Lesson #7: Test the Timing

There's a right time and a wrong time to open a business. This is particularly true when the venture is cyclical in nature or in a seasonal location. And not surprisingly, many shoestring start-ups are small ventures in tourist areas or selling goods of a seasonal demand.

The ideal opening date is about one month before the peak selling season begins. The month's lag gives you time to work out operational problems before the bustle of the season, yet the launch coincides with the positive cash flow of high sales. And you need that positive cash flow to get you through the dry seasons.

While it may be common sense, many entrepreneurs overlook timing's importance and begin the business based on their own convenience or when a location becomes available. Bob Braunstein, a bankruptcy attorney practicing on Cape Cod, reports, "Any business can make it through a Cape Cod summer. But come October half the businesses are gone. It's amazing to see how many new bootstrap ventures quickly take their place and fold before they even reach the summer season."

I share the same observation. Many of the ventures that withered on the vine with an ill-timed start might have had the staying power if they started strong with a strong beginning cash flow. Momentum is the best word for it, and when you don't have the cash to play the waiting game you wait until you can bring in the cash.

Opening at the right time is only one part of the "timing" strategy. The second objective is to smooth out cash flow by structuring payments to coincide with income. For example, a business may open on Cape Cod and have plenty of money to cover expenses and financing payments. When you ride the crest of the wave there's always plenty of money to go around. Then the tide ebbs and cash slows to a trickle, but the heavy note payments continue. When the cash reserves are frittered away, the business heads for trouble.

Handling a cyclical business requires both planning and discipline to reap the harvest and save it for the off-season. Even squirrels know that much. It's a point overlooked by too many entrepreneurs. For this reason I suggest structuring note payments and other fixed obligations to parallel income. Few lenders will refuse and it can keep your cash flow on a steady course.

Lesson #8: Prime the Pump

Since your venture faces a cash drain from the moment you open your doors, make it a goal to build sales as rapidly as possible *before* you open as well as after you open.

Many ventures have an exceptionally slow sales curve. How long it will take to reach respectable (if not profitable) sales depends on the nature of your business, location, competition, and your own ability to prime the pump through promotion.

Of course, every sensible business person wants the fastest increase in sales. The difference with the shoestring entrepreneur is in what he or she will do to achieve it. More than an objective, it becomes a business-saving necessity.

When I opened a retail pharmacy, I estimated the business needed $6000 a week to break even and cover note payments. We couldn't wait the eight months or a year to gradually build sales. Up to our neck in debt, we had to quickly turn dollars. Every week was another promotion. Flyers advertised "specials" at our net cash price and coupons for a $5 savings on prescriptions. We probably lost 5 percent on sales, but we quickly grossed $10,000 to $12,000 a week. We could afford a paper loss of $500 a week, but what we couldn't afford was an income of $4000 a week while we were obligated to pay out $6000 a week. So our objective was to turn dollars.

Priming the pump before you open can pay dividends. It was handled the right way by a friend of mine who planned an awning installation business. Before he set up shop he had over 100 orders guaranteeing him a fast income of over $40,000. His cash flow began to roll the moment he opened his doors. It was smarter than opening his doors and chasing his first dollars while the bills began to mount.

Creating fast sales is so important that we allocate twice as many dollars to a launch promotion as is standard in the discount industry. Make your own commitment "to go after those fast nickels—particularly when you can't afford to wait for the slow dimes."

Lesson #9: Plan on a Lean Year

Since cash flow projections are only a "guesstimate" of what you *think* will come in, measured against what you know will be going out, it's wise to hedge by planning on a lean year.

Any cash flow statement can look rosy on paper if you want to be the confirmed optimist expecting to start with a boom. That's typically the anatomy of a failure. The entrepreneur says to himself, "The business will gross $500,000 the first year and $700,000 the second." With these self-deluding numbers in mind he takes on financing to match. One year later the venture sputters to a stop, grossing $200,000. Nine out of ten entrepreneurs are optimists, which explains why there are so many entrepreneurial ventures and so many entrepreneurial failures.

The right way to project sales is to ask yourself, "What's the *least* the venture can gross?" Make it a worst-case situation. Check industry averages and comparable businesses. You may be a better butcher, baker, or candlestick maker, but few of us are the geniuses to defy the odds.

Underestimating sales has a pleasant cure. You can always take surplus cash and reinvest for faster growth. The process is not reversible. Being locked in with excess financing and expenses predicated on higher sales requires either very understanding creditors or a journey to the Bankruptcy Court. Since the first is improbable and the latter unthinkable, plan on a *very* lean year.

Lesson #10: Don't Choke on Receivables

Few shoestring firms are sufficiently capitalized to sell on terms and wait for their money while watching accounts receivables build. It's the fastest way to strangle cash flow.

If your business is in an industry that typically sells on credit, this puts you at a decided competitive disadvantage. It may even be the controlling factor in not selecting a particular type of business—with plenty of justification.

Fortunately, most shoestring ventures are retail or service firms that can limit sales to cash. Manufacturing and distributing start-ups are another story. Their ability to finance the launch depends on their ability to either operate without extending credit—or make arrangements to finance the receivables.

The common method to finance receivables is by factoring the receivables to a factor who will pay you up front, while holding back a reserve for bad debts. Despite the liquidity the arrangement does offer, it still places an added strain on the thinly capitalized firm. Factoring receivables can be expensive both in terms of interest charges and bad debts that you eventually have to absorb. Cash receipts can still be delayed for 30 to 60 days while you wait for the factor to take over the receivables and pay you. And even a "hold-back" on 20 percent of the receivables as the factor's cushion for bad debts puts a sizable crimp in cash flow.

Lesson #11: Keep Fixed Costs Down

For the small start-up, fixed costs are dead weight. You can't afford them. To the extent possible, every dollar in expense should be directly tied to income. It's only when income and expenses follow parallel paths that the business escapes a cash drain.

Commission salespeople are safer than salaried. Direct ads with a measurable dollar pull are better than institutional ads that only add to good will. A rent based on a percentage of sales can preserve more capital during the survival stage than will a fixed rent. Every expense item has its own possibilities.

David Dube of Silverman & Co., a Boston CPA firm specializing in small business finance, counsels, "The strategy is always to open with the smallest committed overhead. From that point expenses can grow only when you have a favorable cost-volume relationship."

When I'm called in to rescue a start-up venture, my first step is to evaluate whether there's enough gross profit for the business to be viable. Assuming it has the right margin, the next step is to see how it's dissipating the difference. What I normally find is a venture pregnant with needless overhead expenses eating more dollars than the business can produce.

Above all, the one common characteristic of successful shoestring entrepreneurs is their "lean and mean" attitude. They seldom spend a nickel unless they're sure it will quickly produce a dime.

Lesson #12: Protect Gross Profits

Strategizing gross profits for the bootstrap firm must of necessity follow a different route than that of the well-financed counterpart who can afford to buy on better terms and price lower.

"What it comes down to," say Elliot Galahow, "is being smart enough to know you can't stand head-to-toe with a big boys and slug it out. You need a counterstrategy to corner a niche of your market that allows for higher prices and leaner inventories."

Many entrepreneurs go after increased sales—always a worthwhile objective—but give away too many profit points in the process. The business that should operate on a 35 percent profit structure finds itself crippled with a 20 percent profit on sales. Usually it's an entrepreneur who thinks he'll set the world on fire with the lower prices in town. While one eye is on sales that other isn't focused on gross profit. The profit given away seldom matches the sales increases.

There's always the temptation to recapture margins on discount prices by buying deals to save an extra 5 to 10 percent. The shoestring operation can't afford it, because it only builds inventory and further strangles cash flow already strained by a leveraged beginning inventory.

The priority must be on turnover and buying lean quantities so the goods move fast enough to pay for themselves. Set a minimum price spread that not only insures reasonable sales but also reasonable profits to cover overhead and note payments. Industry averages can show you what your right numbers should be. Try to maintain gross profits at least equal to the industry averages and improve turnover by 20 to 30 percent to give the business the best balance between profitability and turnover needed for cash flow.

Lesson #13: Cultivate Creditors

The shoestring enterprise rarely fails because it starts out with too much debt. It fails because the entrepreneur couldn't cultivate the creditors and put them on hold until the venture gained a financial foothold.

The undercapitalized firm has remarkable staying power. And it can stay alive with beginning debt that would have the financial experts shaking in their boots if it follows common sense strategies.

1. Intelligently structure debt from the beginning. The secret of the leveraged start-up is not the amount of debt you take on, but how long you have to pay it down. Financing an opening inventory on 100 percent trade credit terms becomes a problem only if the payback period isn't logically tied to a cash flow projection.
2. Don't let debt panic you. No matter how carefully you plan, you'll journey through the survival stage with desktops heaped with unpaid bills. It's the price you pay for using creditor money instead of your own to finance the start-up. The cure for your sleepless nights is the reality that the stack of bills is dwindling as cash flow and profits take hold.
3. Communicate with your creditors. Creditors will remain patient, provided you keep them abreast of the venture's progress. If you can't stay on schedule let them know about

it before you default. You may begin the venture with one idea on how the debts can be liquidated and be forced to renegotiate several times before the reality of the situation dictates how you *can* pay.

4. Future business and even a dribble of cash toward older bills can keep a creditor satisfied. Creditor problems become serious when you buy on credit only to shut them off and ignore what's owed.

5. When you lay your problems on the line with creditors, you'll have to accept the risk that one or more nervous creditors will go for the jugular and try to push you over the brink. Try to get your major creditors behind you. They can be very persuasive in controlling the smaller creditors who are likely to be more troublesome.

6. Set up a pecking order to give certain creditors priority. Essential overhead—rent, payroll, and utilities—always comes first. Next come payroll taxes. The IRS plays rough. Suppliers selling the essential lifeline merchandise for your business also stand at the head of the line. Banks and other lenders holding security also require priority because they do have the immediate remedy of foreclosure. Cash flow problems are invariably handled by delaying payments to secondary suppliers.

The goal of the shoestring entrepreneur is to make it through the survival stage, albeit under considerable pressure of trying to make ends meet. Many don't succeed because they can't find the path to a profitable business. Others manage to create a company heading in the right direction, but give up too easily under mounting creditor pressure. Staying power is the realization that drastic problems demand drastic solutions. Thousands of small struggling start-ups have made the grade only through a major restructuring of their debt. It may be an out-of-court composition settlement or a Chapter XI reorganization through the Bankruptcy Court, but saving the business may be a logical sequel to starting the business.

Lesson #14: Take Total Control

Most entrepreneurs, being creative types, dislike accounting and finances, preferring to make "seat of the pants" decisions or, as I sometimes say, "decisions from the gut," instead of from the cerebral cortex. Nobody who has been in business will suggest you can run a business entirely by computer, but when your margin of error is somewhere between slim and nonexistent—as it is with the shoestring enterprise—you hedge your decisions with numbers, numbers, and more numbers.

It's all part of taking control—knowing where you've been—where you're going, and how fast you're getting there. What controls will you need?

1. Cash flow statements head the list. Break it down by month, and project ahead at least a year in advance. These pro forma predictions are even more important than past performance records because they help you plan, spot problems, and devise solutions in advance.

2. Work up a tight budget for purchases and your controllable expenses. Without budgeting you're likely to overspend in these areas, destroying the validity of your cash flow projections and profit planning. Don't hesitate to adjust your budget as the conditions change. A new start-up may go through many "ups" and "downs" within a brief period, and you need a budget to control outgo, not restrict growth.

3. Calculate your break-even point. That's the magic number that tells you when the venture crossed the line and is making money. Your accountant can approximate your break-even point with very little work, and it then becomes your target. Plot your growth toward break-even. Monitor the sales curve. It's the easiest way to see if your business is heading in the right direction—and moving fast enough.

4. Profit and loss statements should be published monthly. You can't afford to wait for semi-annual or end-of-the-year reports. The start-up needs immediate corrective

action to cure excess expenditures, sluggish margins, or weak sales. Only up-to-date and timely statements can tell you where you've been and the steps necessary to keep you on track.

5. You should get a readable warning flag report. Program it into the sensitive areas of operations. At a minimum you want constant readouts on working capital, inventory levels, accounts receivable, accounts payable, orders on hand, slow collections, out-of-stock situations, and customer complaints. Keep your finger on the daily pulse of the venture to detect dangerous changes from the norm.

Having the right information is only one part of the equation. It has value only when turned into action. You'll make your mistakes, and the best reporting system won't change that. What it will do is keep your errors down to a manageable minimum.

Check out any small start-up that grows and thrives and pays its bills, and somewhere within you'll find someone who's something more than a creative entrepreneur with an idea. He or she may be one part Scrooge and one part Simon Legree, but it's someone who can keep a cold, calculated eye on the numbers and squeeze every nickel for all it's worth. It's intrinsic to all money management. When you're a shoestring entrepreneur and understand the economics of the situation you squeeze harder.

YOUR SHOESTRING ECONOMICS FINAL EXAM

You've been through a cram course. And there's plenty more to learn, but those lessons will be in the laboratory of your own small venture as you try to turn theory into practice. Are you ready for it? Try a quick pretest.

1. Review the business you have in mind. Is it within a range that's both attainable and desirable?
2. Do you know your true start-up costs, or are you just guesstimating?

3. Do you know how to deploy your capital among assets to create the healthiest start?

4. Are you ready to exploit each asset for its own borrowing power to achieve a shoestring start-up?

5. Do you know your priorities—and the priorities of the business—so you can build the best financial pyramid?

6. Have you tested your financing against cash flow projections?

7. Are you planning to open the business at the right time to quickly tap maximum cash flow?

8. Do you know the steps you'll take *before* you open and *after* you open to maximize sales and help the business to fast sales increases?

9. Have you based your financial projections on sheer optimism or the reality that you may have a lean year?

10. If you plan on selling on credit, have you tested whether you can support the receivables?

11. Are your fixed costs slashed to the rock bottom so you can operate "lean and mean"?

12. Do you have a solid policy of capturing sales without sacrificing needed profit margins?

13. Are you ready to do combat with creditors to keep the business afloat until it is healthy?

14. Are you ready to take total control so you can make "thinking cap" decisions?

Find some interesting answers?

4

STARTING SMART

Entrepreneurship is risk. Starting smart is the awareness that your venture has only a 20 percent chance of making it through the first five years, and taking shrewd steps to protect yourself from the contingency of failure before you start.

HOPE FOR THE BEST—
PREPARE FOR THE WORST

Who ever heard of planning for failure? Open any business book and you'll see rosy pictures of fat cats in plush penthouse suites sipping cognac and "wheeling and dealing" their way to a fortune. They're not the people I see in my office a year or two after they entered the business arena. What I see are discouraged, frightened people who have lost everything they owned and face the prospects of personal bankruptcy.

These people are invariably the full-time dreamers who only see the "benefit" side of the equation and never the "downside" risk. They ignore the possibility of failure until it's too late. Most dreamers don't start smart by taking at the outset the precautionary steps to protect themselves against a less than prosperous business future.

Realists, on the other hand, don't fall victim to the "rose-colored glasses syndrome." Instead they do everything possible to reduce their risks. Realists understand and prepare for possible defeat. They define and prune their potential losses. They objectively weigh the "benefit/risk" ratio of their deal and only move ahead when the possible gains outweigh what they stand to lose.

Whenever I journey into another venture, I pull out a pad of paper and draw a line down the center. In the left column I try to assess the possible financial gain from the deal. In the right column I list my investment and what I stand to lose if the deal goes sour. It's a form of playing "what if," as I try to assess the best and worst case. But I don't stop there. While you can never measure the equation with complete predictability, you can take positive steps to control loss.

Be objective. You have to look at yourself as one entity and the business as another. The relationship between the two must make economic sense. How many times have you seen eternal optimists mortgage their home to the hilt and cash in their savings to move into a start-up? How many ask themselves the two important questions: Can this business possibly provide sufficient return to risk what I am gambling? Are there steps I can take now to reduce what I can lose?

That's what this chapter is all about. It will show you how you can minimize risk because it will:

1. Keep your personal investment to a minimum, protecting what you do invest.
2. Protect valuable personal assets from hungry business creditors.
3. Free you from personal liability on business debts.
4. Put you in the best defensive posture so you, and not your creditors, have the upper hand if the business goes sour.
5. Keep your personal resources intact so you can bounce back and try again.

WHY A CORPORATION IS A MUST

Starting smart means choosing the correct form of business organization and no chapter on risk-reducing strategies would be complete without mentioning that greatest of risk-reducers—the corporation.

About 50 percent of all small businesses are operational as sole proprietorships or partnership forms of organization. Without the benefit of a corporate umbrella, these individuals are literally saying to their business creditors, "If my business doesn't pay your bill, you can come after my personal assets to satisfy the obligation." If you assemble all the nonincorporated entrepreneurs you'll be looking at a long line of dreamers. They never fail, so why do they need the protection of a corporation? Dream on.

If you were to review many of the personal bankruptcies, you'd find they were needlessly caused by the failure of the business person to incorporate. One of my first cases, fresh out of law school, involved a liquor store owner who operated his business for seven years as a proprietorship. His former attorney had said, "Why incorporate and go through the hassles of extra paperwork and tax returns?" It was costly advice several years later when his business finally failed with $200,000 in unpaid bills. With a few quick attachments the creditors had my client's home, and my client moved to a third floor walk-up apartment to ponder the most expensive advice he ever had—"Why incorporate?" It was the first of a long list of similar experiences.

Look at incorporation as just another form of insurance. You may pay $600 to $1,000 to incorporate initially (although later in this book I'll show you how to incorporate for far less), and you may have to pay your accountant another few hundred dollars a year to file corporate tax returns. But those modest premiums isolate and protect all the personal assets you have worked so hard over the years to accumulate. You can't find better insurance.

Every business book seems to dwell on the relative advantages and disadvantages of a corporation over other forms of organization. From my viewpoint it's no contest. The limited liability benefits of the corporation overshadow other considerations. Any attorney who disagrees is an attorney without broad experience in handling business failures.

Aside from the personal protection of a corporation, there are the other advantages. A corporation can provide valuable, tax deductible "fringes," including sick pay, medical and dental insurance, life insurance, and even travel and educational expenses. Workmen's compensation is another big benefit. The only way to obtain personal protection is by incorporating.

The advantages continue to mount. Unlike a partnership or proprietorship, a corporation continues after the death of its owner. No liquidation of the business is necessary. Do you want to bring in partners? Selling corporate stock is the cleanest way to divide ownership. Expansion? Only the corporation offers the flexibility to attract diverse types of financing.

This point is best discussed and decided by your accountant. As an attorney who has seen over 2000 entrepreneurial defeats, though, let me tell you—if you want to start smart, you'll start with a corporation.

SMALL INVESTMENTS MEAN SMALL LOSSES

While optimists always ask how much they can make from a venture, realists ask how much they can lose. And the answer, of course, is in how they formulate and control the investment decision.

That too is what starting smart is all about. Shoestring ventures are not only the creation of entrepreneurs with few dollars to invest, but are equally the creation of people who can invest more but intentionally choose to start with less because they want to risk less.

But even shoestring entrepreneurs can lose a bundle when they lose sight of their objective and begin to make irrational investment decisions. Typically their investment policy is ill-defined to begin with and totally abandoned once the business is under way. It's easier to throw money rather than objectivity into the cash-hungry start-up.

"Unbridled enthusiasm can wreck you financially," admits Pat Dwyer, who parlayed an expected $10,000 investment into a $125,000 loss. Pat's story? "I had my sights on starting a small Syrian-style restaurant in a Detroit suburb. My initial $10,000 investment estimate was workable because I had a fixture company who would lease me the equipment on near 100 percent terms.

But then you become like a kid in the candy store. I decided to upgrade the decor and throw more money into advertising. So my initial investment of $10,000 very quickly became a $28,000 investment. Sluggish sales caused me to mortgage my home for $75,000 to cover operating losses. A start-up can absorb money like a sponge if you let it, and to keep the business afloat I threw in another $60,000 or more over two years before running out of money or ideas on how to get the business off the ground."

It's too common a story. And it's not hindsight or playing "Monday morning quarterback." Uncontrolled losses are always the result of uncontrollable optimism.

The intelligent approach to the investment decision is to focus on four questions *before* you start the venture.

1. How much *can* you invest?
2. How much *should* you invest?
3. How much *will* you invest?
4. *When* will you invest more?

Let's see if we can help you find your right answers with the four-step process.

1. *How Much Can You Invest?*
   This helps define what you're prepared to lose on a venture. Contrary to what many entrepreneurial books suggest, starting smart is not exposing all your personal assets to risk but gambling only with what you can realistically afford to lose. I handle it by dividing my assets into the classical "touch" and "don't touch" piles. For example, I'll confine my entrepreneurial investments to only 25 percent of my liquid assets. That's the formula I'm comfortable with, but you need your own formula. Once you set aside precisely what you are prepared to risk, you know your maximum investment capability while preserving your fall-back position. Setting limits is the only way to control losses.
2. *How Much Should You Invest?*
   Within the limits of what you can afford to risk is the decision of what the business can justify as an investment. Consider

the return on investment the business can offer and make certain it bears a rational relationship to the capital at risk. Many entrepreneurs make sizable investments only to discover the low earning power of the venture. Others understand the financial return won't quite measure up, but go ahead because the business offers psychic enjoyment or a better lifestyle. It's a fair trade-off if that's all you expect from the business. When financial return is important, your goal should be a minimum of 25 percent annual return on investment. The inherent risk of a small business doesn't justify less. What price tag would you put on your venture?

3. *How Much Will You Invest?*

What the business can logically justify as an investment and what you *will* invest are two different numbers. The goal is to prune investment to the smallest possible amount. Cutting investment not only cuts losses but provides a better return on what you do invest. In many of my own ventures I'll target the optimum investment at perhaps $10,000 to $15,000 and then see how I can accomplish the start-up goal with absolutely no money of my own. Why not? Every dollar you invest is a dollar you might lose. Starting smart means investing as little of your own money as possible.

4. *When Will You Invest More?*

Over-investment is most likely to occur after the business is in operation. Many shoestring entrepreneurs start the venture with a reasonably small and prudent investment only to throw caution to the wind as they continuously feed the cash-hungry enterprise. Starting smart is to define the criteria for a later capital infusion.

It takes tremendous discipline to deprive a thinly capitalized business of more owner-provided capital. As Pat Dwyer discovered, you can't succumb to the pressures of what the business needs, but must keep your eye on what is justified investment.

One reason to invest small initial capital is to hold further funds in reserve, feeding them slowly and judiciously to the enterprise once it shows promise. Admittedly, the decision on whether to feed or starve the business is the most difficult of all management decisions. You wonder whether it's "good money after bad," or whether the few extra dollars will propel the business over the start-up hurdles on its way to success.

The only approach to the problem is to set performance standards that can justify adding more working capital. Before I start a venture I project sales. If the business is at or close to its targeted goal, I may loosen my pocketbook to release a few more dollars, but my eyes are always on the financial indicators. If the venture looks like a loser the investments stop. That's the one cardinal error of so many shoestring entrepreneurs. Rather than admit defeat, they think that adding money is the cure. It's expensive medicine.

PROTECT YOUR INVESTMENT

No matter how little you do invest, once you have put together your creative financing package, the next step is to protect even that modest investment so you can recoup it should the business fail.

And there is a right and wrong way to invest money in your own business. The wrong approach is to use your entire investment to buy shares in the corporation. Assume your investment is $20,000. Your investment would be characterized as "equity" or "capital contribution." Should your business fail, you can only recoup investment after all creditors have been fully paid. Considering its improbability, your plight becomes obvious.

Starting smart is splitting your investment so you use a small fraction of the investment to buy the shares, while loaning the balance to the corporation. Not only does this give you creditor status against your own business, but you can repay yourself the loan without taxable consequence, except for the interest charges.

The very best way to protect your investment is to loan the money to the corporation on a secured basis. By holding a mortgage on the business you are the first to be repaid should the business turn sour. With 70 to 90 percent of your investment secured, you have very little to lose.

This strategy requires careful planning. Don't lend the money directly to the corporation. Bankruptcy decisions have disallowed stockholder loans, granting priority to "arm's-length" creditors. The right way to handle it is to lend the money to a close friend or relative who in turn loans the money to the business, taking back a mortgage. Should the business fail, your mortgage-holding relative would be repaid and could then repay his loan to you. A loan from a friendly intermediary is safe, provided he can prove he actually loaned the money.

This strategy is perfectly legal. Should the idea of putting your own economic interest ahead of your creditors shock your conscience, that's morality, not business. You follow your own conscience; however, starting smart will at least give you a choice. Review this point with your attorney and accountant.

ASSETS YOU NEVER HAVE TO LOSE

Turn to the bankruptcy auction pages and scan some of the ads. Look closely at the assets going under the hammer. Many valuable assets could have been saved had the owners used common sense by placing title to the assets in their own name rather than under the business.

Frequently you'll find entrepreneurs prematurely transferring valuable personal assets to their start-up corporation, needlessly exposing the assets to risk of loss should the business fail. It happened recently to a young engineer who developed a patented circuit breaker component and decided to go into business manufacturing the item. Several years later the business folded, and since the patent was now the asset of the corporation, it was sold by the Bankruptcy Trustee for $140,000 to satisfy creditor claims. The shrewd buyer immediately licensed the rights to the product and is now collecting over $30,000 a year in royalties. Had the engineer started smart he would have personally retained ownership of the patent and licensed it to his own corporation. Had he done so he would now be the one collecting the royalty checks.

Business people seldom consider the point, but a transfer of a personally owned asset to the business is the same as a cash investment. It's still an asset at risk. The more common error is made when new assets are acquired. That's when the decision must be made as to whether it's best to buy the asset through the corporation or instead buy it personally and lease it to the corporation.

One entrepreneur who started smart was Cal Sullivan. Cal's venture was a small printing plant in an industry noted for its high failure rate. The key to his operation was a sophisticated piece of high-speed printing equipment that cost $60,000. Cal purchased the equipment in his own name for $15,000 down, financing the balance. He then leased the equipment to his printing corporation for a fair monthly rental fee. Five years later the printing plant collapsed under $100,000 in debt, but all Cal had to do was go in and repossess the machine that now had a $30,000 equity.

In many start-up situations, the tax considerations are the deciding factor in whether an asset will be personally or corporately owned. Frequently an accountant will suggest personal ownership of depreciable assets because it does provide the best tax breaks to the entrepreneur. From my experiences the deciding factor should not be the tax angles but the risk of loss should the business fail. Only in later years, when the business is stabilized, should the decision be based on taxes.

Look over your own situation. If your corporation plans on acquiring real estate, high-cost equipment, motor vehicles, or even a valuable intangible asset such as a patent, trademark, or copyright, starting smart may mean personal, not corporate, ownership of these assets.

SIDE-STEPPING DANGEROUS GUARANTEES

Starting smart means reducing the risk of personal liability and loss by side-stepping personal guarantees. When you are on the personal hook to creditors, it's very much part of the risk side of the equation.

As a shoestring entrepreneur, you may achieve your number one goal of risking little investment capital and still face a mountain of personal obligations should the business fail. Your second objective, then, is to confine the debts to the corporation.

Creditors, for their part, have the annoying habit of always pushing personal guarantees under your nose. Who can blame them? They know that if they extend credit to your corporation, they severely limit their options in the event it goes bust. They're always happier when they have a shot at your personal assets. That's why they want your personal signature on the dotted line.

When I was in law school I had a cantankerous but wise professor who defined a guarantor as an "optimistic moron with a fountain pen." Twenty years and 2000 cases later, I must confess that more times than not his definition fit.

Personal guarantees are an integral part of entrepreneurial life. Banks and other institutional lenders won't lend to a small start-up corporation without the owner's guarantee. Suppliers are equally wary of the new venture without a credit history to rely on. This leaves you in the position of deciding beforehand just how far out you're willing to stick your neck to back up business obligations.

Poverty can be a friend of the shoestring entrepreneur with few assets to lose. The well-heeled entrepreneur is the one with hard decisions to make as he measures the maximum personal exposure he'll submit to.

I look at investment and risk on guarantees collectively in weighing the total risk factor for the venture. For example, I may invest $10,000 in cash and be personally bound on $15,000 in guaranteed debt. The downside on the deal is realistically $25,000. It comes back to the question of whether it's an amount you can afford to lose.

There are several steps you can take to reduce your personal exposure.

1. Structure your financing the right way. In Chapter 6, you'll see the correct procedures in greater detail, but the approach to take is to make certain the bank (or other lenders) loan the money to the business and secure the debt with a mortgage on business assets. In the event the business fails, the bank is first to get paid, decreasing your exposure on

the note. Second, make certain the liquidation value of the collateral is comparable to the balance owed to the bank on the note. You don't want business assets yielding the bank only $30,000 if the note shows a balance of $50,000. They'll chase you for the $20,000 and that's when guarantees become dangerous.

2. If you take on partners, make certain they also sign the guarantees. This is particularly important to remember if your partners come on board after you guarantee the note. Your partners enjoy the benefits of the business so why not the risk? Another point to consider is the ability of your partners to pay equally on a guarantee. You don't want to be the one with the deepest pockets left to pay the creditors. I can tell you one sad story of a 25 percent owner of a restaurant who guaranteed an $86,000 loan without "bothering" the other three partners. You guessed it. When the restaurant failed, his partners walked away, leaving him to satisfy the debt. Overlooking the common sense points can spell financial disaster.

3. Risk is a decided factor in shopping suppliers. Some suppliers will insist on a guarantee while others won't. From my viewpoint, I'll always go with a supplier willing to gamble on the business alone, even if his price is slightly higher or other terms less attractive. If you want to substantially reduce your risk, you'll shop around, negotiate, and even bluff suppliers—but you won't put your signature on their guarantees.

4. Learn the negotiating points to avoid guarantees. A supplier may be willing to accept a mortgage on business assets in place of a guarantee. It's a wise trade-off. If you must, provide a guarantee and then insist on the supplier accepting a mortgage to shield you from excess exposure. Conversely, you may be able to bypass a guarantee by negotiating a smaller credit limit. You may also agree to a postal guarantee confining your liability to a fixed amount.

5. Make it your policy never to guarantee an *existing* corporate debt. Why should you? You have nothing to gain.

When your shoestring venture falls behind in supplier
payments, credit managers will chase you for a guarantee
to solidify their position, and that's when the unwitting
entrepreneur is most likely to place his or her personal assets on the line.

6. Always monitor your risk. If you have personal guarantees
    outstanding and the business shows signs of a false start,
    then begin to think of reducing risk by reducing the per-
    sonally guaranteed debts. Your objective is to pay them
    before the business collapses so they (and ultimately you)
    will incur no loss.

Entrepreneurship may be risky, but it doesn't have to be a
game of excess risk. And the distinctions between the two are
your guarantees.

HOW DEEP ARE YOUR POCKETS?

Smart players realize that no amount of care or caution can prevent personal liability and lawsuits from following them home
once they've closed down a defunct business.

You never know what creditors will come knocking on your
door. It may be creditors holding your personal guarantees or
the IRS chasing you for unpaid withholding taxes. It may even
be your partners with an invented claim against you. In fact, it's
a rarity when an entrepreneur can shutter a business without a
few skeletons lurking in its closet.

So starting smart is starting poor and staying poor so would-be
creditors can't find any personal assets to take once the lawsuits
begin. The strategy is to "judgment proof" yourself by deploying
your assets so they always lie beyond the grasp of creditors. You
may be a multimillionaire, but if none of your assets is in your
name, you enjoy the financial vulnerability of a pauper.

Whenever I represent an entrepreneur about to embark on a
business venture, my very first move is to "judgment proof" him
or her so personal assets are fully protected no matter what happens in their business pursuits.

People are surprised to find there are numerous—and perfectly legal—ways to insulate what they own from business disaster.

Looking ahead and planning for the contingency of failure is the key. As I write this book I'm wrestling with the problems of a businessman who stands to lose over $300,000 in personal assets because he never did quite plan for defeat. As a partner in a mid-sized manufacturing plant going through liquidation, he now knows what trouble really is. As typically happens, the business fell behind in federal and state taxes, and he now has over $200,000 in tax liens against his property. A creditor holding a $50,000 guarantee has an attachment on his bank account and on his vacation cottage. Several other creditors are suing him personally on $20,000 to $30,000 for bad checks and are also moving in to attach his property. In the final tally my beleaguered client will lose virtually everything he worked so hard to accumulate over the years.

Could it have been avoided? Certainly. Had he started smart he could have:

1. Deeded his home or cottage into a real estate trust that he could control as trustee. As trust property it would have been free from creditor attack.
2. Taken advantage of the homestead laws provided by many states. These laws protect all or a share of the equity from creditor claims if you follow the requisite steps.
3. Transferred stocks, bonds, and even cash to either a trust or perhaps a specific corporation set up for that purpose.

These are only a few of the common techniques available to achieve the goal of staying rich while you appear poor. On paper you should look so poor that creditors are more likely to send sympathy cards than subpoenas. The quickest way to defuse a rambunctious creditor is to convince him he's spinning his wheels, chasing a worthless judgment.

Timing is critical. Don't expect to incur substantial debts and try to protect your assets two days before the sheriff comes calling. Creditors can successfully claim it is a fraudulent transfer and set aside the conveyance. That's why you judgment proof yourself *before* you go into business and incur debts.

Discuss this with your counsel. Request that he or she take all necessary steps to protect and insulate what you own. Nothing obligates you to be a debtor with deep pockets. You can legally, safely, and morally shield your assets. Starting smart means having nothing to lose.

YOUR STARTING SMART SELF-EXAM

It's time to test yourself. Take a few moments and review your situation, then ask yourself these questions:

1. Did you look at both sides of the coin, preparing for success *or* failure?
2. Do the potential benefits of the deal outweigh the risks?
3. Have you taken every known step to keep your investment as low as possible?
4. Will you operate your business as a corporation?
5. Is your investment to be protected by a loan against business assets?
6. Have you defined the maximum liability you will accept as a guarantor of business debts?
7. Have you taken all the steps to reduce liability on personal guarantees?
8. Have you defined the assets you will own in your own name rather than under the business?
9. Have you protected your personal assets by judgment proofing yourself?
10. Have you carefully reviewed these points with your attorney and accountant?

If you answered "no" to any of these questions, you have work to do. It won't take long to prepare for the worst. Then you can spend all your waking moments planning and working for success.

5

PREPARE A WINNING BUSINESS PLAN

A well-prepared business plan is mandatory when dealing with prospective investors or lenders. The first thing they look for is a complete, concise, and thorough business plan for your shoe-string venture.

You may tire of hearing about the necessity for planning when starting or expanding a business, but the importance of a sound business plan cannot be over-emphasized. It is essential if you are to have any chance for obtaining business financing. Yet the sad truth is that most people poorly plan their business ventures. Frequently it doesn't occur to them how a business plan can help. Let this chapter guide you through the intricacies of developing a sound business plan.

A GOOD BUSINESS PLAN
CAN BE YOUR ROADMAP TO SUCCESS

The process of creating a solid business plan forces you to take a realistic, objective, and detached look at your business in its entirety. It is important to see your venture as a whole. Most people who have business ideas deal with them in an unorganized manner. Designing a detailed business plan gives you the opportunity to evaluate your business logically and in more concrete terms.

A business plan is also an operating tool that will help you better manage your business and work toward its success. The final, completed plan is the chief tool for communicating your ideas to others—the SBA, business people, bankers, partners, and other potential financiers. If you seek financing for your business, the plan is the foundation for your loan proposal.

Moreover, by taking an objective look at your business, you can identify areas of strength and weakness. You can pinpoint your needs or highlight details you might normally overlook. A good business plan will give you enough information to help you spot problems before they arise. In sum, planning helps you determine how you can best achieve your business goals as it allows you to:

1. Identify precise objectives.
2. Develop clear strategies to meet those objectives.
3. Red-flag problems (and suggest ways to solve them).
4. Create a structure for your business by defining activities and responsibilities.
5. Obtain the necessary financing to start your business.

Many people use their business plan only to obtain financing. Nevertheless, a business plan provides information needed by those who will evaluate your venture for other purposes as well.

There are many types of lenders and investors, but you won't obtain financing from any of them unless they're confident that your business is going to be both secure and profitable. Keep in mind that lenders have not been thinking about your business as you have. They are seeing it on paper for the first time. You must therefore present a plan that clearly, succinctly, and reasonably gives them confidence that you're going to make money, not lose it.

Once people reach the point of needing a business plan, they usually have already thought about the money needed to start their venture. These entrepreneurs generally share two common problems: They desperately need financing, and they face the frustration of rejection by conventional lending resources. Large lenders do not anxiously seek small businesses to finance.

Moreover, shoestring entrepreneurs seldom have either the time or the financial expertise to find the right sources or package their business plans in a manner that will convince such lenders to finance them. Still, whatever type of lender you finally find, you must first present a cogent business plan, regardless of the type of financing you seek.

A good business plan can be therapeutic. Once you thoroughly research and put your business plan together, you will have at your fingertips an enormous amount of valuable financial and operational information about your business, which promotes business knowledge and thus confidence. Confidence, in turn, promotes enthusiasm and makes you a convincing salesperson for your business. The bottom line is that if you're going to use your business plan for the purpose of raising money, you must be able to sell your idea, your plan, and your business enthusiastically. If you don't know everything about your venture—all the ins and outs, ups and downs, pros and cons—you're not going to be the super-salesperson you must be. This doesn't mean you have to be a super-salesperson to obtain financing, but the owner of any business must be able to talk benefits and risks to a financier in an intelligent, convincing, and straightforward manner. Anyone can achieve this level of know-how once he or she has diligently worked through a business plan.

Take the time to put your plan together correctly. Some people take weeks, others months. If you work full-time, you'll find it's almost impossible to put a plan together quickly, because it takes time and effort if you're serious about your business and plan it thoroughly and wisely.

If you're at the planning stage for your business, a good plan will, first and most important, tell you if your business idea makes sense. It can also reveal whether there is enough net profit in your idea to make it an enterprise worth time or investment and hence worth pursuing. A business plan will force you to analyze your market from your perspective as a business operator as well as from your potential customer's point of view. You must determine the potential demand for the product or service you plan to offer and whether you can competitively provide that product or service. Your plan should disclose whether your idea has a reasonable chance of succeeding in the marketplace. Finally, a business plan can help you decide whether you're physically, mentally, and emotionally capable of taking on the chore of setting up, running, and operating such a business, over the long term. Once you know more about the business, you know more about what the business will demand of you.

In review, the business plan, first, can be used to develop ideas about how the business should be conducted. Second, a plan is a retrospective tool against which you can assess the company's actual performance over time. Third—and most obvious—a business plan will help you raise money. Think about your business plan with those purposes in order of priority and your business plan will indeed be your roadmap to success.

HOW TO DESIGN YOUR BUSINESS PLAN

If you read a well-written business plan, you'll find it to be comprehensive, with the information grouped into logical sections so the reader can find precisely the information needed.

A strong business plan holds few surprises for its reader. It conforms to generally accepted guidelines concerning form and content. Aside from the introductory material, a business plan typically has 10 to 13 sections. Each section includes specific elements to clarify your business goals. The following is the basic recommended organization of a plan for submission to the Small Business Administration, but it can be successfully used for any plan:

1. Cover page
2. Statement of purpose and summary
3. General description of business
4. Market analysis
5. Market strategy
6. Design and development plans
7. Operations plan
8. Management structure
9. Timetables and schedules

10. Financial data
11. Supporting information

Each of these sections may be organized according to the following outline:

1. *Cover Page*
  a. Name of company and status
  b. Address
  c. Phone number
  d. Submitted to (personalized for each lender)
  e. Prepared by, or person to contact

2. *Statement of Purpose and Summary*
  a. Company name and type
  b. Amount of financing needed
  c. How the money will be used
  d. Impact of financing on the business
  e. How the plan will be implemented

3. *General Description of the Business*
  a. Industry
  b. Specific type of business
  c. Products or services
  d. Age and growth
  e. Success factors

4. *Market Analysis*
  a. Customers
  b. Market size and trends
  c. Competition
  d. Estimated market share and sales
  e. Market opportunities

5. *Marketing Strategy*
  a. Overall plan
  b. Pricing
  c. Sales
  d. Customer service
  e. Distribution
  f. Advertising and promotion

6. *Design and Development Plans*
    a. Product status
    b. Development risks
    c. Product improvement and new products
    d. Impact on business
7. *Operations Plan*
    a. Location
    b. Equipment needs
    c. Distribution
    d. Personnel
8. *Management Structure*
    a. Organization
    b. Key personnel and background
    c. Compensation
    d. Professional advisors
9. *Timetables and Schedules*
    a. Growth plans
    b. Overall schedule
10. *Financial Data*
    a. Personal capital to be invested
    b. Application of proceeds
    c. Break-even analysis
    d. Balance sheet
    e. Projected two-year cash flow analysis
    f. Projected five-year profit and loss statement
    (For existing businesses, additional)
    a. Current audited financial statement
    b. Tax returns for prior three years
    c. Any other significant historical information
11. *Supporting Information*
    a. Letters of intent
    b. Purchase orders
    c. Letters of recommendation
    d. Job descriptions
    e. Newspaper and magazine clippings
    f. Special awards, achievements

MAKING YOUR BUSINESS PLAN COME ALIVE

Prepare yourself well to develop your business plan. This means intensive research. You must think about the type of business you have, your needs, and what is critical to the success of your business, as well as your overall goals. Be sure, for example, to say not only how much financing will be needed but when. Mention time frames when you talk about targets. Be clear about the scope and limit of your business: financial, manufacturing, distributing, marketing, retailing, wholesaling. For example, if your plan is oriented toward operations, explain your goals for research and development, engineering, manufacturing, and distribution. Consider your marketing—advertising, promotion, and sales force. In general, ask the tried-and-true research questions—who, what, where, when, why, how—and then add how much.

Complete your research before you write your plan. Begin by gathering a range of information about your industry in general and the business in particular. Keep yourself open to discovery. You may slightly shift your business emphasis as you discover new facts.

Talk to prospective competitors and others in the business you plan to enter. Of course, choose business owners who aren't directly competitive. Perhaps they serve a different geographic area or sell products or services to a market slightly different from yours. This network of competitors who can become business confidants is not difficult to find, but you may have to call several people before finding those who will candidly discuss business.

Trade associations serving your industry can be of assistance. Many such organizations publish trade magazines or journals. You can find associations suited to your needs by checking the *Encyclopedia of Associations,* found in most libraries. Trade associations are as near as your telephone.

When preparing your plan it's important to give yourself time and privacy so you can do some creative thinking. Once you have gathered information and know quite a bit about your business, give yourself sufficient time to build the facts into a sound, clearly stated business strategy. This is your opportunity to set up your

planning goals, develop a marketing outline, and prepare an operations outline and financials. Only then can you decide what kind
of money you'll require, when you're going to borrow it, and the
time frame you'll need to break even and repay your financing. An
important fact to keep in mind when preparing your plan is that
you will not necessarily be writing it in the same order that it is
presented. Handle the basics first; the details can come later.

Cover Page

A business plan should have a cover. Make it neat and of adequate size to hold your material. Include a title page also and
place on it the name of the business, the name(s) of its principals, and the business address and phone number. Consider
dressing up your title page with a professional or businesslike
logo. Why not personalize the cover for the particular lender it
will be presented to? Doing so adds dramatically to its impact.

Statement of Purpose and Summary

Next comes a statement of purpose and summary. The summary provides the reader with an overview of your plan and
the financing you require. This is very important. All too often, the financing needs are buried in the middle of the plan.
Make clear what you are asking for in the statement summary.
Although the statement of purpose cannot be completed with
actual numbers until you've calculated your capital requirements, you can write a draft sentence with the numbers to be
filled in later. The summary should state the nature of the
business; the legal form of operation (sole proprietorship,
partnership, corporation, limited partnership); the amount
and purpose of the loan being requested; the repayment
schedule requested; the equity contributed by the borrower;
and the equity-debt ratio after the loan, security, or collateral
is offered. You see the idea. Make it easy for lenders to learn
your wants and capabilities so they can determine their interest immediately and waste neither your time nor theirs if your
business is not a suitable investment for them.

Whether the plan is to be used for financial or operations purposes, its statement of purpose should be kept short and businesslike, preferably no more than a page. It can be longer depending on the size of the loan or how complicated the use of funds may be, but try to condense what you have to say.

With more financially oriented business plans, the statement of purpose might include a table that shows how loan proceeds will be distributed, as well as the source and the use of funds.

Following the statement of purpose is the table of contents. You will ordinarily prepare this last, but be aware that you do need to include one. When others look over your plan, they should be able to find specific information quickly.

Before we get into a detailed description of the business plan, notice that the table of contents follows the statement of purpose. This is important. When you open your plan you first see the cover sheet with the name of the business. Turn the page, and the summary statement of purpose appears—not your table of contents. You can readily see that it's necessary to have a detailed table of contents, but you should first give the reader some idea of the business itself, in the summary, before presenting potentially confusing numbers and facts. Once the business is summarized and the reader knows what you want, it becomes logical for him or her to next read the entire plan or turn to specific sections of greatest interest.

With the statement of purpose completed, you are ready to begin writing the core of your plan.

General Description of the Business

Is the business a middle-of-the-road concept or specialized? Is it a start-up, a franchise, buyout, or an expansion? Describe the industry in which your business will be involved. Include its present outlook as well as its future possibilities. Discuss all the various market segments within the industry, including any new products or developments that will benefit or adversely affect your business.

Classify your business and note whether it's a wholesale, retail, manufacturing, or service-oriented operation. State the status of the business—existing or new—and its form—sole proprietorship, partnership, limited partnership, or corporation.

If you are buying a business, describe it thoroughly. Detail when it was started, who started it, why they are selling, and how you can improve the business.

State the business operating days and hours. Mention seasonal fluctuations and how you will address the manpower variations and other pitfalls they present.

Remember, at this point you want an overview rather than a detailed description of the products or service you intend to market.

Market Analysis

Obtain the required information for a market analysis by conducting a thorough market survey. Many published sources provide market-related information, and there may be a statistical study already published that offers exactly what you need to know about the business you're planning. You need to make a judgment about how complete, accurate, and specific your data is. Typically, one informational source leads to others. Use those most suited to your needs and cross-check them.

There is a multitude of government reports available to you. Other sources include advertising agencies, market research firms, and banks. After you've checked out these secondary sources, consider whether you need to do your own direct market research to verify or complete the data you need.

Inform the lender about your specific customer base. Who are the potential customers for your product or service? Where are they located? What are their characteristics? What is the size of your market? What percentage of that market is yours? How will you attract and keep your market share? Is the market growing or shrinking? How volatile or stable is your market?

Carefully research your market. Specify the aggregate statistics for your business from published accounts of the industry. Emphasize the growth potential of your specific market or other favorable demographic factors.

Once you determine that your market can adequately support

your business and make it profitable, check out your competition. List your four or five nearest competitors, and include their business names and addresses. Your competition is often a better source of information than any library or consultant because through your competitors you can see firsthand how the industry operates. This is useful not only to those who will be reading and evaluating your plan but also to you. Learn from those who have traveled the road before you.

Answer several important questions. How do your competitors' operations differ from the one you plan? How can yours improve upon theirs? How successful are they? Talk to their suppliers. Talk to their customers. Talk to their business neighbors. Are their operations steady? Are they increasing or decreasing? Why? What are the strengths and weaknesses of each major competitor? What can you do to take advantage of their weaknesses? How will their weaknesses work to your advantage?

Use the results of the competition analysis to highlight how your business will differ from your competition and how your operation will give you greater profits. You may imitate your competitors, or you may improve on them while avoiding their errors. Tell why and how you will do so. As you discuss your competition, reveal one or two competitive businesses that perhaps aren't doing well. Rather than scare a lender, such candor will show you're a realist and recognize that some businesses don't perform as well as others. This is your opportunity to show how you will outperform your competition.

Be specific when you show how you will give your business a competitive edge. For example, your business may be better than the others because you will supply a full line of products; competitor A doesn't have a full line. You're going to provide service after the sale; competitor B doesn't offer such support. Your merchandise will be of higher quality. You'll give a moneyback guarantee. You'll provide parts and labor for up to 90 days after the sale. Remember, your company must offer a competitive advantage if it is to penetrate an already competitive market, and bear in mind that few markets are anything but competitive.

Marketing Strategy

If your market research has been completed properly, you should have at your fingertips the foundation for your overall business strategy. Begin with a brief summary of your marketing analysis and cover a minimum of three years.

The overall plan sets the marketing policy. It conveys to the lender exactly how you will proceed with your marketing effort, what tactics you will utilize, and what is different about your business that will enhance its acceptance in the marketplace.

Investors will also want information about pricing in this section of the plan. Factors influencing your pricing strategies include the type of operation you have—wholesale, retail, up-scale, and so on. It's important to be knowledgeable about pricing structures in your industry, and to be able to justify your particular pricing policies. Provide commission structures and short-term as well as long-term plans, and cite examples of your competitors' pricing practices.

A selling schedule and sales budget will come in handy in this section. It will help you illustrate when sales will begin, delivery time, marketing costs, and any projected slowdowns.

Depending on the type of business you enter, customer service may be of great importance to your marketing efforts, or of no importance whatsoever. Customer service includes return policies, warranty periods, or guarantees. Emphasize these points as marketing tools when they are essential to the success of your venture.

To round out your marketing effort, describe the most appropriate forms of advertising and the type of promotions you plan. Advertising and promotion are too important to any business to be ignored. It may be that your promotional program alone makes your business unique and attractive as an investment.

Don't attempt to detail the exact costs of advertisements or the expense of a promotional campaign in this section, but do provide an estimated advertising budget and a breakdown of the various media you will utilize in your advertising campaign.

Design and Development Plans

If you have already developed a product or a service concept and have all the components at a point you consider marketable, then this section will not be necessary.

Be prepared in this section to discuss not only the status of your product or service concept but also any costs associated with the production of the finished products, timelines for completion, and any foreseeable problems that may be encountered in the development of your business. Always let potential lenders know the current status of your product or service concept.

If you have developed the idea but not the product, or have plans to improve an existing product, or if you are a growing company with plans to introduce a new product, this section will be extremely important to the business plan. Investors will want to know the development progress of any product or service concept, costs associated with making it a marketable item, and the estimated time it will take to bring it to market. Be certain to pinpoint patent rights or other legal steps taken to protect any proprietary rights.

Operations Plan

Your primary objective in the operations section will be to describe how your proposed company will conduct its business. You need to discuss such factors as what will be required in the location of the physical plant, the equipment required, and the purchase and management of inventory. In sum, outline how the business will come together and how it will function on a daily basis.

This part of the business plan is very important because it illustrates your philosophy and shows the operating policies for your business. Your reader can thus see the direction your business will take over the next several years, which means that everything else in your plan must be consistent with these plans. Anyone lending money will look for consistency, and the basis for that consistency is contained in the description of how the business will operate in light of the objectives it hopes to achieve.

Within this section include a thorough location analysis, particularly if you plan a retail business. This is essential to a strong business plan. Begin the analysis by stating exactly where you plan to establish your business or where it is presently located if it is an ongoing operation. Note the community within which the business will be located, the trading area the business will serve, and why this is a preferred location.

Give a detailed account of the operational strategies that will make your business run more smoothly. If it's a manufacturing business, provide information that describes all the procedures at every level of production and distribution. Emphasize the purchasing and retail processes if it's a retail operation and, of course, the service procedures if it's a service concept. Cover subjects such as inventory financing, available labor, and any vendors as examples.

Discuss the wages you plan to pay for inexperienced and experienced workers. Note whether you are going to use independent contractors or have people on payroll. If you plan a commission schedule, what will it be? What employee benefits do you plan to offer? Be specific.

Management Structure

Include a chart illustrating the company's key management positions and who will fill each. Elaborate upon each individual's past experience and any work relation he or she has had with other management personnel.

Basically, you're providing job descriptions of those closest to the business. Clarifying who does what, where, how, and why is essential for any business to run smoothly and profitably. Complete résumés of each person on the management team should be included in an appendix to the plan. Watch executive salaries! Excessive salaries will doom any chances of financing. If you include elaborate salaries for yourself and your management team, the lender will rightly conclude that you and they lack the commitment and maturity to make the business a success. Emphasize management skills, prior experience, and accomplishments. Remember—investors invest in people more than they do in business.

Timetables and Schedules

Include a schedule detailing precise timetables for start-up, expansion, and capital fund requirements. These schedules should show the timing and interrelationships of the major events necessary to launch your venture.

Highlight the start of the business and your expected growth over the next three years. Only novice entrepreneurs begin a business with no idea of how and when it will evolve. Clarify your strategy in terms of sales and profit growth. If you're starting a small hardware center within a department store, for example, and plan to grow into an independent housewares store within three years, detail how this expansion and transition will occur. Since you'll obviously need more space, more money, more inventory, and more support personnel, let the lender know how these resources will come together to insure this future growth.

Make certain the schedule also includes any deadlines or major events or contingencies that are critical to the success of the business. This will help convince the reader your plan has been carefully conceived.

Financial Data

Every business, large or small, new or old, needs a financial plan to guide it. Whether you call this an operating plan, a forecast, or a projection, it must show your potential profit or loss and your cash flow during the first several years of operation. Coming up with these estimates will probably be the most difficult part of preparing your business plan. You may want to enlist the services of an accountant for this phase.

When you draft your projections, it isn't unusual to recalculate several times. Let's start first with the income statement so you can see, step by step, how this financial information comes together.

Income Statement

Revenue (sales).   Total sales include both "cash" and "on-account" sales; net sales are total sales minus returns and refunds. If your business has separate departments or key product lines, estimate sales for each department or product line separately. Be conservative when you forecast sales. Remember, too much optimism can quickly lead to a failed business.

Cost of Sales.   Calculate the cost of merchandise sold. If your estimates of sales are by department or product, then your cost of sales will also be by department or product.

Be certain cost of sales reflects freight or transportation charges you pay on incoming merchandise. If employees are paid sales commissions, the commissions should also be included in your cost of sales.

One method for estimating your cost of sales is to use industry averages. For example, if you know that cost of sales in your type of business averages about 63 percent, you should apply that percentage unless you can show why your business will vary.

Gross Profit.   Gross profit, sometimes called the "gross margin," is the difference between net sales and cost of sales. This is a simple calculation to make.

Expenses.   Estimating operating expenses involves less guesswork than does estimating sales. Begin by estimating each expense individually. Use industry averages as a benchmark for what you will spend on each expense category. If the sum of your individual estimated expenses is greater than your estimated gross profit, you probably need to re-evaluate all expenses and revise several downward.

Salary Expense.   Base your estimate of salaries on the number of employees you will need, the number of hours they will average each week, and their rates of pay. Include overtime wages if you anticipate high seasonal or peak demands. Don't include your own salary draw if you list it separately as officer's salary. It is usually a good idea to separately disclose the pay you intend to draw from the business.

Include both payroll taxes and paid benefits you will provide your employees—such as vacation, sick pay, health insurance, and so on. A conservative estimate would be 10% for payroll tax, 2% for vacation, 5% for sick pay, and $400 plus a month per employee for health insurance and related benefits. These items can add up, so don't forget them.

Supplies.   Include all stationery supplies and business cards, as well as pens, pencils, staplers, computer supplies, and so on. Also include postage expense here along with all other items purchased for use in the business (not for resale).

Repairs and Maintenance.   Total all extraneous labor and material charges for upkeep of the business premises or equipment. Don't include those normal charges already within the payroll and supplies categories.

Advertising.   Consider this item carefully. Identify the kinds of advertising and promotion you will require—TV, radio, newspaper, magazines, handbills, direct mail, and so on. Estimate the frequency of use, and obtain costs based on these estimates. Don't forget special promotions and the separate costs for a grand opening sale. Remember yellow pages advertising! This can be quite costly.

Car, Delivery, and Travel.   To calculate total estimated business travel, estimate the number of trips, air fare, and a per diem cost for meals and lodging. Include any business vehicle monthly lease payment. Figure gasoline and vehicle maintenance based on estimated mileage. Consult your accountant or the IRS for the permissible mileage charge that may be deducted as a business expense.

Accounting and Legal.   Include estimates for accounting/bookkeeping services, both monthly and for preparing year-end financial statements and tax returns. Add an additional $500 a month to cover occasional consultations with your attorney as well as an estimate of initial organization costs.

Rent.   Real estate rent, lease, or mortgage payments can usually be accurately determined but don't overlook other occupancy costs such as insurance, real estate taxes, repairs, or other charges you will incur.

Telephone.   Account for both local and long distance charges. Your phone company can provide estimates.

Utilities.   Electricity, gas, or oil for heating; water; garbage collection; cable TV; and sewer charges are all examples of utilities. Call the firms or agencies that provide these services and ask for approximate costs. Since utility charges constantly increase, never rely on old figures.

Insurance.   Check with your business insurance broker for a quote on casualty and liability coverage. Don't forget to include any special coverage needed for your particular venture.

Taxes.   Local authorities (city, county, and state) can provide tax estimates, or you can check recent bills for applicable taxes on your business license, inventory tax, sales tax, excise tax, and personal property tax. Don't include income tax or payroll tax in this category.

Depreciation.   For tax purposes, the IRS allows you to deduct a certain percentage of the cost of various fixed assets as a non-cash expense. This deduction varies according to the type of asset and it frequently changes under the tax laws. Call your local IRS office or your accountant for guidelines when computing your depreciation expense.

Interest.   Don't overlook interest on loans. Be certain to distinguish between your personal and business debts as only business debts should be included. Don't include the portion of your debt that covers principal repayment.

Other Expenses. Identify other expenses not included in one of the aforementioned categories, and then enter their annual cost. For example, entertainment to promote your business interests, subscriptions to trade publications, membership dues in clubs and business organizations, and small expenditures for which separate accounts would not normally be prepared are all examples of miscellaneous "other" expenses.

Total Expenses. The sum of all individual expenses.

Net Profit. Subtract total expenses from gross profit.

Cash Flow Projections

When estimating your projections, you must understand that profits and cash availability are not the same thing. It isn't unusual for a business to encounter shortages of cash even though sales and profits may be high. Therefore, it is necessary to prepare a separate schedule specifically to project cash flow, which illustrates total cash inflow and outflow, month-by-month, for a 12-month period. This can be readily figured once you have prepared accurate projections for sales and expenses.

A cash flow projection is necessary for you to successfully manage receipts and disbursements so that adequate cash is always available to meet expenses and loan payments. Thus, projections must pay close attention to timing and take into account the time lag between sales and the collection of accounts receivable as well as certain loan obligations that are not reflected on your income statement.

Your accountant should be recruited to prepare a 12-month cash flow statement. No particular form is required, provided you follow these steps:

1. **Cash on Hand.** List the sources and amounts of cash you can expect to receive in each of the first 12 months. For a new business, cash will be provided by your investment, loan proceeds, and sales the business will generate.

2. **Cash Receipts.**
    a. *Cash sales.* If your "Total Sales" estimate is primarily cash sales, enter those monthly figures. Many small businesses do not offer charge sales; if this is the case, total sales equal cash sales.
    b. *Collections from credit accounts.* Credit card sales are considered cash sales (deduct the 2 to 5 percent credit card expense charges).
    c. *Loan or other cash injection.* For example, short-term loans or seasonal loans.
3. **Total Cash Receipts.** (sum of 2a, b, and c.)
4. **Total Cash Available.** (sum of 1 and 2.)
5. **Cash Paid Out.** List all cash to be paid out each month. Include payments for monthly expenses as well as the purchase of capital assets.
    a. *Loan payment.* Include payments on all loans and equipment purchased on time payment. Include interest and principal.
    b. *Capital purchases.* Nonexpensed (depreciable) expenditures such as equipment, building, and vehicle purchases, and leasehold improvements.
    c. *Other start-up costs.* Expenses incurred prior to the first month projection and paid for after the start-up occurs.
    d. *Itemize* operating expenses *except* depreciation.
    e. *Owner's withdrawal.* Should include payment for such things as owner's income tax, social security, health insurance, executive life insurance premiums, and so on.
6. **Total Cash Paid Out.** (sum of 5a—e.)
7. **Cash Position.** Total cash available *minus* total cash paid out. If monthly disbursements are greater than the total cash available, you will have a negative cash flow. Serious or prolonged cash flow shortages show a significant weakness in your plan and will probably require the assistance of an accountant.

Take the time necessary to prepare a reasonable and realistic projection of your month-by-month sales, expenses, profits, and cash flow. Be prepared to defend each. In spite of your efforts, a reasonable and realistic estimate remains an educated guess. Nevertheless, the better documented your estimates, the better your chances of securing the funding you need.

Supporting Information

Finally, there is a catchall section for your supporting information. This is the section that allows you to dress up your business and use your charm, personality, and creativity to land financing. Think of all of your supporting documentation as icing on the cake. Two things are important: The documents must be relevant, and for best results they should be thought of as a marketing tool. If, for example, you have commitments from prospective clients, include their letters of intent to do business with you. Even better are in-hand purchase orders.

Include several letters of reference from people who know you. These can be business or community leaders, friends, or business associates. Reference letters should be short, indicating how long the authors have known you and in what capacity, and how they evaluate your skills in relation to the business.

Other items can be added to your supporting documents, including patents, promotional material, census or demographic data, insurance requirements, and license requirements. Feel free to include whatever else you think evidences the potential success of your business.

WHERE TO FIND HELP

Don't let the process of preparing a business plan intimidate you. You can find help from numerous sources. Check out the several excellent computer software programs specifically designed to produce business plans. These are available in most computer stores for under $200.

The Small Business Administration can also provide you with a list of professional loan packagers and business plan designers. Many entrepreneurs applying for SBA loans use professional loan packagers. You may also obtain free assistance from

SCORE (the Service Corps of Retired Executives), which, under the auspices of the SBA, consults to small business owners.

Oftentimes you will need assistance with only one or two parts of the business plan. Possibly your accountant or banker can help in the financial areas. Involve your attorney on matters of corporate organization or in other legal areas. Just as a business necessarily depends on a number of specialists, a business plan requires the input of those same specialists.

There are many excellent books on the subject of business plans. These books usually offer sample business plans that can be easily followed in the preparation of your own.

KEY POINTS TO REMEMBER

1. A solid, well-designed business plan is essential for any shoestring start-up.
2. Your business plan must be used for more than financing. It is your roadmap to success because it guides you in the design, operation, and growth of the business.
3. Tackle problem areas the business plan discloses *before* you begin the business and those same problems become costly.
4. Be realistic in your planning. Overly rosy projections will make you look like a rank amateur to seasoned lenders and investors who know new companies rarely perform as predicted.
5. Involve your accountant, attorney, banker, or other specialists. They should approve the plan in advance of its disclosure to potential lenders.
6. Preparing a business plan is not a once-in-a-lifetime event. As your business grows, planning will become a continuous activity.

6

FINDING THE MONEY

Wearing well-worn jeans, running shoes, and a T-shirt, he sports a full blond beard nestled beneath over-sized sunglasses. A frayed Brooklyn Dodgers cap sits tilted on his bushy blond hair. Scrambling from thought to thought, he reminds you of Woody Allen while constantly pushing his glasses on his nose. Cradled in his left arm is a large, gray, contented cat, in sharp contrast to his animated master.

Would you lend $100,000 to this man?

Thirty-seven bankers said "no." So did the SBA, nine finance companies, and a slew of prospective private backers. They just didn't know Bernie Simon, the youthful chairman of the board of Simon Industries, grossing several million dollars annually in the laser light entertainment field.

Chairman Simon now occupies a spacious suite overlooking Boston's waterfront, and you'll still find the Dodgers cap perched on his head as the link to his Brooklyn past. But to the kids who storm the halls to have their eyes strained by psychedelic laser lights and their ears punctured by local rock bands, he's still "Big Bernie." Indeed, Boston's young have made "Big Bernie" a very wealthy man.

Boston's financial community was less enthusiastic. "You can't take some guy in a pinstripe suit hiding behind a mahogany desk and expect him to understand what your deal is all about. Not when it's an untried idea, and they can't back the loan up with hard collateral," explains Bernie. "Bankers aren't gamblers. So they warily shake your hand like you're a Martian and wish you well. Two minutes after you leave they're spraying Lysol around their office."

So who was it that gambled on "Big Bernie" and his "Magnificent Laser Light Show"? Quite a few people. Ten investors each shelled out $5000 for 4 percent of the business. Bernie was halfway there with $50,000 and still owned 60 percent of the company. With some fancy footwork, Bernie talked the equipment supplier into loaning him $10,000 and another $10,000 loan came from the concession operators promised the opportunity to hawk hot dogs and Coke to the adolescent appetites. The final $30,000 loan came from another entrepreneur who had recently struck gold in a high-tech business. With the $100,000 in hand, Bernie's "Magnificent Laser Light Show" opened in three suburban theaters and can now be seen in cities dotting the East Coast. Bernie remarks, "You need your own style to find money. Willie Sutton, the famous bank robber, did it with a gun. I do it with enthusiasm. Sometimes it's contagious."

Can you infect a financial backer with the "contagious enthusiasm" to fork over your start-up capital? Successful entrepreneurs agree that the answer depends on three essential ingredients:

1. How long you look.
2. Where you look.
3. What you look for.

Here's a close-up view of each:

1. *How long you look: Check your staying power*
    Finding start-up capital is never easy. Forget the nonsense rags-to-riches books that tell you the streets are lined with deep-pocket capitalists ready to throw money at you. It doesn't happen that way. Not if you're armed with only an idea and lack collateral to back up the loan. "And when you have little or no money of your own to throw into the deal it makes it that much tougher," says "Big Bernie" of laser light fame. "It's not impossible, but your fingers do get tired walking through the yellow pages," recounts Bernie, who struck out 52 times before landing his first few dollars.

Perseverance and sufficient commitment to your idea to knock on still another door are the keys. Too many people with perfectly valid business plans underestimate what it takes to locate leveraged financing, and with a few turndowns, sigh a discouraged note aborting their plans.

Look at it realistically. Financing is a competitive process, and the start-up comes in last in the bid for available cash. First in line are successful ventures seeking expansion capital, followed by buyers of going businesses. When start-ups are considered, priority goes to the venture that is both well capitalized and readily collateralized. Funding an idea alone is always a challenge because lenders are skeptics and every start-up must pierce through a stone wall of skepticism to pierce a lender's vault. And lenders should be skeptics. They know that between idea and successful operation too many things can go wrong.

To turn to a positive note, you only have to consider the hundreds of thousands of new businesses opening their doors this year. It's proof positive that start-up capital is available, and in many of these cases the business idea had little more to offer lenders than entrepreneurial enthusiasm. Bernie Simon was one story. Amy Shapiro is another. Today Amy operates a large restaurant near Groton, Connecticut, but not without the helping hand of a potpourri of lenders ranging from the SBA to a $3000 loan from the cigarette vending firm anxious for Amy's promising location. "It took me almost two years to build my financial pyramid," says Amy, "and that represents 700 days of bending the ear of anyone who could possibly be interested in making a small loan. Most people weren't interested. A few were. But the 'few,' and the perseverance to find them, is what it takes."

2.   *Where you look: Capitalists in the crowd*

Matching your money-making idea to the right financial backer is half the battle. And there are plenty of capitalists in the crowd who don't sport pinstripe suits.

You can't stop with banks, the SBA, and other conventional lenders. Sometimes it's a waste of time to even start with them—particularly if you don't have strong collateral or a heavy personal investment to wave before them. As Bernie Simon says, "Banks don't gamble. And what can be a bigger gamble in someone short on cash and collateral dreaming of his or her own business?"

So where does the seed money come from to start your boot-strapped money tree? Noninstitutional lenders. Friends and relatives are obvious candidates. Others are high tax bracket individuals looking for a high return buttressed with the consoling thought that the IRS will share their losses. Still others are suppliers, customers, and even landlords with a vested interest in having you open your doors. The list is endless.

Andy VanBuskirk, with a string of successful businesses behind him, endorses the point. "I didn't have a dime to open my first donut shop, but I had the tenacity to nibble away at plenty of people who did. A bank loaned $10,000 against the value of used equipment, three suppliers each chipped in $3000, and a finance company backed me with $4000 credit. Sharpening my bite, I landed $5000 from the boys at my poker club and another $2000 from a college chum who would never have made it through Chem 101 without me. But that's how it is when you need money. You don't leave stones unturned."

3. *What you look for: Dealmaking*

Just as you have to abandon your idea of conventional sources, you'll also have to abandon your idea of conventional terms. In reality there's no such thing as "conventional" loan terms when you talk about shoestring start-ups. Your deal is what you can bargain for.

"To tap the money sources you have to be a bit of a wheeler-dealer," says Mark Winn, who specializes in financing leveraged start-ups. "Every lender has his own motivations and expectations, and you have to talk and think in their terms to cement a deal. Too many people can't roll with the punches."

Private backers, for example, won't settle for 18 percent interest if a profitable loan is their objective. They want the high 24 to 26 percent interest proportionate to the high risk. Some want a piece of the business as a bonus. Suppliers are sold on the basis of a profitable account. Interest is secondary. Friends and relatives are yet a different breed. You never know what will make them happy.

It all points to one word: salesmanship. As Mark Winn adds,

"The successful borrower targets a prospect and knows how to put together a proposition and sell it like you would any product. And when you know the right words, it invariably leads to a 'yes.' "

Keep these ground rules in mind as you go through the next several pages and learn to play the game to win your needed financing. Then see the next two chapters for other sources of capital.

YOU CAN'T BEAT BORROWED MONEY

Walt Disney once said, "I must be successful; I owe seven million dollars." So you're not Disney, but that doesn't suggest you shouldn't go after as much capital as you need. In fact, the cornerstone of shrewd financing is to borrow 100 percent—or as close to it as you can—while using little or none of your own money. And contrary to what theorists preach, it's both workable and advisable. Here's why:

1. You need your money as a reserve. Typically, a start-up will be financed by an owner depleting his or her cash reserves and borrowing the balance to complete the capital needs. But you can never estimate with total accuracy what your business needs for a successful start. During the first year or two, you'll have cost overruns and a host of unexpected expenses. It's too soon to go back to your lenders for more cash, and with your own money tied up, the cash bind begins. A higher debt level to begin with would allow you to hold your cash as a "cushion" to clear the unanticipated hurdles.

2. Taxes are another factor. With funds borrowed by your business, the interest payments are deductible. If you plow money into the business, you can only take it out as taxable income or interest.

3. Debt is a safety net. It's difficult for laypeople to understand but the more debt your business has, the more patient

creditors will be with you. The reason is simple. If your business fails, creditors stand to see little or nothing. A business with a high liquidation value in relation to secured debt will yield a healthy dividend to creditors and make you a more vulnerable bankruptcy target.

4. Emotion is part of it. When your own money is at risk, you may make warped business decisions—worrying more about what's "safe" for your money than what's "right" for your business. Of course, when your home or savings account passbook backs up a loan, it's still money "at risk," but with further shopping and bargaining you may find ways to finance while keeping your cash and assets intact. It's the best of all worlds when you're finally in business with everything to gain and have nothing to lose in the process.

If you follow the 100 percent-leveraged philosophy, you'll be in the strongest of all positions. You can sit back and objectively assess the performance of the business. If it's going well but needs periodic cash infusions, you have your cash reserves to handle it. But now you're making the investment decision based on performance and not projections. It's far safer.

How will financial backers take to the notion of 100 percent financing as you jockey to avoid putting any of your own money into the business? It depends on the backer and your reasons. When lenders are convinced the reason is that you don't have the cash to invest, you retain credibility, but your backers will take an even more skeptical look at the validity of your business plan. Obviously suspicion reigns when you do have capital and let it be known that you'd simply prefer to play with everyone else's.

There are several ways to handle either situation. Honest disclosure of your limited finances is a start. Don't allow lenders to think you're holding back and afraid to risk your own capital. If you do have available capital, then explain that your cash is committed for working capital and can't be used for fixed start-up costs. It won't be of primary concern to private lenders whose loan decision is usually independent of owner's capitalization; however, institutional lenders are another matter. In fact, most institutional lenders require that an entrepreneur put up at least half the start-up capital from his or her own funds. Many banks don't really care how much you actually invest, provided their loan does not exceed 50 percent of the needed financing. That leaves the door open for secondary financing and subordinate lenders and your own "no cash" investment. Others are satisfied if you pledge personal assets as collateral for the loan.

Many entrepreneurs overcome the "owner's capital" question by contributing personally owned equipment, vehicles, or patents to the business. It satisfies most lenders, testing your commitment to gamble on your own business. "But commitment doesn't necessarily have to be in the form of owner's cash," admits one New York banker. "We look for other clues. How much effort went into the planning? Is the applicant leaving a high-paying job? How serious about the business does the applicant appear to be? It all comes under the heading of 'sweat equity,' and it may mean more than some clown toying with a half-baked idea and a pocketful of cash."

NEGOTIATE YOUR WINNING TERMS

Buying money is no different than buying any other commodity. You want the best terms available, and to win the best terms, take a short course on the bargaining points to watch for and negotiate in your favor.

Many a lender will tell you that "eager beavers" entering into their first business are so intimidated by the lending process— or so thrilled about obtaining a loan—they never think to haggle. It's a mistake. Even a few fine points bargained in your favor can add up to big savings. And it's all part of one-upmanship. Beggars don't land financing.

So whether you're negotiating with a bank, finance company, supplier, or your next-door neighbor, keep this negotiating check list before you.

1. *Do* structure the loan properly. And this means the loan is made directly from the lender to your corporation.

Don't have the loan go to you while you in turn invest it or loan it to your business. You may have to personally guarantee the loan or perhaps back it up with personal collateral, but the business should be the borrower. Consider the advantages: With the loan directly between the lender and your corporation, the lender will have recourse against your business, which may shield you from needless or excess personal liability. Taxes are a second reason. With the business paying the loan directly, you have no adverse personal tax liability as you would if you had to take money out of the business to pay your loan. Review this advice with your attorney and accountant.

2. *Do* ask for more money than you need. Many lenders arbitrarily cut you to a smaller amount, so by starting high you may end up at just the right amount. A good rule of thumb is to ask for 25 to 30 percent more than what you hope for. The danger in going beyond that is that you lose credibility if the loan request is obviously in excess of what the business demands.

3. *Do* negotiate interest. With institutional lenders you should start by checking prevailing interest rates to comparable start-ups. Available collateral will greatly influence interest rates, so take this into consideration. Here are a few specific tips to follow. Always try to bargain a lender down 2 to 3 percent from the offered interest. Most banks, for example, start with flexibility, expecting your counteroffer. Another strategy is to reduce the interest as the loan balance is reduced. Why not? The lender's risk is now reduced. Watch interest based on an inflationary high prime rate. Bargain for a "floating prime" rate that cuts your interest when the prime rate comes down. A point or two on interest can appear in significant, but doesn't one percentage point on a $100,000 loan put $1000 in your pocket each year the loan is outstanding?

4. *Do* demand the longest loan possible. This is a critical point with all business borrowing, and it's particularly important with a shoestring start-up. A bank, for example,

may offer a three-year note. Can your business pay it
down in three years? Forget rosy projections. You need
loan payments that coincide with a conservatively
drafted cash flow statement prepared by your accountant. Some lenders have a maximum three- or five-year
loan as a matter of policy. One alternative is to schedule
payments on the basis of a longer loan and be obligated
to pay the balance upon maturity of the loan. By then
your loan should be low enough and your business stable enough to refinance. But in the meantime you may
cut your monthly payments by 30 to 40 percent. Extending this same strategy a step further, see if the
lender will accept interest only for the first year or two.
Retaining the payments on principal can do wonders
for an anemic cash flow.

5. *Do* pledge business assets as collateral if you personally
    guarantee the loan. Auction proceeds may satisfy the
    lender, so he won't go after you personally. Conversely,
    don't use personal assets as collateral without a fight.
    Lenders are collateral hungry and will demand whatever
    you own to reduce their risk, but it's always a negotiable
    point and you may be surprised how much you can bor-
    row without fear of losing your home.

6. *Don't* settle for the first loan offer. There are plenty of
    lenders once you know where to look, and they're all in
    competition to "sell" you money. Having spent the time to
    put together your loan proposal, shop it around. You'll see
    some surprising differences among the offers.

PROPOSALS THAT CREATE CASH

Now the fun begins. You know what you want for a loan, and
suddenly you find yourself sitting across the lender's big mahogany desk proposing a $100,000 loan to start your money-
maker. You ramble on about what a great deal it is and how
much money you're going to make when he politely shows you

the door—without the cash. Where did you go wrong? The answer is simple. You acted like an amateur and lenders don't lend money to amateurs. If you have a pile of collateral they may overlook your inadequacies as they glance at your assets. But not if you're the entrepreneur going on nothing more than a wing and a prayer. That's when you must think like a pro, act like a pro, and sell like a pro.

So how do you become a pro? You don't. You hire one. The plain fact is that business people may be great butchers, bakers, or candlestick makers, but that doesn't make them the financial genius to package a loan proposal that sells.

If you intend to knock on the doors of a few hard money lenders, the best advice is to find a consultant who knows how to put the numbers together. Your accountant may be a logical candidate, particularly if he has solid loanmanship experience. Business school professors are another good source. They live in a world of business plans. I was fortunate in finding a retired bank president who enjoys moonlighting by helping entrepreneurs turn ideas into financial logic. Money finders or loan brokers lurk in every newspaper but be cautious; many are con artists anxious for a fast retainer who never seem to place loans. Give them a close check.

You'll need the pro to be in the trenches with you and field the tough questions:

1. Why do you need the amount requested?
2. What will you do with it?
3. How do you know it's enough?
4. How much less can you live with?
5. Who else will you borrow from?
6. How do you propose to repay it?
7. How can you prove you can?
8. What collateral can you offer?

No matter what lender you approach, the questions are always the same. What's important to one may be less important to another, but you'll still need answers to them all. And each question is likely to give rise to five more, probing the legitimacy of your answer.

Martin Stone, a Cleveland money broker, objectively says, "Novice entrepreneurs don't anticipate the questions, and when they do they can't come up with puncture-proof data. They rely on overblown words—rosy adjectives and adverbs. It doesn't inspire lender confidence."

No two loan proposals are identical in form, but they all answer the essential questions and have the financial projections to back up their answers.

You have your own spade work to do before a loan proposal can take shape:

1. Calculate your start-up costs and document them with cost quotes and written estimates. Lenders are always interested in how the business will come together.
2. Show how the loan will be used, breaking it down by expenditure. If the loan will be used for working capital, tie it in to a carefully prepared cash flow statement.
3. Don't overlook your lease. If location is a factor, your financial projections are based on the location. Without a location in mind you can only talk in generalities.
4. If you plan to collateralize the loan, then define the business or personal collateral you'll offer. Go further. Have appraisals ready so the lender knows what the security is worth.

Concentrate on the three "Cs" of all lending—character, collateral, and cash flow. Lenders, unlike partners, aren't as interested in the phenomenal growth you plan for your business as they are in the likelihood of being repaid.

Harry Nickolaow, who specializes in loan placements for leveraged ventures, says it best. "The chances for obtaining a loan go up by 70 percent when an applicant shows up with a well-thought and well-presented proposal. Lenders who may know very little about the proposed business usually can't challenge the numbers, but they can certainly detect an amateur at the game."

OPEN THE RIGHT DOORS

What's the best source of start-up capital? In truth there is no one best source. As common sense will tell you the best source is the one who'll give you the most money on the best terms. And that, in turn, depends on the venture and what you can offer in return.

Banks and the SBA are best for the larger long-term loans if you can offer collateral. They typically form the base of your financial pyramid.

Private lenders, and even friends and relatives, may be best once collateral is exhausted; however, they usually offer intermediate-term (one to three year) loans.

Suppliers, customers, and business affiliates may help you out with short-term unsecured loans to get you started, and are natural candidates to form the peak of your financial pyramid.

Since you will probably go after several sources—and layers—of financing it pays to know the specific strategies for approaching every type of lender.

BANKS CAN SAY "YES"

Even though you can find them on just about any street corner, banks still remain the most misunderstood and intimidating of businesses.

Why all the mystery? It's a rare person who hasn't dealt with a bank. You have a checking account and, chances are, a savings account or two. And you may be one of the bank's favorite people, lending them your money at low rates while they loan it back to you much higher. How do you think they pay for their fancy buildings?

Business loans are another ball game. Lending to a start-up venture is quite unlike borrowing for a home or auto. It can become so complicated even bankers can become confused.

To begin with, banks offer a menu list of loans. That's one advantage of banks over other lenders—banks have the flexibility to shape the loan to your needs. For example, if you're a direct-mail firm, you may be in the market for an accounts receivable loan. A cyclical business will shoot for an open line of credit. An inventory or equipment intensive business may select a five-year secured loan. For working capital you may need a revolving short-term loan. The combinations or possibilities are countless; to add fuel to the fire, each bank has its own menu board to offer.

So keep an open mind as to the loan package that's right for you. You aren't an amateur if you ask the bank to help design the right loan package for you, provided you have the information needed. Even the most sophisticated businesses rely on their banker to be a financial architect.

The wide range of loans should qualify you for some money. As asset-based lenders, banks typically won't lend long-term funds in excess of pledged collateral. Suppose your business will have $40,000 in equipment, inventory, or receivables. A bank will probably advance 60 to 75 percent of the collateral value. But this isn't a fixed rule. If you have a strong track record, a bank may lend in excess of collateral values. For example, in my first Discount City store the best I could land from a bank was $35,000 against $100,000 in collateral. For my second store I was able to finance $90,000, even though my second store only offered the same $100,000 in collateral. The difference was in the bank's perception of risk.

When you're at the idea stage, it's best to confine your loan request to the collateral you can offer. Because collateral is the bank's primary concern, you might as well retain credibility by starting out on the same wavelength. But don't hesitate to knock on the banker's door a year or two later for more money, even though the collateral may be unchanged. You too will have a track record to sell and that's collateral in itself.

Banks do make unsecured loans and your signature alone may be worth more than you think. Here the bank is relying on your personal credit rather than the business finances. But many times this dribble of cash is enough to start a small business. Lay the foundation to build your personal credit rating before you apply. If you have credit blemishes, then straighten out your accounts and try to have the black marks removed from your credit report. Build your credit standing. If you don't have a credit history, you won't have borrowing power. Take out a small loan well in advance of starting out and repay it on time. Now repeat the process, borrowing more each time. You may start out with a $10,000 credit line and gradually build it to $50,000 in a year or two through a series of consecutive loans. And many a successful business has been started on less than $50,000.

Multiple bank loans are another possibility. Your signature may be worth $5000 to a bank, but that means it's worth $20,000 to four banks. The way to handle it is to apply for the four loans simultaneously. In that way you can legitimately ignore the other loans on the application since the loans have yet to be granted.

CHARGE YOUR BUSINESS TO MASTERCARD

Ambition has no bounds. I didn't believe it either at first, but I know one gutsy individual who actually started a business on his MasterCard. Now I know we usually think of MasterCard as a convenient way to charge a fancy meal, a new suit, or even a vacation, but who ever heard of charging an entire business to MasterCard? My friend Bob Kuzara did, and was proud enough to have it written up in the *Boston Globe* as a featured story in the business section. Bob calculated he would need $80,000 to launch his furniture factory, and within 30 days had five MasterCards from four different banks, each with a $20,000 credit line. As Bob tells it, "Plastic credit is the easiest credit to get, and when you have enough 'plastic' in your wallet you have your start-up capital."

It makes you wonder. How many ways are there to make a bank say "yes"?

PRESS THE RIGHT BUTTONS

The right bank—and the right banker—can make a whopping difference in your chances for success. No two banks or bankers are alike. Watch where you shop.

To start with, you want commercial banks rather than savings banks or cooperatives who specialize in home mortgages or consumer loans. If you're pledging your home as security, these banks may be interested, but they're still the wrong choice because they can't offer you the loan flexibility your business will need.

Bank size is another factor. Stay with the small banks, and the smaller the better. As a small start-up you mean very little to the large metropolitan banks catering to the Fortune-500 firms. They may have slick ad campaigns to lure small businesses, but few will give you the service or consideration of a smaller bank whose lifeline is the small business.

Consider location next. Banks do give preference to businesses in their immediate area. One reason is that they want you as a depositor.

Timing is also important in shopping banks. Money is a bank's inventory. You want to hit the bank when it has the money to lend and will be most lenient. One way to find out who has the money to spare is to check with the financial community. Heavy ad campaigns are another clue.

Of all the considerations, the philosophy of the bank is most important. Some banks, particularly newer banks, have a reputation as "high flyers," abandoning strict asset-based formulas in favor of a "gut" reaction to a business that will make it. At least five Boston banks have been known to cast big dollars on big ideas and little collateral. And these were loans the conservative pinstripes wouldn't touch. Your city has its share of high rollers. Ask around.

The banker within the bank is your next target. And contrary to popular belief, bankers are people and that gives them their own philosophies, personalities, and prejudices. The chemistry between you and the banker can add points to the win column.

I won't do business with a banker I'm uncomfortable with. I want more from him than a loan. I want candid advice. I expect him to be my financial consultant and one of the architects of my success. When business is slow or takes a wrong turn I want to be able to approach him and work it out over a cup of coffee. If I need expansion capital or money for yet another venture I look forward to my banker throwing his feet on the desk and sharing my entrepreneurial dreams—or calling me a stupid S.O.B. for even thinking about it. In short, he's part of your team. If you don't think you can develop the right chemistry with your pinstriper behind the mahogany desk, then move on. You want more than money.

One last pointer in finding the right banker: Try to locate one with experience in your type of business. It's a big plus. My own banker has years of experience as a comptroller for several large retail chains. He knows retailing, and his advice means something to me. Make yours work for you.

WHEN THE BANK SAYS "NO"

Rejection can be beneficial. It can pinpoint a weakness in your loan proposal or a fatal flaw in your business idea.

Don't take a loan turndown and stroll on to the next bank until you find out why the loan was declined. Some banks hedge on a candid answer because they neither want to offend nor engage in long conversation. But push for an honest answer. I can tell you about plenty of loan turndowns that saved me a bundle on half-baked ideas. Sometimes it takes some fatherly advice from a banker to set you straight.

Problem proposals are easy to cure. You may apply for a $70,000 loan only to be turned down. Will the bank consider $50,000? Counteroffer. It may trigger a compromise.

Your banker isn't an adversary, but an ally in evaluating the soundness of your plans. He may see weaknesses you overlooked or questions other lenders will raise. Listen closely. Pick his brain. If he raises some doubts in your own mind then move on and pick a few more brains. There are thousands of success stories thumbing their noses at bankers who said "no." For alternatives to banks, see Chapters 7 and 8.

A FRANCHISE CAN MEAN FINANCING

Thinking of a fast food business, retail shop, or even a motel? Name it and you'll find it franchised. And one benefit of a franchise is the financing. That may come with the package.

Many franchisors will finance 60 to 70 percent of the total start-up cost. Generally they'll guarantee your bank loan, charging you a few extra percentage points on interest, but in some cases they'll make a direct loan.

One reason franchisors can offer generous finance terms is because the collateral has a high value to the franchisor if you default and he has to step in and foreclose. A franchisor of donut shops explains it this way, "Our franchise package costs $130,000. This covers the equipment, opening inventory, and the franchise fee of $40,000. We require our franchisees to put down $30,000 and we finance $100,000 at six points above prime. It's usually better than a franchisee can get from a bank, since most banks won't lend more than $30,000 to $40,000 against fast food equipment. However, the equipment can always be resold by us for the same $100,000."

Watch the economics of the deal. In many cases you may have high built-in financing because the franchise package allocates a large part of the price to the name rather than equipment or inventory.

If financing is the controlling factor, evaluate a franchise in this light. Could you start an independent business with less of your own capital than what a franchisor wants as a down payment for a franchised unit? In many instances you can. Besides the fact, you're no longer financing the franchise fee. You also have nobody to answer to but yourself, which gives you a clear field to bootstrap the operation with used equipment and other cost-cutting techniques. Weigh the alternatives by checking out several franchises.

SUPPLIER FINANCING: YOURS FOR THE ASKING

Suppliers can be a generous bunch. In Chapter 12, I show you how to tap suppliers for an opening inventory on 100 percent credit terms. Perhaps you don't need much of their inventory, but can use a few dollars of their cash instead. They'll be equally generous and for the very same reasons—they want your business.

Who will your suppliers be once you're in business? Concentrate on the two or three largest suppliers. Forget the secondary suppliers. You don't offer enough profit potential to win their financing. But let's assume you project buying $100,000 annually from a primary supplier. Why shouldn't this justify a $10,000 to $15,000 start-up loan?

Your best bet in attempting supplier loans is to go after suppliers most anxious for your business. You may not mean much to a conglomerate, but a local privately owned firm may consider your account vital to its own growth. Another reason. Publicly owned firms have rigid policies and although they grant credit they don't lend money. These constraints don't tie the hands of smaller privately owned firms.

How do you sell the proposition? Use the same selling points and safeguards for obtaining credit in Chapter 12. The strategy is precisely the same.

I've used supplier loans to terrific advantage in many of my own deals. They're right up there on my shopping list. Discount City, for example, was helped along by a $5000 working capital loan from its photofinishing supplier and $3000 from its tobacco jobber. Why be embarrassed to ask? These suppliers now sell over $800,000 a year to Discount City stores. Your supplier may see it the same way.

A FINAL WORD

Will you find your money? Whether it's a dribble of dollars or several million in start-up funds, you'll have to clear a few hurdles. Despite small business financing cutbacks, high interest rates, and an uncertain economic picture for the years ahead, lenders can still be induced to make the old risk—and reward—calculation and place their bets on an attractive deal.

Old Casey Stengel was a perennial optimist. When his New York Yankees returned from a disastrous road trip he simply announced, "You can't win them all."

That message should ring loud and clear in this chapter. You may not find the cash on your first try. You may have to beat the pavement and accept terms that will make life somewhat harder. But regardless of how you borrow—or whom you borrow from— it will put you in your own business. The best part is that some- day the loans will be paid off and the business will be yours free and clear. And it may have started without a dime of your own.

KEY POINTS TO REMEMBER

1. There's no magical formula to finding money. It takes the right sources, the right terms, and the perseverance to put it together.
2. Pinpoint the loan you want before you go shopping.
3. Structure the loan so you get the best protection and tax benefits.
4. Banks are like snowflakes—no two are alike. Match your deal to the right bank.
5. Draft your loan proposal so lenders know you're a profes- sional.
6. Can you clear the financing hurdle with a franchise?
7. Suppliers will lend, money and can be the easiest source of start-up capital.
8. If you strike out on financing, ask yourself the important question—do you really have a solid plan?

DEALING WITH THE SMALL BUSINESS ADMINISTRATION (SBA)

Want a helping hand from Uncle Sam? Consider what the U.S. Small Business Administration (SBA) has to offer.

I'll be blunt: the SBA has a mixed reputation as a source of business funding. Some entrepreneurs mistakenly consider the SBA to be a good place to find capital for business start-ups. Others believe that the SBA is so tangled up in red tape that it's pointless to deal with the agency at all. Both opinions are off the mark.

The truth is, the SBA has plenty going for it. You'll have to pick carefully, however, to make good use of its resources. That being said, here are some starting points for entrepreneurs who believe they can benefit from this agency's resources.

THE SBA—A POTENTIAL ALLY

During the early 1950s, Congress created the SBA to nurture the formation of new business enterprises. The SBA's mandate is to serve small businesses by providing information, financial backing, and an advocate for small business on Capitol Hill.

Do you qualify for SBA help? Here's the agency's definition of a small business:

- Service businesses and retailers with annual revenues of $3.5 million or less
- Manufacturers with fewer than 500 employees
- Wholesalers employing fewer than 100 workers

So far so good. This definition covers more than 95 percent of the companies in the United States. Keep in mind, however, that despite a broad mandate, the SBA is a small agency—with only 4000 employees and limited resources. The result is a bureaucratic good news/bad news joke.

The good news is that the SBA can offer you lots of help if you know where to look and (here's the catch) *if you reach the right people.* Among the resources available are financing guarantees, direct loans, workshops, individual counseling, publications, and videotapes.

The bad news? Dealing with the SBA can severely try your patience. If you hope to benefit from the SBA's programs, you must be clear-headed, well-organized, and exceedingly persistent. It's not sleek efficiency that has earned the SBA such a mixed reputation within the U.S. business community.

What can the SBA do for you? There are all sorts of possibilities. Most often, the SBA helps you obtain conventional financing through loan guarantees or loans made by private lenders. Among the available programs for financial assistance are:

- Small loan guarantees
- Export revolving line of credit guarantees
- International trade loan guarantees
- Energy loan guarantees
- Seasonal line of credit guarantees
- Pollution control loan guarantees
- Handicapped assistance loans
- Venture capital
- Loans for disabled and Vietnam-era veterans
- Long-term loans
- Development company loans
- Access to surety bonds through guarantees on bonding for small and emerging contractors, including minority members

In addition to these programs, the SBA offers training, technical help, and counseling with three partner organizations:

- Service Corps of Retired Executives (SCORE)—free training and one-on-one counseling from volunteers.
- Small business development centers (SBDCs)—training, research, counseling, and other kinds of assistance at more than 600 locations nationwide.
- Small business institutes—free management studies provided by business students under faculty direction at more than 500 universities.

GETTING INFORMATION FROM THE SBA

Before we examine any of the specific programs, let's have a look at more general sources of information you can obtain from the SBA.

SBA Web Site

The easiest way to obtain information about SBA programs is to visit the agency's web site at www.sba.gov. Data posted on the site includes FAQs, a start-up kit, shareware, and pages about research, training, assets for sale, business plans, outside resources, and contact links to the SBA staff.

Catalogs

One of the best resources is the *Catalog of Federal Domestic Assistance,* which is a U.S. Government Printing Office publication. The *Catalog* describes the types of loans that various agencies offer to small businesses. It includes the requirements for each type of loan, as well as the amount of financing typically provided. You can probably find this publication in your local public library.

Meanwhile, the 59.000 series of catalog listings of these programs and their originating agencies includes the SBA loan programs, among them the agency's two primary vehicles—guaranteed loans and direct loans. Sorting through the information in these catalogs is a good first step in dealing with the SBA.

Publications

You can also benefit from the SBA's numerous publications and Web pages for home-based businesses. Topics include:

- Dealing with venture capitalists
- Borrowing money
- Writing a business plan
- Cash management
- Accounting and bookkeeping
- Leasing equipment
- Choosing a retail location
- Managing a construction company

Most of the publications are free. Check out the SBA's web site at www.sba.gov/library/pubs.html. Alternatively, call the SBA's Answer Desk at (800) 827-5722.

SBA-Affiliated Organizations

What I've mentioned so far suggests quite a bit of information you can obtain from the SBA. Even if you don't obtain SBA information or funding directly, though, you can find assistance from other sources. Among these sources are SCORE and SBDCs, two partner organizations affiliated with the SBA.

Service Corps of Retired Executives (SCORE). Volunteers from the Service Corps of Retired Executives (SCORE) help SBA applicants determine their objectives and prepare business and financial plans. They also serve as business consultants to people running small businesses. Their assistance is free.

A word of warning, though: most SCORE volunteers have no consulting background as such. They are well-intentioned, but their advice isn't always reliable. In addition, some of them are private consultants using their volunteer status to find new clients. In short, you should acquire and apply their advice with caution. The value of the information you receive from SCORE depends on what you already know and whether you end up with an advisor who meets your specific needs.

Small Business Development Centers (SBDCs). The SBA's Small Business Development Centers (SBDCs) are the result of a collaboration between universities, the federal government, state and local governments, and the private sector. There are 650 SBDC branches throughout the United States. One possible drawback: most are located on college campuses, so access to an SBDC isn't a sure bet everywhere. Services include low-cost seminars, workshops, courses, and individualized consultations with the business school's faculty and students. SBDCs focus on providing management training.

Here's an example. Let's say that you need advice on finance, legal issues, marketing, exporting, or government procurement. When you contact an SBDC, someone will match you up with an expert. For a modest fee, this consultant can help you with aspects of a small-business start-up, including financing, writing a business plan or marketing plan, assessing cash flow, and so forth. The likely result? An abundance of helpful, inexpensive information.

HOW THE SBA WORKS

Here's a brief rundown of how the SBA works. There's a common misperception among entrepreneurs that SBA loans and guarantees are ideally suited to small business start-ups. True? Hardly. If you don't have a track record yet, the SBA probably won't lend you money or guarantee your loan.

SBA officials claim that they decide each case on the basis of merit alone. The SBA does, in fact, provide some loan guarantees to start-ups. The catch: Equity for start-ups must be more substantial than that for established firms. Also, the SBA states outright in its current loan packages that it isn't actively seeking loans from businesses that are less than one year old. In short, you should probably be in business for at least a year or two before you seek financial assistance from the SBA. Otherwise, you're probably wasting your time.

Now here's another caveat: The SBA is a huge, politically motivated bureaucracy, and its bureaucratic nature will inevitably affect the application process. It's not hard to see the consequences. Whereas a bank has lending officers who collaborate with you to provide financing, SBA loan officers have a different set of incentives. A typical SBA loan officer has little experience in loan or risk analysis. His or her expertise is in following SBA procedures and properly completing the agency's forms. A bank's lending officer will earn a commission if your loan goes through, which is a big incentive for helping you. For an SBA loan officer, though, offering you a loan merely means more work for the same pay. The result: You may experience many delays throughout the SBA loan process.

SBA PROGRAMS

Here's a quick rundown of the most popular programs that the agency offers.

7(a) Loans

7(a) loans help small businesses with credit problems. They aren't direct loans—they're loan *guarantees*. A commercial bank supplies the funds. The bank must participate 10 percent for loans up to $155,000 and 15 percent for loans between $155,000 and $750,000. Interest rates can't be more than 2.25 to 2.75 percent over prime. The material to be purchased may serve as collateral, although personal guarantees may be required.

The SBA's basic program includes the following:

- Regular business loans
- Certified lenders program
- Special loan programs

- Surety bonds
- Development company loans
- Small business investment companies (SBICs)
- Minority enterprise small business investment companies (MESBICs), also known as special small business investment companies (SBICs)

In short, the SBA offers many programs and service available through the 7(a) loan program. You can request detailed information through your local SBA office, or by calling the Small Business Answer Desk at (800) 827-5722 (in Washington, DC, call (202) 653-7561). A directory of information is available from the SBA at www.sba.gov. The SBA's web site will help to answer your questions about how to start, operate, and manage a business, and about where to get SBA financing and assistance.

Basic Eligibility Requirements

Depending on your type of business, certain standards determine your eligibility for SBA financing:

- **Manufacturing.** Total number of employees: up to 1500, though the actual number depends on the specific industry.
- **Wholesale.** Total number of employees: up to 100.
- **Service Companies.** Maximum annual sales: from $3.5 to $14.5 million, depending on the industry.
- **Retail Companies.** Maximum annual sales: from $5 million to $21 million, depending on the industry.
- **General Construction.** Maximum annual sales: from $13.5 to $21 million, depending on the industry.
- **Special Trade Construction.** Average annual receipts: cannot exceed $7 million.
- **Agriculture.** Annual sales receipts: cannot exceed $500,000 to $9 million, depending on the industry.

The SBA recently issued an "alternate standard" ruling regarding the 7(a) loan program. Under this ruling, a company can qualify as a small business if its net worth is up to $6 million, and if it had an annual after-tax net income of up to $2 million in each of the past two years. This alternate standard ruling opens the program to a much wider group of businesses. On the other hand, it makes no mention of providing additional funds to compensate for the influx of these larger small businesses.

Ineligible Businesses

The Small Business Act excludes some forms of businesses from receiving loans. These include:

- Not-for-profit organizations, except sheltered workshops
- Book publishers
- Newspapers and magazines
- Movie theaters
- Radio and television stations
- Theatrical productions and dinner theaters
- Businesses involved in the creation, origination, expression, or distribution of ideas, values, thoughts, or opinions
- Film, record, or tape distributors
- Manufacturers, importers, exporters, retailers, or distributors of communications such as greeting cards, books, sheet music, pictures, posters, films, tapes, broadcasters, or other performances and recordings of musical programs
- Businesses engaged in floor planning, gambling, speculation of any kind, and illegal activities
- Businesses for which the applicants are incarcerated persons or persons on probation or parole for serious offenses

To determine your eligibility, contact the nearest SBA office or your bank.

Other SBA Loan Requirements

Before the SBA will guarantee a loan through a lender, you must demonstrate that these conditions apply:

- Your business will be able to repay current debts in addition to the new loan requested.
- There's a reasonable amount of equity invested in the business or collateral that the borrower can pledge for the loan. (The actual percentage is determined by the lender and the SBA; this differs for new versus existing businesses.)
- Your company's past track record has been good and/or its financial projections are realistic and supportable.
- Your company's management has the expertise to conduct business operations adequately.

To determine if an SBA-guaranteed loan is appropriate to your financing needs, call your banker for an appointment. (Remember, you must be turned down by at least one bank anyway before you can qualify for SBA assistance.) The bank may end up refusing you a direct loan; if that happens, ask if the bank would be interested in participating in an SBA-guaranteed loan. If the answer is yes, give the bank all the information it requests. Bank personnel will help you complete the loan application and forward it to the SBA for approval. The entire process can take just a few weeks.

Guaranteed Loans

The heart of the 7(a) program is guaranteed loans. These are loans from private lenders, which the SBA then guarantees for a percentage of the loan amount, up to $750,000. To obtain a guaranteed loan, submit a loan application to a lender participating in the SBA loan guarantee program. The application must meet the SBA's eligibility and credit requirements, in addition to all of the lender's own requirements. If the lender approves your application, the SBA then receives it as a submission for approval. The SBA usually makes a credit decision on loans within ten working days. Obtain an application from participating lenders.

Here are some subcategories of guaranteed loans within the 7(a) program. They are governed, for the most part, by the same rules, regulations, fees, interest rates, and so on, as the regular 7(a) loan guaranty. Your lender can advise you of any variations.

Low Documentation Loans (LowDoc).   LowDoc is one of SBA's most popular programs. Once you have met your lender's requirements for credit, LowDoc offers a simple, one-page SBA application form and rapid turnaround on approvals for loans up to $150,000 (for loans over $50,000, you must also provide a copy of U.S. Income Tax Schedule C or the front page of the corporate or partnership returns for the past three years). The SBA will guarantee up to 85 percent of the loan amount. Completed applications are processed quickly by the SBA, usually within two or three business days. Proceeds may not be used to repay certain types of existing debt. Business start-ups, as well as businesses with average annual sales for the past three years not exceeding $5 million and with 100 or fewer employees, including affiliates, are eligible.

SBAExpress (formerly FA$TRAK).   SBAExpress loans are available for up to $150,000. The program authorizes SBA-preferred lenders to use mostly their own forms, analyses and procedures to process, service, and liquidate SBA guaranteed loans. The SBA guarantees up to 50 percent of an SBAExpress loan. Loans under $25,000 do not require collateral. This is a change from the FA$TRAK requirements. Like most 7(a) loans, maturities are usually five to seven years for working capital and up to 25 years for real estate or equipment. Revolving lines of credit are allowed for a maximum of five years. Contact your local SBA office for the names of approved banks.

CAPLines.   This specialized umbrella loan program is designed to help small businesses meet their short-term and cyclical working capital needs. The CAPLines can be used to finance seasonal working capital needs; finance the direct costs of performing certain construction, service, and supply contracts; finance the direct cost associated with commercial and residential construction performed on a speculative basis (without a firm commitment for purchase); finance operating capital by obtaining advances against existing inventory and accounts receivable; and consolidate short-term debt. SBA provides a 75 percent guarantee. There are five distinct programs under the CAPLine umbrella:

- The Contract Loan
- The Seasonal Line of Credit
- The Builders Line
- The Small Asset-Based
- The Standard Asset-Based Loan

The Export Working Capital Program (EWCP). The Export Working Capital Program is a line of credit for financing foreign accounts receivable. It is a transaction-based program and can be revolving or nonrevolving. The SBA provides a 90 percent guarantee to the lender. The business must have been in operation for at least 12 months prior to the application, and the proceeds can be used to finance materials and labor needed to manufacture or purchase goods and services for sale in foreign markets, including such items as consulting services, overseas travel to establish a market, and participation at trade shows. Funds cannot be used to refinance existing debt or purchase fixed assets. The maturity is generally 12 months or less, but can be renewed up to a total of 36 months.

U.S. Export Assistance Center (USEAC). The U.S. Export Assistance Center (USEAC) provides assistance and information on a wide variety of export programs including the SBA's Export Working Capital Program (EWCP). In addition, the center promotes and markets the agency's International Trade Loan (ITL) programs. The USEAC provides a mix of marketing assistance available through the Department of Commerce, the state SBDC network, and the financing assistance available from participating agencies including the SBA and the Export-Import Bank.

Under EWCP, the SBA guarantees up to 90 percent of the loan, up to $750,000 of working capital. Loan maturities may be for up to three years with annual renewals. Loans can be for single or multiple export sales and can be extended for preshipment working capital and postshipment exposure coverage or a combination of both. Proceeds can only be used to finance export transactions. The SBA can guarantee up to $1.25 million on an ITL for a combination of fixed-asset financing and working capital.

International Trade Loan.   This program provides short-term and long-term financing to small businesses that are engaged in international trade, preparing to engage in international trade, or adversely affected by competition from imports. The SBA can guarantee up to $1.25 million for a combination of fixed-asset financing and permanent working capital.

Defense Loan and Technical Assistance (DELTA).   DELTA is a joint effort of the SBA and the Department of Defense to provide financial and technical assistance to defense-dependent small firms affected by defense reductions. The goal is to help these small firms diversify into the commercial market while remaining a part of the defense industrial base. Reductions affecting business may be the result of any number of actions, such as cuts in defense spending, termination of defense contracts or the closure or realignment of military installations. The SBA may guarantee 75 percent of a loan up to $1.25 million under the 7(a) program, or $1 million under the 504 program. Technical assistance, including help in preparation of a business plan and loan application package, is available through SBDCs.

Energy Loans.   These are available to firms engaged in manufacturing, selling, installing, servicing, or developing specific energy-saving measures.

Disaster Assistance Loans.   When a specific area is declared a disaster area, the SBA offers two types of loans:

• Physical Disaster Loans—for homeowners, renters, businesses (large and small), and nonprofit organizations within the disaster area. Loan proceeds can be used to repair or replace damaged or destroyed homes, personal property, and businesses.

- Economic Injury Disaster Loans—for small businesses suffering substantial economic injury because of the disaster. Loan proceeds may be used for working capital and to pay financial obligations that the small business could have met if the disaster hadn't occurred.

Pollution Control Financing.   If you need long-term financing for planning, designing, and installing pollution control facilities or equipment, the SBA can help. The SBA provides financing through its loan guarantee program: a maximum of $1 million per small business with a guarantee of up to 100 percent.

The SBA can guarantee 100 percent of the payments due under qualified contracts for eligible small businesses to plan, design, finance, and install pollution control facilities or equipment.

There are no special eligibility requirements. To apply, you must meet the eligibility criteria that apply to 7(a) loans. Do you think your business is or will be at an operational or financial disadvantage as a result of government pollution control mandates? Are you at a disadvantage in obtaining financing for such facilities? If so, you should apply.

For additional information and details, contact:

U.S. Small Business Administration
Pollution Control Financing Staff
1441 L Street, N.W., Room 808
Washington, DC 20416
(202) 205-6600
www.sba.gov/financing/frpollute.html

8(a) Minority-owned Business Loans.   The 8(a) Business Development Program helps disadvantaged small businesses obtain federal government contracts. Under this program, the SBA acts as a prime contractor and enters into all types of federal government contracts with other government departments and agencies. The SBA then subcontracts that contract to small businesses participating in the 8(a) program.

To be eligible for the 8(a) program, you must demonstrate that your firm is at least 51 percent owned and managed by one or more people who are U.S. citizens and who are regarded as socially and economically disadvantaged. In addition, your firm must also have been in business for at least two full years.

The SBA also has a women's business ownership program. (According to the SBA, a woman-owned business is a "business that is at least 51 percent owned by a woman, or women, who also control and operate it.") The SBA offers a series of business training seminars and workshops for women already running a firm as well as for those wanting to do so. These seminars and workshops, which are part of the 8(a) program, focus on business planning and development.

Small General Contractor Loans. Designed to help small construction firms with short-term financing, Small General Contractor Loan proceeds can serve to finance residential or commercial construction or rehabilitation of property for sale. However, you can't use proceeds for owning or operating real estate for investment purposes.

Seasonal Line of Credit Guarantee. Seasonal Line of Credit Guarantee loans provide short-term financing for small firms with a seasonal loan requirement resulting from a seasonal increase in business activity.

Export Revolving Lines of Credit (ERLC). Offering guarantees to provide short-term financing for exporting firms already in existence for one year or more, ERLC loans also help provide financing for the purpose of developing or penetrating foreign markets.

International Trade Loans. The SBA has developed various programs to encourage small businesses to export their products and services overseas. The means to this goal include guaranteed loans to exporters of up to $1.25 million ($250,000 for working capital; $1 million for facilities or equipment to be used in the United States in the production of goods and services involved in international trade), and the ERLC (see above). Through the ERLC, the SBA can guarantee up to 90 percent of a credit line extended by a bank to an exporter. The SBA also offers referrals to other agencies involved in exporting; it sponsors regular export seminars and workshops; and it has free counseling available through SCORE.

The 504 Program—Certified Development Company.   The 504 Loan Program links the SBA, a certified development company, and a private lender in a 10- to 20-year financial package. Although similar to the 502 program, the 504 program provides assistance for projects costing well above $1 million, most of which involve acquiring land, buildings, machinery, and equipment, or constructing, modernizing, renovating, or restoring existing facilities.

A 504 certified development company (CDC) is a private, public sector nonprofit corporation set up to contribute to the economic development of its community or region. Specific rules govern the CDC, its structure, and its operation. A CDC is responsible for assisting at least two small businesses a year, injecting 10 percent of the funds necessary to complete each project, and ensuring that the debentures are correctly closed and secured. It must maintain a place of business open to the public during business hours and listed under a separate phone number. The CDC is also responsible for submitting an annual report containing financial statements, management information, a full activity report, and an analysis of its assistance to small businesses.

If you're interested in this program, make appointments with loan officers from a bank and with a CDC. The CDC will usually guide you through the process from start to finish. To locate the nearest CDC, contact your SBA field office.

DIRECT LOANS

As I've stressed throughout this chapter, the SBA generally grants loan guarantees rather than loans as such. Does this mean that a direct loan is out of the question? Not necessarily. You may be able to obtain a direct loan in a few specific circumstances.

Guidelines for Direct Loans

To apply for a direct loan, you must prove that funds are unavailable elsewhere at reasonable terms. This means providing evidence that you have been denied funding by your bank or other lending institutions capable of providing the kind of funding you have requested. If your city has a population greater than 200,000, at least two such institutions must have refused your request. Each bank must explain in writing what circumstances prompted its officers to refuse credit. Try to obtain a loan through all the standard sources before approaching the SBA.

The Odds for Obtaining a Direct Loan

Even after you've met the SBA's eligibility requirements, you've taken only the first step in obtaining a direct loan. This is especially true if your business is new and lacks a track record. Rest assured that the SBA will closely review your personal financial record, including whether you've ever declared bankruptcy or defaulted on a financial obligation. Any history of having been a principal in a business bankruptcy proceeding at any time will minimize your chances of receiving a loan. Other considerations are your ability and willingness to provide collateral in addition to whatever money (if any) you intend to invest in the new business.

Ten Reasons that the SBA May Deny Your Request

Here are the most common reasons given by the SBA for denying direct loan requests:

- **Reason 1:** You can, in fact, obtain funds from private lenders on reasonable terms.
- **Reason 2:** You intend to use your loan to pay off existing debt, to pay off the principal(s) of the business (as in a management or partnership buyout), or to replace capital already used for such purposes.
- **Reason 3:** Your business is a nonprofit organization.
- **Reason 4:** You intend to use the loan for lending or investing.
- **Reason 5:** You intend to use the loan for speculation in property.
- **Reason 6:** You intend to use the loan for relocating your business for unsound business reasons.
- **Reason 7:** Your company is a newspaper, book publishing house, magazine, or similar enterprise (excepting TV, radio, or cable broadcasting firms).
- **Reason 8:** The loan promotes a monopoly or is inconsistent with the accepted free competitive standards of the U.S. economic system.
- **Reason 9:** Some of the applicants' (or principal owners' or shareholders') gross income comes from gambling (except for small concerns that obtain less than one-third of their income from the sale of state lottery tickets in a state where such activities are legal).
- **Reason 10:** You are acquiring or starting another business (if you already own a business) or expanding to an additional location.

Incidentally, the SBA will judge your competence partly by the various financial statements included with your loan application. If more than a few inaccuracies appear in your cash-flow statements, cost estimates, and profit projections, the SBA will probably reject your application on the grounds of questionable management ability. After all, the SBA's aim is to promote sound business enterprises. You'll also hurt your chances with the SBA if you purposely underestimate costs or overstate sales and profits.

DEALING WITH THE SBA

If you decide that one or more of these SBA programs suit your purposes, your next step is to tackle the application process. Here's an overview of what you'll face.

Seeking SBA Financing

In applying for SBA guarantees, you normally work directly with a lender, not with the SBA itself. For this reason, you should select a bank you're comfortable with—one that also has sufficient experience with SBA programs.

The SBA divides banks into three categories:

- Level 1—"regular" banks, which help applicants prepare SBA loan applications and submit them to regional offices for approval
- Level 2—"certified" lenders, which conduct the financial analysis necessary to expedite SBA loans
- Level 3—"preferred" lenders, which have sufficient experience with SBA requirements that the SBA lets them act in its stead

Being turned down for a regular business loan is the first step in qualifying for SBA financing. If you lack sufficient equity or experience but your idea and approach are sound, you may then apply for an SBA loan guarantee. Most banks will apply for you once you provide enough details in an application.

The SBA's collateral requirements are strict. Generally speaking, you'll have to pledge one-third to one-half of the assets needed to launch a new business. You may also have to make personal guarantees. Remember: *SBA loans are totally and completely secured.* If you have a small, struggling company and lack collateral, you have only minimal chances of getting a loan.

Part of your submission will be a business plan describing your company's market, products or services, marketing plan, and long-term goals and objectives, in addition to a balance sheet that lists your assets, liabilities, and net worth. You should also submit income (profit and loss) statements for the current period and, if available, for the previous three years. Include monthly cash-flow statements, too.

New business applicants should prepare an estimated balance sheet, including personal start-up funds as of the day the business was (or is to be) started. You should also include detailed projections of earnings and expenses for at least the first year of operation, plus estimated monthly cash-flow statements. In short, you should provide a short, detailed package describing why you need the money, who you are, and how you perceive your financial profile and projections.

Finally, prepare a personal financial statement for each owner. List the collateral you're offering as security for the loan, including estimates of each item's present market value. State the size of the loan you're requesting and what it's for. If you're unsure how to prepare these documents, seek assistance from a financial professional.

SBA approval takes up to four months; the average is usually half that.

Preparing a Loan Proposal

It's fairly simple to prepare a loan request and application for an SBA loan. Just follow these three steps:

- Collect the necessary information
- Utilize the information to prepare the application and forms
- Present the application to your bank

You have two main choices in applying for an SBA loan: (1) prepare the loan application and additional forms yourself, or (2) retain a professional financial analyst to prepare the application for you. The second choice is easier in some ways. But is it the best? In fact, you have the best chance for approval if you prepare the application yourself. The reason: working through the documents yourself helps you gain a better grasp of all the managerial and financial aspects of your enterprise. By contrast, hiring someone to make the application for you means that you risk losing an opportunity to understand crucial aspects of managing your business. Furthermore, preparing the papers for your loan yourself may impress your bank officer by showing that you know how to do it. (It doesn't hurt, either, that this method often costs several thousand dollars less than the alternative.)

Here's the recommended procedure for completing an SBA loan application:

- **Step 1:** Contact the commercial (SBA) banking officer of your bank and request an SBA loan package.
- **Step 2:** Review the SBA requirements for a loan proposal [items 1 through 20 of the Application for Business Loan (SBA Form 4)] and familiarize yourself with the requirements as they pertain to your loan request.
- **Step 3:** Prepare the business plan narrative (operating plan forecast).
- **Step 4:** Prepare the financial exhibits:
  —12-month income statement (profit and loss statement)
  —12-month cash-flow forecast
  —Other relevant financial projections
- **Step 5:** Complete the loan application documents as required. Pay special attention to required signatures and documents. This is important in expediting your loan request.
- **Step 6:** Schedule an appointment with the commercial banking officer at your bank to review the loan application and discuss your loan request.

As part of the application process, the SBA will investigate your character and standing in the community. Written character references from friends, business associates, and community leaders carry considerable weight. The SBA will investigate your background, including whether you have a criminal record. Don't lie about your past. Having a criminal record doesn't automatically disqualify you for a loan; however, deliberate misrepresentation of facts will almost certainly rule you out. An ideal way to provide the SBA with a clear picture of your character is through a professional-style resumé attached to your loan application.

Procedures for New Businesses (Start-Ups)

The application process differs for new versus established businesses. Here's the sequence of steps if your business is a start-up:

- **Step 1:** Explain in detail the type of business you want to establish.
- **Step 2:** Point out your experience and management capabilities.
- **Step 3:** Prepare a current personal balance sheet; indicate all personal assets and liabilities.
- **Step 4:** Estimate how much money you or others have available to invest in the business.
- **Step 5:** Prepare a detailed statement projecting the business's first-year earnings.
- **Step 6:** List the collateral (if any) that you intend to offer as security for the loan. Indicate the current market value for each item.
- **Step 7:** Present the documentation to your bank to support a request for a private commercial loan. If the bank denies your application, ask the bank to make the loan in accordance with SBA's loan guarantee plan or to participate with the SBA in a loan. If the bank is interested, ask the loan officer to contact the SBA regarding your loan application. The SBA usually deals directly with the bank concerning guaranteed or participation loans.
- **Step 8:** If the SBA guarantees or participates in your loan, you'll be required to complete SBA Form 4, "Application for Loan," and other related forms. You will also be required to provide certain exhibits as supplementary information.
- **Step 9:** If you can't find a bank willing to participate, then you should immediately write or visit the nearest SBA

office. The SBA has many field offices, and its officers visit many small cities on a regular basis.

Procedures for Established Businesses

By contrast, here's the sequence of application steps for established businesses.

- **Step 1** Prepare a current balance sheet, indicating all *business* assets and liabilities. Don't include personal assets or debt on this statement.
- **Step 2:** Provide an earnings (profit and loss) statement for the previous full year of operation as well as for the current (up-to-date) period.
- **Step 3:** Prepare a personal financial statement for each principal, partner, or shareholder holding 20 percent or more of the business.
- **Step 4:** List collateral to be offered as security, including an estimate of each item's current market value.
- **Step 5:** Indicate the exact amount of the loan needed; clearly specify intended uses.
- **Step 6:** Present the documentation to your bank to support a request for a private commercial loan. If the bank denies your application, ask the bank to make the loan in accordance with the SBA's loan guarantee plan or to participate with the SBA in a loan. If the bank is interested, ask the loan officer to contact the SBA regarding your loan application. The SBA usually deals directly with the bank concerning guaranteed or participation loans.
- **Step 7:** If the SBA guarantees or participates in your loan, you'll be required to complete SBA Form 4, "Application for Loan," and other related forms. You will also be required to provide certain exhibits as supplementary information.
- **Step 8:** If you can't find a bank willing to participate, then you should immediately write or visit the nearest SBA office.

The SBA has many field offices, and its officers visit many small cities on a regular basis.

Timing

The government's fiscal year begins October 1 and ends September 30, but government budgets are rarely approved before December. Because the SBA must have budgeted allocations and/or funds available before it can guarantee or fund a loan request, your best time to submit a loan proposal would be December, January, or February.

Dealing with Bureaucracy

There's no question that dealing with the SBA requires enormous patience. After all, it's a huge federal bureaucracy. To keep the issues in perspective, though, remember that the federal government isn't alone in generating bureaucratic rigamarole. There are many stories of bureaucratic blunders at the state, county, and city levels. At the same time, I need to underscore this point: Be ready for a bumpy ride. As I stated earlier, there's no incentive for SBA employees to be responsive to you, the customer. In fact, there's an incentive to do just the opposite. Maybe you'll go away and leave them in peace. That being said, it's true that the vast majority of the SBA's employees are sincere, hard-working people who truly want to help.

What happens if you get stuck with one of the few who help create a dubious reputation for the whole organization? In that case, demand the name of the suspected offender's supervisor; then work your way up the chain of command until you get your questions answered. Document your case thoroughly, including telephone conversations. Send copies of that documentation to the SBA administrator in Washington, DC, your regional SBA director, and your congressional representatives. Ask for their intervention in your case to get the answers you desire. This will inform them of problems at the field office level—and put pressure on the field office officials to look into your specific case. You still may not get what you want, but you're more likely to get results.

Regardless of whatever proclamations the SBA makes about what the agency has to offer small businesses, be ready to work hard as you obtain the available benefits. The SBA is by nature a political organization, so it's in the SBA employees' best interests to play the political game. They'll do their jobs, but only if they have no other choice. What's the bottom line? You must struggle through all the required paperwork and leg-work, and you must be properly qualified for the benefits you wish to receive. Do your part diligently and patiently. Then you, too, will reap the benefits that your government has made available to you.

KEY POINTS TO REMEMBER

1. Your credit rating doesn't have to be as strong for an SBA loan as it must be for a bank loan. The SBA favors appli-cants whose credit cannot meet bank requirements.

2. The SBA favors minorities and women, but that doesn't mean that the nonminority or male applicant doesn't have a good chance to win SBA financing.

3. The SBA will consider loans in distressed areas, which most banks won't.

4. The major SBA advantage is the length of the loan. Most banks limit loans to five years, but the SBA sponsors 7- to 10-year loans. This can help your cash flow in the begin-ning years.

5. The SBA's liberal policies can be a potential disadvantage, however, since the agency prefers applicants who have been turned down by two or more banks, the SBA decision-making process may favor relatively weak and even illogi-cal deals.

6. The SBA is hungry for collateral. If you own it, they want it. Think carefully about what you're prepared to lose if the start-up fails.

7. Expect to pay higher interest for an SBA loan. You'll be paying up to 2 percent more than what a bank would charge on a "straight" loan.

8. The biggest problem: The SBA expects its applicants to contribute 50 percent of the start-up capital from their own funds. This discourages shoestring start-ups whose entrepreneurs hope to win 100 percent financing. However, the SBA has exceptions to the rule and routinely modifies this policy.

8

DEALING WITH VENTURE CAPITAL FIRMS

Are you in the market for $500,000 or more in start-up funds? If so, welcome to the big leagues of financing: venture capital.

A word of caution, though, before you whip up your enthusiasm: Venture capital isn't for every business. Venture capitalists are high-risk, high-stakes money lenders who are on the lookout for capital-intensive businesses with rapid growth potential. And by "rapid growth" I mean 25 percent to 50 percent compounded annually. The front runners for this sort of funding are usually in the more exotic business fields—high tech, computers, and biotech engineering.

Who are these venture capitalists? Usually they're investors who capitalize their firms partly with their own money and partly with government loans. In turn, they help capitalize start-ups with a combination of loan and partnership interest. To understand them, though, you need to know a little more about the different types of venture capitalists and the different ways they go about making their deals.

THE NATURE OF VENTURE CAPITAL FUNDS

Although it's true that some venture capital firms have a preference for early-stage companies, true seed money is hard to find. Venture capital funds (or individual venture capitalists) are gen-

erally looking for two crucial attributes in potential investments. First and foremost, there's what I've already mentioned—extraordinary rates of return. Second, investments that
will become liquid within a short period of time. You may have
a hot business idea, but is it *really* hot? Unless you've developed a wonder drug or made a computer technology break-
through, the answer is probably negative. And that means
venture capitalists won't be stumbling all over each other to offer you money. In fact, venture fund managers often say that for
every hundred proposals they receive, they might talk to the
principals of only ten companies. They end up actually doing a
deal with maybe one of those ten. You can calculate the odds
easily enough.

Over and above the high rates of return and the short investment horizons, the following are the main features of companies that interest venture capitalists.

Proprietary Characteristics

Venture capitalists often prefer to invest in businesses that have
a proprietary edge on the competition. What kind of edge? Typical preferences include patents, licenses, trademarks, or other
forms of legal protection. And since high-tech firms are more
likely to have products with these characteristics than are those
in other industries, likely target firms include those with computer technology, telecommunications, biotechnology, and similar products.

Computer Technology.   There's still some room for growth in
the computer and computer-related industries. That being said,
I'd have to add that investors are increasingly sophisticated and
choosy about what they'll fund. You have to convince them that
your product or service is unique and has a large potential market. What's likely to fly? Pure software ventures are a more difficult sell than those involving hardware or a mix of hardware
and software. You'll need a much more persuasive track record
to make your case. The reason: The issues affecting the protection of intellectual property are fuzzier than those involved

with patents. If you have a proprietary, patentable item as the base of your company, persuading a venture capital firm to fund you will be far easier.

Biotechnology. Venture capitalists remain interested in biotechnology firms, so there's still some investment in the biotech industries. On the other hand, some technologically successful projects have been disappointing from an investment standpoint, since bringing biotech products to market often requires much greater lead times than initially expected. The FDA approval process causes some of the delay. Consumers' anxieties account for much of the rest. The public protests against bioengineered crops, such as genetically engineered corn, are one example. There have certainly been some big success stories, but technical success doesn't guarantee commercial payoff. You can guess the result: Biotech projects aren't an easy sell.

Security. Following the 9/11/01 terrorist attacks, companies that develop and manufacture innovative security products may warrant venture capitalists' attention. Hardware or software that helps increase transportation security—bomb detection devices or biometric scanners, for instance—could be promising to investors. Precisely because the post-9/11 crisis is so uncertain, however, venture capitalists will be picky in which projects they back, and their terms will be severe.

Healthcare. Investment in healthcare currently takes two main forms: funding of managed care companies, and funding of new healthcare-related products and services. The first of these two generally involves investment in firms that organize health maintenance organizations (HMOs) with the intention of growing the company, then selling it off after a relatively short period of time. The second can take any number of forms. For instance, a company called VisionScience has developed a new technology for removing discolorations from the vitreous humor within the eyeball. Another active area is made up of companies that produce computers and software for healthcare management—both for administrative and patient care purposes.

Potential for Strong National or International Expansion.   In addition to a preference for funding proprietary products and services, venture capitalists have a second main investment goal: finding products and services that won't be limited to a specific geographical region. Investors don't want an arbitrary limit on the expansion capabilities. Sometimes the limits might be cultural, such as a food product that wouldn't appeal to consumers outside a particular part of the country. Sometimes the limits might be legal, such as restrictions on distribution. Either way, investors want as few constraints on your corporate growth as possible.

Huge Market Potential.   Similarly, there's the question of market potential. Even if you have no geographical constraints, what is the inherent potential for growth in your target industry? The limits may be demographic. That is, there are issues of how large your consumer population is and how much it will grow in the future. These concerns reflect venture capitalists' desire to obtain 5 to 10 times their initial investment within a relatively short period, generally about 3 to 7 years. Vulture capitalists (more about them shortly) will have an even shorter focus, usually 2 to 3 years. With this goal of 40 to 50 percent annualized rates of return, venture capitalists will expect you to demonstrate high rates of expansion in your potential market.

Proven Management Talent.   No matter how promising the target market, potential investors won't fund you if they're not confident in your skills as a manager. Do you have the ability to grow your business to the size necessary to meet their investment objectives? If not, even the most promising new product won't be persuasive. And although a venture capital investment contract will probably allow the investors the right to take over your company if you fail to meet certain performance objectives, that option is always a last resort. Investors would almost always prefer *not* to take the driver's seat. They aren't operating managers. They aren't interested in any real likelihood of getting involved in managing your company on a day-to-day basis. The takeover clause is mostly a sword they'll hang over you;

what they really want is for you to run your own show well enough that the company will thrive and yield a high return.

The following are some of the qualities that venture capitalists associate with companies capable of generating exciting returns.

The Quality of the Individual Entrepreneur.   You'll need to demonstrate evidence of maturity and experience in similar businesses you've started or run in the past. What defines a high-quality entrepreneur? The answer is somewhat subjective and intuitive, of course. That being said, however, I have to offer this caveat: Don't kid yourself about investors' intuition. Just because venture capitalists are intuitive doesn't mean they won't check you out from top to bottom when they evaluate your business. This is as true for individual investors as for corporate fund managers. These people don't make money by taking dumb gambles. The degree of latitude they express in making their decisions will depend on the particular fund. Some have more strict due diligence requirements than others. If the money comes from wealthy private investors, for instance, the fund managers may have more leeway than otherwise. If the money is coming from pension funds, there will be very little latitude.

Functionally Balanced Teams.   Venture capitalists look for entrepreneurial teams that meet the human resource needs of your company. Fund managers don't have time to help you structure your management or oversee day-to-day operations. Hence the one-man show is less attractive than the professional and aggressive team. The quality and synergy of your people will swing a lot of weight in encouraging or discouraging investors' interest.

Exit Strategy.   Something you'll need to show prospective investors early on is how they'll be able to bail out of a deal with you. All venture capital investments are relatively short term. As I mentioned earlier, venture capitalists want to make an investment, multiply their money by five to ten times, and get out. But how long will they be stuck with this investment? And where's the exit? This is what they want to know.

The two usual means to that end are (1) an initial public offering (IPO) of stock, and (2) outright acquisition by a big industry investor. The ease by which a venture capitalist can exit from an investment will be a pivotal aspect of how that investor decides whether to fund you. You don't stand a chance unless your product is attractive enough that you'd have an easy time promoting an IPO or selling a business with an obvious role to play in an fast-growing industry.

FIERCE COMPETITION

Now for the nitty gritty. Let's say that each of the criteria we've discussed checks out. You have an appealing, innovative product or service in a high-tech industry. There's no limit to your market's geographical range. The market potential looks good in other ways, too. Your company has a strong management team. You've designed a workable exit strategy. Given all you have going for you, what are the odds of finding someone to fund you?

The truth is—not good. In fact, the odds of finding a venture capitalist willing to put some money on the line are still less than 1 in 100. Competition for venture capital is extremely fierce. Even getting investors' attention is difficult.

What can you do to improve your chances? I have no magic answers to this question. Here are some issues to consider, though, that may help you find someone willing to consider what you have to offer.

The Key to Success: Finding the Right Venture Capitalist

This sounds obvious, but you'll greatly simplify your task and increase your odds simply by focusing on people interested in what you're doing. Too many entrepreneurs waste their own time—not to mention investors' time—by barking up the wrong tree. If you've developed a new cardiac catheter, don't approach venture capital firms that specialize in telecommunications. Zero in on funds with a record for going after your kind of company.

Another point is less tangible and largely a matter of chemistry. There's no point in beating your head against the wall if your particular proposal doesn't excite much interest in a particular company. Despite all the formulas, guidelines, and procedures for evaluating proposals, you have to reach one of the partners in a venture capital fund who specifically has a knowledge of your industry and a favorable predisposition toward your proposal. If you haven't made that kind of contact, you can forget the rest. The means to this end isn't a question of mailing out a bunch of business plans. You have to narrow down your search, arrange one-on-one meetings, and establish a rapport.

Networking

This brings us to the inevitable issue of networking. You can go about making contacts by any means that works. Approach potential investors through mutual friends. Play golf with them. Go to their parties. Wine-and-dine them. But keep in mind that anyone with money to invest will be getting a dozen proposals a week. Don't expect to be welcomed with open arms.

Other approaches may be more promising. Most mature market areas have occasional venture capital conferences in which a number of firms get together and let new companies present themselves. Some of these companies will be invited to present short summaries of their businesses in the conference papers. Others will have an opportunity to get up on stage and make a presentation about why they are attractive candidates for investment. The way to get into these programs is probably through an accounting or investment firm in your area. This can be a great opportunity to show your wares before a group of 10 to 50 venture capital firms—a method that's obviously more efficient than networking one contact at a time.

Agents

There's another tempting possibility: agents. As soon as you start actively going after money, dozens of people will approach you, offering to act as a go-between, make introductions, and smooth the way for you. This isn't a possibility you should reject right away. Some agents do, in fact, serve a good purpose. But you should be very, very skeptical and cautious about dealing with agents.

How do you know which agent to avoid and which to consider? There are no hard-and-fast rules. One rule of thumb is this: avoid anyone who wants an up-front fee to make an introduction for you—unless, of course, you have a reliable referral about that person indicating that signing up with him will produce a 99 percent chance of success. On the other hand, what if someone offers to represent you on a contingent basis? What do you have to lose? Maybe nothing. Even so, you'd better be sure that this person would be able to make a credible presentation of your company. If agents don't come across as knowledgeable, organized, and articulate, there's a pretty fair chance they'll do more harm than good.

KINDS OF INVESTORS

Within the venture capital industry, there are a variety of investors to consider approaching. Here are the main kinds and my suggestions about how they work, what interests them, and how to approach them.

Private Investors

Private investors—the so-called angels—are generally wealthy people willing to put their money into new businesses. Some don't have enough funds to get into a venture capital fund but still enjoy the challenge (and can tolerate the risk) of venture-type investments. Others want a hands-on approach to their investment decisions. A few may even be gizmo-obsessed dilettantes looking for the next Rube Goldberg invention. But don't get your hopes up. Although a fair number of angels are out there in the investment world, you should never count on being able to find them. They aren't going to make themselves any more conspicuous than necessary. In fact, most of them will keep a decidedly low profile. As a result, there's no simple methodology for approaching them.

Like institutional investors, angels will go through a review process to evaluate your proposal. This may or may not be a more limited review than what you'd experience from an institutional fund, though individuals may make decisions much faster than institutions. How much faster? That's hard to say, but a process of two or three months isn't out of the question. However—as I noted earlier but need to repeat again—you shouldn't suffer any delusions about their intuitive decision-making. These people didn't get rich by making rash decisions. Almost all of them will have professional investment advisors who will evaluate prospective investments. And you can assume that the evaluation process will be rigorous.

On the other hand, working with private investors has a distinct advantage over some of the alternatives. One such advantage: The deal can be structured any way that you, the investor, and your respective lawyers prefer. You're much less constrained under these circumstances than you would be if you were caught within an institution's guidelines. Here are just a few of the questions that influence what shape a deal might take:

- Does the investor want an active involvement in your company?
- Does he or she want to sit on the board, or not?
- Does he or she want to lend money or have an equity position?
- What sorts of conditions would be put on the money?

Institutional Venture Capitalists

In addition to wealthy private investors, venture capital funds are available from institutions. Some of these institutions are companies that focus entirely on venture capital investments; others are subsidiaries of corporations with a variety of products.

Venture Capital Partnerships

This is the predominant form in the industry. When people think of venture capitalists, they normally mean professional venture-capital fund managers who make the decisions about which companies to invest in. These venture capital funds are usually limited partnerships. The professional managers are the general or controlling partners. They generally put up a small proportion of the fund's capital, often as little as one percent. Limited partners provide the rest of the fund; they put their money at risk and can receive great rewards, but they have no say in the fund's day-to-day operations. Many of the limited partners are financial institutions, pension funds, and corporations.

Funds of this sort don't put all their eggs in one basket. Since they're looking for such extraordinary returns, venture capitalists expect a certain proportion of their investments to turn out badly. That's just the reality of gambling on making an outrageous return. For this reason, they have to make sure that their exposure on any given investment isn't so great that it could sour the whole fund's performance. Hence it would be unusual for any one investment to be more than 10 percent of the whole fund.

There are a number of ways for venture capitalists to lower the level of risk. One is by not making an investment alone. To spread the risk, they often find other funds to share the investment. Several venture capital funds pool resources to spread the risk. A single firm will be the lead investor and will be ultimately responsible for the go/no-go decision; other investors depend partly on that lead investor's due diligence. The lead investor might not necessarily be the biggest investor in the pool.

Using this method, two or more firms will often combine their resources to limit their exposure. That's not something that you, the entrepreneur, should concern yourself with. Your primary task is to identify one venture capital fund that's interested in your product. That firm will then go and find other partners that may be interested. You don't broker the partnership. You might mention to ABC fund, which is interested in you, that you've also spoken with the XYZ fund and you know that XYZ might be interested. But that's about all you have to do. Besides, you can assume that the venture capital firms you're speaking with have better contacts than you do throughout the industry.

Is there any correlation between the number of companies that pool their funds and the likelihood of your getting funding? Not necessarily. It still depends on the quality of the product you have to offer, the appetite of the fund, and the fund's size. You won't be in an immediate position to influence how many firms will be involved. You'll be signing only one contract.

Two issues you should consider, though: industry preferences and life-stage preferences. These will influence a fund's interest in what you have to offer.

Industry Preferences.   In any venture capital company there will be partners with special interests. One may be an expert on healthcare who knows what's hot in the industry, who the players are, and so forth. Another may specialize in telecommunications. Yet another may focus on computer technology. Although funds often have overall preferences for specific industries, individual fund managers may also have their own individual biases. The upshot: a big key to your success in approaching a fund will be to get to the right contact person. That will take some research. If you're going to make a pitch about what makes your business special, you may as well be pitching to someone who knows what you're talking about.

Life-Stage Preferences.   By contrast, the issue of life-stage preferences is a matter of risk and the planning horizon. The earlier your company's life stage, the riskier you are as an investment. Probably the biggest predictor of your long-term viability is how long you've stayed in business so far. For this reason, it's not uncommon that if you approach a venture capital firm in, say, January, the fund manager will say, "Well, what you're doing is interesting. I'll think about it. See you next January—we'll talk some more." The firm is just checking on your survivability. Typically, the earlier you are in your life stage, the longer the investor will have to wait to get his money out. All funds have their guidelines about what they expect—three years, five years, whatever. So they'll be looking at your stage of corporate life very closely.

Corporate Venture Capitalists

Many large companies have their own venture capital funds. These funds often serve primarily to help finance firms that will contribute technology to the parent corporation or a company within it, or that are compatible in some other way. Sometimes the corporate venture company even wants entrepreneurs to create companies that the larger company will then acquire. Still others are purely independent in their mission; their purpose is simply to run a profitable investment business.

For example, Allstate Insurance has a venture capital fund. A certain amount of their portfolio investment goes into high-risk ventures. Just because Allstate's venture capital subsidiary is part of an insurance company, though, you shouldn't assume that the venture capital firm is looking for investments in the insurance industry. The fund managers will be looking for investments purely in terms of strategic financial criteria. They could be as interested in high-tech health products as anything else.

As an entrepreneur with a small company, are you better off dealing with a corporate venture capital firm or with a private investor? There's no easy answer to that question. The core issue is still what you have to offer. You still have to tell a persuasive story. The difference between the two kinds of organizations is chiefly that your contact with a corporate venture capital fund will be an officer in the company; the criteria for how he's judged on his performance will differ from how a partner in a venture capital fund will be judged. What's the upshot? It's probably fair to say that a corporate venture capital fund officer will be more constrained to do things by the book than will a partner in a venture capital fund. It's more methodological than goal-oriented—a question of following certain criteria.

Investment Bankers

When doing venture capital deals, investment bankers won't be investing money that they control directly. Their interest will be in doing some kind of offering, either private or public, and their compensation will be fee-based. In most cases, they'll want the fee up front. So unless you're in a situation in which you can afford money for up-front fees, investment bankers aren't a very attractive source for venture capital funding.

SBICs

Small Business Investment Companies (SBICs) can provide you with a way to obtain money from the usual kinds of places, but with the advantage to the lender of having government guarantees on the investment. Because of the loan guarantees, a large proportion of the lender's risk is minimized.

Here's how it works. A venture capital fund borrows money from a funding source; because that loan is guaranteed, the fund obtains its loan at a low rate. Then they invest it or loan it, usually by means of a convertible kind of investment—most often a debenture—that gives them the right to convert into equity. They get a high rate of return on that investment while it's still debt, which is how they make their money. It's an instance of the old adage of "borrowing cheap and lending dear."

The advantage for you as an entrepreneur is that you probably have better odds of getting funded through an SBIC than by most other means. In addition, SBICs (unlike many sources of capital) are easy to find and contact. You can reach them through local development agencies. The size of their investment may be small—a few hundred thousand dollars—but the money is relatively easy to get to in the first place. For this reason, you shouldn't look down your nose at SBIC funds. This is especially true because there really isn't a strict dividing line between SBICs and "traditional" venture capital funds. Many venture capital funds have SBIC operations as well.

Is there a clear downside to this sort of funding? Isn't it possible, for instance, that applying for loans through an SBIC will lead to all sorts of government rigamarole? Not necessarily. The truth is, looking for funds *anywhere* will require you to jump through a lot of hoops; the SBA doesn't hold a patent on rigamarole. No matter where you go, you'll need to have a well-done business plan and well-prepared financial projections that can stand up to a lot of scrutiny. Dealing with the SBA won't be any more onerous than dealing with a reasonably prudent venture capital fund.

Ad-Hoc Venture Pools

In addition, some private investors will band together to create informal investment groups or investment pools. Sometimes one private money source will turn to other private investors to obtain the money for investing in a venture. In addition to SBICs, here are some other examples of these ad-hoc venture pools:

- Minority Enterprise Small Business Investment Corporations (MESBICs)
- Economic development groups (sometimes called "economic development corporations" or "business development corporations") administered on a federal, state, or local level
- Private foundations and universities that invest a small percentage of their endowment portfolios in small, risky ventures
- Mutual funds that invest in start-up and small, growth-oriented companies

Vulture Capitalists

Now for a controversial topic: the so-called vulture capitalists. The controversy isn't whether there are people in the venture capital business who demand returns and conditions that sound extreme even by industry standards. These people are out there in the world, no doubt about it. But is this particular breed of capitalist as onerous as their reputation suggests? That's where opinions vary.

Strictly applied, the term *vulture capitalist* refers to an investor who makes an investment with terms that allow him to take over the company under circumstances that aren't at all unlikely. I mentioned earlier that most venture capitalists are content to avoid an operational role in your company; they want *you* to succeed in running your business, since that's the quickest and most hassle-free means for them to earn the high rate of return they desire. By contrast, a vulture capitalist is definitely interested in the possibility that you'll fail in meeting the terms of your agreement. Then they can sell a larger proportion of the company than would be possible otherwise.

Here's a typical vulture capitalist scenario. The fund offers a million dollars if you agree to various terms, one of which is that your company must become profitable within 12 months. If you fall short of this goal, then the vulture capitalist has the right to acquire a controlling interest in the company's stock. Then he can do whatever he wants with it. If your company owns a promising patent, for instance, the vulture capitalist may cut his losses by selling the intellectual property to another company rather than staying put for the long haul. There's a much more predatory aspect to what funds of this sort require— and much more drastic consequences if your efforts to run the company fail.

Does this mean that you should avoid dealing with funds of this sort altogether? Not necessarily. But you certainly have to evaluate your options very carefully, and you have to face the potential consequences of fulfilling—or not fulfilling—the terms of your contract.

The Corrupting Influences of Big Money.   There's another dimension to look at closely. This is the issue of how easily a big infusion of capital can be corrupting. I don't mean corrupting in the sense of unethical or illegal; rather, it's something subtler but still potentially devastating to your business.

Deciding how much money you need for an investment is tricky. You don't want to guess low on how much money you need, because that could leave you scrambling for more funds later, or perhaps even defaulting on the agreement you made. You need a clear sense of what will get you where you want to go, whether that means "break-even" or making an IPO. On the other hand, you don't want to ask for too much, since getting it may leave you with difficulty providing a return to the investors. One way of getting yourself into trouble is to accept $5 million when $4 million would do the job. If you take $5 million, you may have to generate $1 million in returns instead of $150,000.

Vulture capitalists enter the picture because they may, in fact, offer you more money than a regular venture capitalist might provide, but with more difficult—even impossible—conditions to meet. Your product may have a very successful likelihood of attaining sales of X-dollars, but the odds of attaining sales of Y-dollars may be virtually nil. But if you obtain funds on the basis of attaining Y, you'll get yourself into a lot of trouble. What's the solution? First and foremost, you have to know what you need and what use you'll make of the money. Run your numbers as accurately as you can. Don't delude yourself with a belief that paying off your debts will be easier than it really will be.

Other Companies

There's one last possibility for obtaining funds: using the companies you deal with as ad-hoc sources. The companies I'm referring to include your suppliers and your customers.

Let's say your supplier of widgets has an interest in your success. Their company may not be able to support you with an equity investment or a loan as such, but they might be persuaded to be more generous in their credit terms. Alternatively, they might be convinced to bear the inventory holding costs themselves rather than expecting you to purchase inventory from them for resale. Those are two ways that a supplier could help a small business. It's a form of mutual backscratching.

Likewise regarding customers. One of your customers might

want to have a very close relationship with you in a given area, rather than doing everything by tenders. So a customer might actually be willing to make a substantial advance payment for the procurement of something that you're going to install. That advance payment might be sufficient for your company to hire a new employee, who would then be dedicated to that process.

Forms to Use.   Here are some of the business structures that might lead to advantageous arrangements of these sorts:

- **Joint venture**—a separately incorporated company owned by two or more partners formed for the specific purpose of entering a new market or developing a new product.
- **Strategic alliance**—similar to a joint venture, but not as formal.
- **Loan guarantee**—from a supplier, for example.
- **Cooperative advertising**—shared underwriting of a portion of your advertising for your market.
- **Licensing of intellectual property**—putting together two or more technologies by means of a licensing agreement. (The terms of the licensing agreement can be anything you want—either fees up front, all royalties, or some combination.)

THE NEED FOR A BUSINESS PLAN

You'd probably rather be on the business battlefield racking up victories than behind the lines planning your assault. You may also feel less capable of articulating business concepts than acting on them. If so, then you're probably the sort of person who dreads preparing and writing a business plan. Don't hold it against yourself—you have lots of company. But no matter how difficult and unpleasant you find this task, a plan is absolutely crucial for your business. I said this elsewhere in this book and

I'll say it again: You won't get anywhere with venture capitalists without a top-notch business plan.

You already know that a business plan serves three functions:

1. It helps you develop ideas about how you should conduct your business.
2. It serves as a retrospective tool to assess your company's actual performance over time.
3. It's a tool to help you raise money.

Most lenders or investors wouldn't think of investing money in your business without seeing a business plan. If you present an idea to a venture capitalist without a business plan, he or she would ask you to come back only once you'd drafted one. That is, *if* you're lucky. Many investors might never take you seriously again after that. How could you even think of approaching them without an articulate, well-thought-through plan put to paper?

Given the importance of a convincing plan, you might want to seek professional assistance for the task of writing it. You have a number of options to consider. One is a business consultant. Another is an accountant. Whatever means you use to produce the plan, though, there's no avoiding the reality of this situation: *If you have any hopes of someone taking your venture seriously, you* must *prepare a suitable document.*

How to Structure Your Plan

In Chapter 5, we discussed what makes for a good business plan. All of the general principles there apply to the specifics of approaching venture capitalists. Your plan is still a hybrid document—part pragmatic projection and part sales tool—that must walk a fine line in content and tone of presentation. The information contained there must be accurate, yet it must express your optimism and excitement. You need to acknowledge risks, yet you shouldn't dwell on them. The tone must be—well, businesslike. After all, the people who read business plans are practical people.

They'll respond to a positive, clear-headed, enthusiastic, interesting presentation, and they'll be turned off by one that's uncertain, foggy-headed, or just plain boring. An imaginative (but not flamboyant) presentation style may work in your favor. Keep your target audience in mind, though: Investors are ultimately most interested in what your business offers them. If you wax poetic about how wonderful it looks for you and forget your investors' needs, you'll lose your chance. Also, don't assume that appearances don't count. Even minor spelling and grammatical errors may work against you—and therefore against your enterprise as well. Hire a freelance editor or proofreader to double-check your documents and eliminate these minor blemishes, since they may have a disproportionate impact on how investors perceive you.

Business plans follow a standardized formal structure that reviewers will expect in any document you submit. There's room for creativity within this structure, but you should stick to the standard form if you want to avoid confusing your reviewers. For further information about how to structure your plans, review Chapter 5.

Here are three final issues I need to emphasize:

- **Be brief.** Write a document that's only long enough to get the job done right.
- **Be thorough.** Although you don't want to rattle on *ad nauseum,* you shouldn't skimp—or investors may think you're hiding important facts.
- **Be aware of your investor's needs.** Your plan's whole purpose is to persuade a venture capitalist that your business works to his or her advantage.

KEY POINTS TO REMEMBER

1. Don't overestimate the novelty or 'sex appeal' of your product or service. If the world isn't going to beat a path to your door, venture capitalists probably aren't interested in what you have to offer.

2. Venture capitalists may he intuitive, but they're not stupid. You must present yourself *at least* as persuasively to them as you would to other investors.

3. Network widely but choose carefully which venture capitalists to approach. There's no point in courting an investor who has no interest in your industry or product in the first place.

4. Make sure you clarify how the investor can bail out of the investment.

5. Consider the flexibility and accessibility of SBICs.

6. Be wary of agents, but don't rule them out.

7. Don't sell the family farm. You may be eager for funding, but take the long view, especially with potential investors who might be quick to take over your company.

8. Don't get your hopes up. Venture capital money is *extremely* competitive.

9

PARTNERS FOR PROFIT: YOUR BRAINS, THEIR CASH

Yes, there are investors out there—cash-toting partners anxious to lend an ear to a proposition to earn them even more money. You'll find them in all shapes and sizes. Some want to be "silent" partners watching their money work, others want to roll up their sleeves and work beside you. Some look for existing businesses on their way to the next plateau, others like nothing better than to take a flyer on an exciting idea. Some can offer you only a few scrimped dollars, while others are an endless river of gold. Some will work with you to create wealth, and some will work against you to create ulcers and headaches. So whatever you find, you'll find it an interesting relationship. It's either paradise or purgatory. Seldom is it in between.

WHO NEEDS PARTNERS?

According to the SBA, the guru of business statistics, 70 percent of all small business start-ups need partners. That's just about the percentage of businesses started with "friendly" partnership money coming from friends and relatives all the way up to sophisticated venture capital firms.

Why are partnerships so popular? There's no one reason. Overestimating start-up capital needs is probably the most common. A hesitancy to go after *less costly,* but harder-to-come-by loans, is another. Some of the myths we exploded in the first chapter help explain it. What it boils down to is a willingness to trade a piece of the pie for a few start-up dollars to complete the financing package. And it's usually faulty thinking. Why? Two reasons:

1. Partnership money is the most expensive money you can buy. And it's particularly expensive when you usually don't need it in the first place.
2. Partnerships have the highest failure rate because success depends not only on the success of the venture, but on the success of the relationship as well.

The idea of a partner *should* make you think twice. Here's a closer look.

HOW FRIENDLY IS "FRIENDLY" MONEY?

"Not very friendly," if you ask Nancy and Bill Tyler. In 1979, the Tylers signed a franchise to open a videotape sales and rental shop in a Philadelphia suburb. The franchisor was willing to finance $25,000, but the Tylers needed another $15,000 to complete the financing package. "We could have easily taken out a second mortgage on our home to raise it," remarked Bill Tyler, "however, a neighbor agreed to invest the $15,000 for a 50 percent partnership interest. Looking at it as a terrific alternative to borrowing, we grabbed it. We discovered it was like taking money from the Philistines. Three years later we had expanded to four stores grossing close to two million dollars and it cost us $200,000 to buy back our partner's interest. It was a foolish decision to take on a partner when we could have achieved our goal by paying a few thousand dollars in interest."

When you talk about faulty economics, the Tylers don't stand alone. One of my closest friends tells an even more bizarre story of how he took on a 30 percent partner to start a computer software journal. All the partner invested was $30,000, and now his interest is worth over $300,000. "The crazy part is that I didn't even need his $30,000 to start," my friend admits. "I had enough of my own money into the deal to effectively launch the journal, and advance subscription payments always gave me a healthy positive cash flow for growth."

So the point is made. From a financial angle, a partner may be an expensive idea. It is for most start-ups who reach for a partner's helping hand. But it's also easy to understand why it happens. It's always tempting to reach for a few partnership dollars when you start without asking what it will cost later.

Dig deep. If you want a partner for his money alone, you also want to move slow. If you can raise most of the start-up capital without a partner, then beg or borrow the rest from wherever you can, or pare down costs to match what you have. You may start with less, but at least it's all yours.

Do you still need a partner?

MORE THAN MONEY

It's an interesting fact of life that money is not the motivator behind most small business partnerships. People join together, believing two heads are better than one. Sometimes they're right and sometimes they're wrong. It always depends on the heads in question.

Let's look at the bleak side first. Once you have a partner on board you no longer work for yourself. You're suddenly accountable to your partners as well. They can influence or even control every decision you want to make. Say goodbye to being a loner.

It's difficult for some people to accept. Many a maverick has welcomed a silent partner or two—and their money—only to discover the silent partners weren't so silent. The Tylers of video fame learned that bitter lesson, too. That's why they finally bought back the partner's interest. The Tylers wanted to expand into a videotape wholesale distributorship instead of more retail outlets. "No way," screamed the partner. Who was right doesn't matter. The Tylers couldn't move without the partner's blessing, and the partner wasn't about to give it. Two heads rarely think alike.

I discovered the same thing in a few of my ventures. Years ago I believed the best formula for success was to make a manager a working partner by giving him a 20 to 30 percent partnership interest. I figured he'd work harder and steal less as a co-owner while I still enjoyed control. It didn't work that way. When I ordered a new Cadillac through the business my partner gave me the jaundiced eye. Another partner took a tantrum when I took a business trip to New Orleans. It taught me a lesson, forcing me to buy back their shares for a healthy price, but I too was learning what you'll learn. Either it's your own business or it's not. And when you have partners it's never quite your own business.

Is this antipartner talk? Absolutely not. There are thousands of strong, successful partnerships at work proving two heads can indeed be better than one. A synergy is created while the partners achieve what they could never accomplish individually.

Confidence is what a partnership means to Mildred Pendergast of Amy's Fashions, a Providence-based chain of ladies apparel shops. Mildred is the first to admit she could never muster the confidence to go it alone, and neither could her equally timid partner whom she met at work. But the ladies did meet, struck up a friendship, and built on their common goal while feeding confidence and courage to each other. I constantly see it. Two prospective partners will tell me about their plans, each buoyed by the support of the other. The partners may be wrong for each other, or it may be a nonsense idea, or a foolish financial arrangement. What does it matter? The venture may fold or the partnership may break up, but the partners have been in business. They know what it's about and are no longer afraid to go it alone. Sometimes it takes a partner to make you an entrepreneur.

Management? It was the key ingredient for John Miller at Southland Food Commissary of Dedham, Massachusetts. John knew he was a great outside man able to hustle accounts for his start-up catering service, but he needed an inside partner to handle internal operations. Along came Ken Berman with years of experience in food service management to fill the bill. Today Southland grosses over $3 million a year.

Looking to augment skills is only part of the equation. Sometimes it pays to assess your own personality weaknesses and take on a partner with a corresponding strength. It creates terrific partnership marriages. I call them "Mutt and Jeff" operations.

One partner may be the idea man while the other puts the plan into play. One may be the resident good guy while the other is the resident S.O.B. One may be the perennial optimist while the other is the realist with both feet on the ground. It's more than management. It's chemistry. And the right partner can be a powerful ingredient in your business formula.

"Just plain old-fashioned fun" is how Becky Gavitas and Sarah Talini describe their gift shop partnership. Close friends for years, they decided to flap their entrepreneurial wings in a small venture to extend their social relationship into a business relationship. "We don't make a heck of a lot of money," confesses Becky. "And from a financial viewpoint the business should really be a one-owner operation," adds Sarah. "But money alone isn't our reason for being in business. We make fewer dollars, but have many more laughs working together." Who can call them wrong?

Several years ago the *Boston Globe* ran a series of business columns along the Dear Abby lines. Someone wrote asking whether he should take in a partner for a proposed car dealership. The reply said it all. "It's like getting married. If you have to ask, you've answered your own question." It's food for thought.

WHERE THE MONEY LURKS

A solid business idea will attract potential investors like bears to honey. Would you believe more people are looking for good investments than there are good opportunities? The trick is to plant your honey pot of an idea outside the right bear caves.

Where do you begin?

1. If you're looking for a "working partner" with capital, the emphasis will be on the career opportunity rather than the financial return. Precisely define the skills you need and seek out prospects just as you would an employee.
2. "Silent partners" kicking in small money in the $5000 to $50,000 range are generally high-income individuals in

the over-40 age bracket with spare investment dollars. They are constantly on the prowl for small business deals that can create enormous long-term gains not offered by conventional investments, hedged by the reality that the IRS will share their losses if the business doesn't make it. Professionals, executives, and business owners fall into this category.

3. Hunt for candidates who have been in your type of business, have succeeded, and are now retired. They are quicker to invest because they know your business, have more confidence in it, and often enjoy reliving their career through your venture.

4. Don't overlook people who can not only benefit from the profits of the business, but can equally benefit from doing business with you. Suppliers come under this category as I explain in Chapter 6, and so do distributors or potential customers.

5. Put your accountant, banker, and lawyer to work. They have plenty of clients with investment money and can oftentimes sell a deal on the basis of favorable tax angles alone.

6. Advertise. Partnership money is "bought and sold" like any other commodity. Place a simple ad in the classified section of your newspaper, describing your deal and the cash needed. The *New York Times* prints an entire column of "capital needed" listings every Sunday. So will your metropolitan newspaper. While you're at it, scan the bulging columns marked "Capital Available." It shows just how many people are anxious to exchange money for a partnership interest.

7. Promote your deal. Mention it to your barber and you may end up with his father-in-law as a partner. Many marriages come about through word of mouth.

Don't limit yourself. Set up an active campaign to network your deal. The objective is to have 20 to 30 interested partners. That's the only way to keep the upper hand, bid one against the other for the best deal, and find the right partner.

Beware! Hiding in some caves sniffing your honey pot are some creatures you *don't* want as partners.

1. Avoid close relatives. They're the easiest people to tap for money and that's precisely why it's a mistake. Business is business. It's difficult for relatives to say "no," and they seldom bring objectivity to the deal. Lose $50,000 for a stranger and you lost an investor. Lose it for your mother and you become the black sheep of the family. Don't risk family relationships over money. The same goes for anyone else whose relationship with you means more than dollars.

    Money is a peculiar commodity. I have seen soured business deals turn brother against brother and father against son. Keep them out of it. Should your business go bust you can still show up with the clan to enjoy Easter Sunday.

2. Avoid little old ladies in tennis shoes. Sometimes you'll spot them wearing Guccis instead while clipping AT&T dividend coupons. Plenty of people have loads of investment capital but are programmed toward the safe, predictable blue chip investments. Your idea for a pizza chain may excite them, but rarely do their investment objectives or expectations match those of an entrepreneur.

3. Run away from crybabies. Unless your business becomes another IBM, they'll be nipping at your heels. First-time investors who only remember the bright rosy picture but never contemplated the risk fall within this category. So too do investors who can't afford the loss or expect a quick cash payoff. You need a seasoned partner who understands what business is all about, can afford to risk capital, and is practical about what it can accomplish.

4. How about friends? They seem to be a logical choice but seldom are—particularly when you're scouting for a working partner. What you prize in a social friend is far different from what you may need in a working partner. This is probably the most common error in selecting partners. In my younger days, I ventured into a partnership with my closest friend. Why not? We had a ball, playing poker and

chasing the girls together, so why wasn't he the perfect candidate to connive with me for a quick fortune? I found out why when I saw his sub-zero management mentality at work. Fortunately we are still good friends and poker partners, but it's never easy to find out that your best friends can be your worst business partners.

PUT YOUR PARTNER TO THE ACID TEST

Pull out your magnifying glass and give your potential partner a thorough working over. I don't care how much money he's about to hand you, your job is to make certain you're marrying a swan and not an ugly duckling.

It's easy to act in haste and repent in leisure. Mr. M. spent less time screening partners than he did a minimum-wage stock boy. Mr. M. operates a retail and wholesale bakery business. He had a simple set of standards for a partner—$20,000 and the willingness to spend eight hours a day at the oven. His first partner physically ousted Mr. M. from the premises, and it took six months of expensive litigation to finally throw the partner out. His second partner walked away with $18,000 and was last seen heading west. Undaunted by his first two defeats, he now has partner number three, who spends half his time drinking bourbon and the rest of his waking hours at Alcoholics Anonymous. Partnerships are a people game. Finding them is the easy part. Picking them is a bit tougher.

Marty Colburne, a successful entrepreneur with several partnership start-ups under his belt in the Miami area, claims he can spot the "right" partner in one hour. "In the first 30 minutes I know how smart he is, and in the final 30 minutes I know what he knows about the business. And while he's talking I can tell whether he's someone I can work with and build with," says Marty.

Try Marty's checklist.

1. *Check the track record:* With a working partner you want a "doer" not a "drifter." Past performance counts. Educa-

tion, experience, career growth, and success in other ventures are all tallied on the scorecard.

2. *Investigate personal history:* Chronic illness, gambling, alcoholism or other personal problems have their telltale signs and can be fatal to a working relationship.

3. *Probe prior partnerships:* How did they work out? What do prior partners say about him? This is important even with "silent" partners, to test if they worked cooperatively or are chronic troublemakers.

4. *Meet the spouse:* He or she may be the real power behind the throne. You can never quite tell unless you see them together. And the last thing your business needs is a partner with a meddling spouse.

5. *Examine the lifestyle:* A shoestring start-up needs every penny it can get, and that means profits being plowed back rather than being harvested by a high-roller living for today.

6. *Talk about the business:* What does he know about it? Let him give you his ideas. Listen carefully. It won't take long to find out whether a partner can match your management mentality—or you his.

7. *Do you think alike?* This is the key. Check whether his ideas are compatible with yours on important issues such as growth, operations, responsibility, and financial planning. The blending of ideas is indeed the key to every successful partnership.

Above all, a good partnership is still chemistry. And to test that chemistry demands more than a pleasant chat. It needs a courtship. It's the ultimate acid-test as you constantly meet to discuss plans, check out competitive businesses, get together socially, and really get to know him or her as a person. As with any courtship, you want to know whether you have the foundation to build a future.

"HAVE I GOT A DEAL FOR YOU"

Money, money, money. It always comes down to money—how much you need and what you're prepared to give up in return.

Let's say your grand idea is a pizza parlor which will hopefully expand to dot the land as Happy Harry's Pizza Emporiums. All you need is $50,000 to launch your first. Since you can't swing any more loans and since your cash is nil, you approach an old college chum who made it big in plastics saying, "Have I got a deal for you!"

Standing there in his smoking jacket is your buddy patiently mixing his first martini. "So what's your deal?"

Maybe you'll tell him that for $50,000 he gets a piece of the action. Of course, he does. But what's fair—20 percent? 40 percent? 50 percent? 51 percent? Maybe you haven't thought about it.

Plasticman may like your idea, but as he stirs his second martini he suggests his own proposal. He'll loan the business $40,000, secured by assets of the business payable over five years at three points over prime, and also backed up by a mortgage on your home. For the other $10,000 he wants 1000 shares of preferred stock at $5 par value and 51 percent of the common stock with a right to convert $10,000 in debt to an additional 20 percent of the common stock. "Oh yes," he adds munching on the martini olive, "my attorneys will insist on a simultaneous registration of my shares so I can sell out if you go public." Plasticman concludes by spitting out his olive pit.

It's all so depressing. All you wanted was $50,000 to start Happy Harry's Pizza Emporium and now you're thoroughly confused while you suddenly realize how your buddy made his millions.

Look at it logically.

1. You need your accountant and lawyer to decipher the legal mumbo jumbo. Better still, you want your accountant and attorney to prepare a proposal *before* you call on prospective partners. Don't show up as a rank amateur begging for a handout. That's not business—it's charity. You want to look like a pro as you toast plasticman with your own martini.

2. You have to think about the deal from the investor's viewpoint. And he has plenty of questions going through his mind. How can I reduce my risk? What control do I have?

How does my investment evolve over time? How soon can I get my money out? How can I increase my return? When can I cash out? What are the tax angles? If you find a prospective partner overlooking these and perhaps 101 other interesting questions, you don't want him. He's too dumb to be your partner.

3. Here's the most important point. There's no such thing as a fair deal. Don't look through books or expect a computer to punch out the formula. Your partner will fight for as much as he can get while you jockey to give up as little as you can. The final deal will depend on many variables, the most important being whether you need his money more than he needs Happy Harry's Pizza Emporium. So while your buddy is shopping other deals to bury his money in, you'll be out shopping other investors. The reality of the marketplace will eventually show you the right deal.

PACKAGE YOUR PROPOSAL TO SELL

Everything to be sold is packaged to sell. You have to make it attractive. That's why new cars in a showroom are buffed to a shining gleam each morning and why my publisher will hopefully spend a fortune designing an appealing jacket for this book. It's no different when it comes to selling a piece of your business. You want the most for the least and you must package it to sell. How do you do it? Put on a prospective investor's eyeglasses and look at your idea the way he would.

1. *Sell Your Business Idea:*
Make it come alive. Paint the picture so the investor can visualize it. Why will it be successful? That's the key question. Explain the market, the competition, and precisely how your business plan will turn projections into profits. Show how you plan to operate the business in as much detail as possible, backing it up with costs, financial projections, and plans.

It doesn't have to be an exotic business idea to be a winner. Common, everyday businesses can show exciting profits. In my first Discount City store I sold a 20 percent interest for $30,000 to an industrialist. Now there's nothing particularly interesting about a discount store. America needed it like it needed another recession. But the town I had my sights on needed it and I could prove the business would show an $800,000 gross and $50,000 profit. A three-inch-thick file packed with facts and figures backed it up. We weren't far wrong. Investors are buying profits. Your job is to prove that the profits will be there.

2. *Sell Yourself:*

Investors don't really buy a piece of a business. What they do buy is a piece of its management. That's you. So you have to sell yourself. Once you've convinced investors you know what you're talking about, they'll have the confidence to buy whatever business idea you're selling. Watch a shrewd investor in action. He'll ask plenty of questions and try to punch holes in every answer. He will if he's a shrewd investor, and frankly I haven't come across any with that perfect combination of stupidity and money.

Blow your own horn. Play up your education, special skills, experience, and your own track record. Your first start-up will be the toughest sell and you'll probably end up on the short end of the deal. Once you have a success or two behind you, start mixing your own martinis. You'll have a pack of investors at your door crooning, "Have I got a deal for you!"

3. *Sell the Deal:*

This is the tricky part. Don't suggest the proposed split. Let that come from the investor. Simply provide the basic information he needs to frame an investment offer. What will he want to know?

The amount of capital needed.
How it will be used.
The other sources of capital.
If and when additional funds will be needed.
How profits will be utilized.

Your investor will be able to put it all together in his mind and, glancing over his shoulder at potential gain versus possible risk, make an opening offer. And it may be a far better offer than you imagined. It will be if you packaged your proposal to sell.

BEWARE THE BOOBY TRAPS

There are plenty of them out there. But three deals are particularly dangerous. Here's what to watch out for.

"The Glorified Employee Deal"   What's a "glorified employee"? Someone who thinks he's an owner but is in reality only an employee. And that's just what you are if you settle for less than an equal 50/50 partnership interest. A minority stockholder (owning less than 50 percent of the company) is powerless and is in control of nothing. Your partners with the majority interest control the business because they control the votes. They decide who sits on the Board of Directors, who the officers will be, and whether you keep your job. And if they boot you out, you can decorate your walls with the stock certificates.

Check around. You'll find plenty of fuzzy-thinking founders who trade away a majority share of the business for the start-up dollars. Somewhere down the line there's a fork in the road on how the business should be run and guess who's out?

Make it the one *non*-negotiable point in your partnership deal. Never, never accept *less* than an equal partnership and an equal say. It may be your partner's money at stake, but it's still your deal. If you're not worth as much as their money, head the other way.

"The More Is Better Deal"   If one partner is good, two or three is *not* better. It's worse. You want a business not a political club, and a political "back biting" club is just what you're likely to have when you have more than one partner. Finding two people who can think alike and get along is difficult enough without compounding it by bringing in more.

Not long ago a client picked up a four-store hobby shop chain started by three working partners and a wealthy angel who bankrolled it with $140,000. Within a year, two working partners ganged up on the third, and the third ran to the investor to put the squeeze on the other two. It wasn't a business. It was a battlefield. What they lost in sales they made up for in combat ribbons. It's a rarity when it doesn't happen. Usually it starts with each partner trying to call the shots and ends when they shoot each other. Who needs it? Keep it simple. Go with a maximum of one partner per deal. Make it a fair fight.

"The Tourniquet Treatment Deal" A wealthy partner can be a dangerous foe once the business is churning out profits and looks like a proven money-maker. Some partners will reward you for a job well done and give you more money to expand with, while others will decide it's the perfect moment to dump you and take over your share of the business for a song. That's when they turn their financial one-upmanship into a variety of squeeze plays. It may be refusal to help with any additional financing the business may need. A common squeeze play is to call in loans the company may owe the partner. Armed with the staying power of cash he may even start expensive but frivolous litigation to get rid of you. Whatever the tactic, the tourniquet treatment is money man's way of proving that in the battle between your brains and his money the money always wins.

Be patient. It may not happen until that perfect moment when the business is well off the ground. But that's just when your money partners get greedy—when there's something to get greedy about. And like any other poker player, you want a pile of chips to match theirs when the bluff is called.

It can also work in reverse. Without even realizing it, you may be walking your own less financially endowed working partner into a tourniquet treatment. Let's suppose you team up with a partner, each throwing in $10,000 to start the business. Two years later the business is expanding and needs another $30,000. You don't want to mortgage your house while your penniless partner whistles. A mismatch in your financial resources will inevitably lead to either stagnant growth, uneven contributions, or the reality that the financially stronger partner should take over.

Watch out for these three booby-trap deals. They spell trouble with a capital "T."

SEVEN TIPS ON THE CARE AND FEEDING OF PARTNERS

Why is it that some partnerships are whopping successes while others are miserable failures? It's always the case of people knowing how to handle people. And you don't have to be a master politician to keep a smile on your partner's face. A few commonsense tips will do:

1. Don't overestimate potential profits. A novice may sell an investor on the promise the business will show a $40,000 first-year profit, and then faces a lot of explaining when he comes in with a $2000 loss. Be realistic and stay on the conservative side. Always underestimate the good and overestimate the bad to look like a genius.

2. Keep your partners involved. Make them co-conspirators in the success—or failure—of the business by having them join in the decision-making process. You are looking for trouble to keep silent partners in the dark and then hit them with major problems. Regular meetings to track the progress of the business are a must.

3. Don't rely on standard corporate books and bylaws to document your deal. Supplement it with a written agreement on all major points, including salaries, bonuses, expenses, and division of responsibility. Remember, once you're a partner you're also an employee. Know what you're entitled to. It can avoid plenty of arguments later.

4. Don't make up your own report card on how the business is going. All financial information on the business should come only from your accountant, and let him verify your figures. As part of the reporting process, you may be inclined to put together your own financial data to show silent partners. A year or two later when the business fails, your partner begins to wonder about the accuracy of your numbers. It can create some nasty lawsuits.

5. Watch out for side deals, hidden profits, or conflict of interest situations. Nothing can turn a partnership into a vendetta faster than a partner who thinks you double-timed your obligation to make money for him. If you're involved in deals that can even remotely impact on your partnership arrangement, bring it out into the open and square it away before you start.

6. Don't let minor feuds or irritations mushroom into major battles. If you have areas of disagreement, then meet and resolve them before they get out of hand. If you check many of the failed partnerships, you'll find it was the small annoyances rather than a substantial disagreement on policy that caused defeat.

7. Listen, listen, listen. It's not just your business. Your partners have a say and many times what they have to say makes a lot of sense. It comes back to what I said at the beginning of the chapter. If you want to be the "loner" or the entrepreneurial maverick and call all the shots, then forget partners.

"DIVORCE"—PARTNERSHIP STYLE

Strive for the best, but prepare for the worst. The pessimistic facts are that 70 percent of all partnerships do break up within two years of formation. And don't look for any one reason. It may be the inability to get along, disagreement on the future direction of the business, or simply an alternate career opportunity for a partner. Whatever the reasons, the dismal statistics prove it's difficult to keep two or more on the same track to build a longterm business future. It's even more difficult with a shoestring start-up with its embryonic problems of poor capitalization and a "touch and go" daily operation.

If "divorce fever" sets in, it may be too late. You must set up the deal so you control it and maintain the upper hand. Otherwise you may find yourself on the outside looking in as your partner walks away with the business.

The best way to handle it is to structure the arrangement so you have the option to buy your partner out. For example, you may need a partner's investment of $20,000 to launch your business. In return, you agree to give him 50 percent ownership. Perhaps your partner would sign an option to acquire his interest for $35,000 within two years? A silent partner may go along with it, considering it a far better investment than a safer but low yielding savings account.

I successfully used this technique in several of my own start-ups. Silent partners realize a stalemate can only lead to dissolution of the business and perhaps loss of investment. Conversely, if the partnership isn't working out, he's certainly entitled to his share of the net worth of the business and a healthy bonus for risking his capital to start it. So the buy-out figure is both speculative and negotiable. Sometimes it's difficult to precisely fix a fair value in advance. In a few deals I have reserved the "buy-out" option for five years and agreed to let an arbitrator set the buy-out price if and when the option is exercised. But throw an additional ingredient into the deal. When it comes time to buy out your partner, have him finance the buy-out price rather than expect cash. For example, the agreement may provide that 20 percent of the buy-out price will be in cash and the balance paid over a defined number of years with specified interest and security.

A "buy-out" option will:

1. Allow you to dissolve the partnership should disagreement arise. Having a fixed, predetermined (or arbitrated) buy-out figure puts a ceiling on what it will take to dissolve the partnership while retaining complete ownership.
2. Provide you time to work down existing loans and/or build the business so you can borrow to buy out your partner.
3. Insure that you will not have to share long-term profits or gains with a partner.

Essentially, a partnership structured along these lines has the characteristics of both equity and debt financing. Your partner has an ownership interest in the business, but you have the right to pay his investment back with a deserved profit to regain sole ownership. It may be a steep price, but it's seldom as steep as what this same partner would walk away with many years later. Shake your partner's hand when you say goodbye. Don't forget it was his money that got you started.

KEY POINTS TO REMEMBER

1. Partnership money is the most expensive money you can buy. If you want a partner for his money alone, consider it your last resort.
2. Partnerships are not for everyone. Do you really want to answer to someone else?
3. Look for the *right* partner. The right partner will bring more than money.
4. Put your partner to the acid-test: Does he have what it takes to succeed?
5. Package your proposal to sell. No one will invest if he can't see the benefit of the deal.
6. A "fair" partnership deal is the best deal you can derive. Forget magic formulas; they don't exist.
7. Avoid nonsense booby-trap deals that can only cause you problems.
8. Plan for the worst. Cover the contingency by cementing a "buy-out" agreement.
9. A partnership is only another form of "marriage." It's the joining of your brains with their money to start on a shoestring. It can work if you know what you're getting into.

10

SETTING UP SHOP

Setting up shop for Hal and Mindy Oreste is a ten-minute affair. Owners of a unique roadside business, the Orestes operate under the name of "The Teepee." Using a nomadic approach to retailing, the Orestes tote their Indian-style tent to various locations alongside interstate highways slicing through New Mexico and Arizona. Within a few minutes of spotting a likely location, the tent is up and several tables are loaded with Indian handicrafts beckoning tourists to stop. "Our objective is to take in $200 to $300 a day before the sheriff has us packing and on to the next county," smiles Hal Oreste. "And we usually succeed."

Chances are, setting up your show will be quite a bit more complicated. Facing you are two considerable investment decisions:

1. Where to locate.
2. How to find—and buy—the necessary fixtures and equipment.

This chapter will show you several techniques for setting up shop on a shoestring, saving you a bundle of cash in the process.

The place to begin is explaining that it makes sense to consider location and equipment as a package. The two items are very closely related. In the following chapter you'll see how to hunt your inventory to bring the business to life. Let's take first things first and give your business a home and some fixtures and equipment to go with it.

DEVELOPING THE MISER'S TOUCH

Businesses started with the miser's touch usually have what it takes to turn into a pot of gold. It comes down to underspending on rent and fancy frills equipment to build and applying the cash where it will do the most good—on inventory and promotion. It's always a balancing of needs, and what you probably need least for a successful start is an expensive overhead or costly equipment to chew up cash faster than you can generate it.

So you have to think cheap and be cheap to get in cheap. For some people with champagne tastes, it's more than an objective—it's an impossibility. With a few, it's not knowing how to put together a business for less than top dollar. This chapter will help. Others simply overestimate what their business needs, throwing away valuable dollars while they find out. Other big spenders just can't bring themselves to think in Spartan terms when their personal lifestyle is on a high note.

Are you likely to be a big spender? MBA students at Suffolk University Business School think so. They surveyed start-ups to determine the relationship of rent and equipment costs to profits and success. They checked out comparable retail, service, and manufacturing firms with conclusive findings. The most successful businesses had the lowest rent and capital equipment costs. The study went further: 92 percent of the businesses examined could have started on an appreciably less expensive scale, with no anticipated drop in sales but with a healthy jump in profits. The big spenders were everywhere. With a tighter purse string, they would now have a fatter purse.

A few examples. One Italian-style restaurant in the study spent $90,000 on fixtures, equipment, and renovation costs. A restaurant supply firm estimated the same business could be put together for less than $25,000 with comparable used equipment, competitive bidding on renovations, and eliminating some renovations that actually reduced sales potential. You have to sell quite a few spaghetti dinners to recoup the overspent $65,000.

Another big spender was a small journal publisher found in a $25-per-sq.-ft. plush office building overseeing his increasingly shaky 4000-sq.-ft. empire. The "B" students had a ball with this one while they tallied up $90,000 a year in wasted rent and $16,000 a year to finance plush office furnishings. That's big spending to the tune of $66,000 a year from a business that couldn't afford it. Today you'll find the business where it belongs—in a $10,000-a-year low-rent building with the office furnished in modern K-Mart. But the business is now making money.

That's what it's all about—making money. And you don't make money when you're foolishly spending money. And the most foolish money you're likely to spend is in setting up your shop. So forget grandiose ideas or castles in the sky. You need the miser's touch.

HANGING YOUR HAT FOR A DOLLAR A DAY

At what point are you spending too much on rent? The answer is simple. When there's alternative space available to house your business for less. And for service, mail-order, and small manufacturing firms, that cheaper alternative space is your own home. It's where most start-ups in these businesses start, and it's the logical starting place.

I recently read an interesting article on some of today's flourishing businesses started in garages. It told fascinating tales of everything from printing plants to mail-order firms whose beginnings were a common, everyday home garage—and a rent at less than $1.00 a day to cover the light bill and a gallon of kerosene fuel for the space heater. Others move the clutter out of their basement to hang their hat, and others ascend skyward to the attic or a converted bedroom. Wherever you find them, you won't find them paying rent if they can avoid it.

Shrewd investors are always on the lookout for these "start-at-home" ventures, waiting for them to outgrow the corner of a basement and take the important step into larger outside quarters. It signals a pragmatist at the helm of a growth enterprise.

Is it smart for you to start at home? Here are some pros and cons to consider:

The pros are:

1. You avoid rent costs.
2. You avoid lease commitments. It's important when you don't know how successful your business will be—and can't really assess short-term space needs.
3. It's ideal for a space-time venture.
4. It's tax deductible. The portion of your home used for business purposes can be deducted from your household costs. Uncle Sam can be generous here and oftentimes the tax savings actually net you several hundred dollars a year to help your business along.

Why think twice about it?

1. The principal reason is that it's tough to work and concentrate at home. Many household entrepreneurs report the distractions, family interruptions, and the tendency to sneak away for a few moments of creature comforts reduce efficiency to the point where it's false economy. An "at home" venture may be considered more of a hobby than a business. Whether this is an obstacle for you depends again on your own discipline and the ground rules for your family.
2. Space limitations must also be considered. Many household start-ups have such confined space that "set-up" and "break-down" time eat into efficiency.

These reasons aside, many people reject the idea based on imagery—"what customers will think." It's a factor if you have a steady stream of customers knocking on your door, but with most businesses in this category the customers don't come knocking and have no idea the business is a desk in the attic. Prestige mail drop and telephone answering services and communal office space are answers for those that do. For minimal fees you can have the plushest address and telephone number in town, or you can pop into a swank—but shared—office to meet your occasional key customer. Look in your metropolitan paper for listings.

When the patter of approaching customers increases, a split operation may make sense. Typically a start-up will rent a presentable office for sales purposes, while confining production to a bargain basement facility. The merger of the two locations comes about when the two functions must be housed together for operating efficiency and control.

Once the business is beyond the survival stage, a rent ceiling should be based on a percentage of sales rather than dollars per sq. ft. "It's better expense control," reports Jack Manoog, a Cape Cod–based real estate consultant. "Too often business people figure that if they find bargain-priced space it's a bargain for them. It's only true when the total rent is in line with sales."

What are some of the hottest low-rent bargains around?

Retail basement space leads the list and is plentiful. Many of my clients wisely rented space in a supermarket or other retail basement for rents as low as $4 to $5 a sq. ft. while comparable space elsewhere costs vastly more. You may have to spend a few dollars to build a separate entrance, but it's nothing compared to the rent savings.

Older and larger homes can be an ideal rent saver for "paper-work" or light production businesses. A large home may have 3000 to 4000 sq. ft. of usable space and rent for $25,000 to $50,000 a year—depending on the local real estate market. Still, residential homes can cut rent by 50 percent compared to commercial space. One caution: check the zoning before you sign the lease.

Boarded-up service stations can be another bargain. Fix-up costs are small, and stations can be adapted to a wide range of businesses needing up to 2000 feet to operate.

Rental agents and commercial brokers don't usually lead you to the best deals. They're networked into conventional space and conventional space means conventional rent. Since you want cheap rent, it means going after it yourself. You may spend more than a dollar a day, but you'll also save more than a dollar a day.

GOING WHERE THE CUSTOMERS ARE

Retail start-ups are another story. Cheap is out and expensive is in. You need a high-traffic location to make it today in retailing, and high-traffic locations bring fancy rents. A high-traffic location is perhaps even more important for a shoestring start-up than for a well-capitalized business because the shoestring operation must start at a profitable level, and that only happens with a prime location.

Not all shoestring start-ups agree. To an extent they're right. You can start in a low-rent, low-traffic location and bolster traffic with a high-cost advertising program to pull the people to you. But don't delude yourself. When you spend money to draw customers, it's only another form of rent.

The best example of the two methods at work is the Factory Sweater Outlet. Its first location was an abandoned factory building on a secondary road with light vehicle traffic. "The rent was only $7000 a year so we couldn't pass it up," recounts its merchandise manager. "But it costs us over $20,000 a year in billboard ads to let people know we're around—so it really costs us $27,000 a year to pull our $650,000 in sales." Some years ago, the Factory Sweater Outlet opened its second location in an enclosed shopping mall, paying $25,000 a year for 1600 sq. ft. This location is pulling the same $600,000 to $700,000 a year without advertising, so with mark-ups and other expenses equal, the choice of locations is a toss-up.

Given the choice, the preference should be to the high-rent, high-traffic location. Three reasons: First is that many retail operations offer convenience or impulse goods. People won't travel for everyday inexpensive items even with heavy promotion. The pulling power of ads will work with clothing, shoes, furniture, or unusual items that fall into the demand category, but most merchandise needs the steady flow of traffic. The second reason is that a good advertising program takes "know-how"; too many start-ups think they can whip together a high-powered campaign and fall on their faces. The last reason is timing. Even with heavy advertising, it takes weeks or months to create a traffic-building reputation. Usually you don't have the time.

Can you land a prime location? It's not easy. The very best locations are enclosed malls. Just as suburban strip centers crippled downtown stores, the enclosed malls now dominate the strip centers. If a mall is the type of location for your business, you'll have plenty of competition for space. Most developers prefer chain tenants with their recognized name and strong credit rating. In many instances a mall will be locked up by chain tenants a year or two before it's even built. The few remaining spaces usually go to strong independents. So how do you land space in a mall?

1. Consider a co-signer for your lease. Many developers will consider you if you can back up your lease with a strong signature.
2. Lease insurance is another possibility. Some insurance firms will guarantee your lease for a premium, taking you over the credit hurdle. A commercial broker can lead you to them.
3. Kiosk or "island" space is always a possibility if you need only 100 to 200 sq. ft. It's usually idle space for a landlord anxious to make it an income producer. Check some malls in your area and you'll see plenty of shoestring entrepreneurs peddling everything from soft-serve ice cream to stuffed animals in their thriving island locations.
4. Sublets are another possibility. Many tenants want to cut back on the size of their store and will sublet a portion to a related business. Concessioned space is an excellent space vehicle for a shoestring start-up, working equally well in discount stores and supermarkets. Don't overlook the idea.

Some of the most successful start-ups happily pay exorbitant rents to achieve equally exorbitant sales. The Quincy Marketplace in Boston's revitalized waterfront is one example. Rents top the $30-per-sq.-ft. mark, or triple what you'd pay for suburban space, but the tenants aren't complaining. Most report sales are at least twice what another location would offer. It's difficult to find a city without similar opportunities.

Convenience type businesses—food stores, dry cleaners, appliances, drugs—each have their own logical location. Site analysis is beyond the scope of this book, but remember the key point. A low rent isn't necessarily a bargain. You want a location to give you the customers.

TWO MONEY-SAVING POINTS TO NEGOTIATE

Your attorney can walk you through the typical boilerplate on your twelve-page lease. Your job is to negotiate two critical points that can save you a bundle in start-up costs.

1. Deferred rents.
2. Landlord renovations.

Consider the economics.

1. *Deferred Rent:* Your rent will probably be set at a fixed amount for the first several years, increasing in later years to adjust for inflation. And a heavy cash outlay in the beginning months when sales are lowest can positively put a crimp in your cash flow. The strategy? Bargain for lower beginning rent and add the difference to the later months (or years) when you can better afford it. "It's not an insignificant point," suggests Russ Stockwell, who started Stockwell Chicken Ranch, a family-style restaurant in southeastern Massachusetts. "Our landlord wanted $2000 a month rent, which was a fair enough figure— except we couldn't afford it until the business got off the ground," adds Stockwell. "So we proposed starting at $1000 a month for six months to catch our breath, tacking the $6000 savings on to the next 30 months. Keeping the $6000 in our checkbook saw us through a tough start-up period when survival was nip and tuck."

Security deposits are another negotiable item to be deferred or eliminated altogether. With landlords increasingly having the upper hand, the three- or even six-month security deposit can lock you out of some attractive locations. The cure? One is to pledge personal collateral—a car or house mortgage for an equal amount. Another is to find a guarantor whose liability is limited to the deposit amount.

The same strategy can even save you from the first month's rent. One of my clients pulled just that ploy, deferring $7500 in three months' initial rent. The landlord was satisfied, holding a mortgage on my client's computers to secure the later payment of $7500, while my client had the money to use for other start-up costs.

Can you get the keys to a prime location without upfront rent? In large measure it depends on your respective bargaining position. A desperate landlord with a desperate location may give you six months free rent if you're smart enough to push for it. And you always push when you're working on a shoestring.

2. *Pass Renovation Costs on to Your Landlord:* Negotiate this point for all it's worth, for it's worth plenty. What renovation costs are we talking about? You name it. A new store front, ceilings, tiled or carpeted floors, air conditioning, lighting, panelled walls—or whatever else it takes to turn a concrete box into a furnished store. And whatever it takes costs plenty. Betty Tamer, an executive with a leading shopping center development firm, tells it straight when she says, "Cash-poor independents can't afford to take new space in most shopping centers. And it's not the rent that keeps them out, it's the renovation costs—like most developers we provide only a 'shell,' wall-to-wall cinder block. It stops most start-ups cold when they realize it will cost them $50,000 to $100,000 to complete it as a 'turn-key.' "

Worse still, renovation costs can't readily be financed by the tenant. Banks can't repossess wall panelling or a new store front now belonging to a landlord. But a landlord can, often incorporating the improvement costs into his mortgage financing. Of course, you'll pay higher rent for a "turn-key" space compared to a "shell" since the landlord must recoup the costs, but it will save you some serious upfront money.

Negotiating landlord improvements is no game for the amateur. Consider these three tips:

1. List what you absolutely need to make the location suitable for occupancy. Avoid the frills and needless high-cost improvements. Don't forget you eventually pay for the improvements in a stepped-up lease.

2. Obtain bids. An architect or contractor can help. Make sure you know the lowest price so you know what it's worth in a higher rent.

3. Negotiate to split the costs, with your share being tacked
    on to the rent. One advantage with landlord-furnished im-
    provements is their ability to do it at less cost. And don't
    forget, the improvements are to the landlord's property.

THE MILLION-DOLLAR LOOK ON HUMBLE PENNIES

"Cardiac arrest" is what Barry Adler called it when he received
a $48,000 quote to renovate a dilapidated interior into a modern
seafood restaurant on the Cape Cod waterfront. "And that didn't
include the equipment—just the ceiling, floors, and four walls.
With $2600 budgeted I had to be creative—and damn creative—
to give it the million-dollar look," Barry quickly adds.

"I decided to go with a nautical theme, figuring I could pull
together plenty of sea-faring memorabilia to give it the right
feeling. Instead of a $3000 drop ceiling I paid $200 for used
fishing nets, fireproofing them to get by the fire code. Creating
my own 'fishnet' ceiling, complete with used $10 spotlights
peeking through, gave it the right touch. Would-be walnut
paneling was replaced by four high-school kids giving the
walls a fresh coat of blue paint, hurriedly adorned with twenty
seascapes for sale on consignment by local Rembrandts. It not
only produced a few bucks profit but saved me $8000 on pan-
eling. The architect recommended a $12,000 marble foyer. I
had a better idea lining the foyer with floor to ceiling crates
featuring fine wines from every corner of the world, adorning
it with a $20 sign—'Sea Shanty Winery.' Customers loved it
and while lingering for a seat, would select their choice, boosting wine sales by 40 percent. Discarding the $24-a-sq.-yd. car-
peting samples, a rental floor sander returned the floor to its
original high-gloss state. It looked like a seafood restaurant
and a mighty classy restaurant at that," Barry proudly will tell
you. With humble pennies, Barry achieved his own million-
dollar look.

Restaurants aren't the only ugly ducklings to be turned into
swans on a few creative ideas. Walk through clothing stores, gift
shops, and even the corner drugstore and you'll see cost-saving

renovation techniques at work. Consumer Value Stores, a 500-store pharmacy chain, knows how to cut corners while building image. Walk into any one of their stores and you'll see manufacturer-furnished wall murals surrounding the store. Coppertone, Alka-Seltzer, etc., form a continuous billboard boosting their sales while brightening the walls. It's a clever idea. And there are thousands of equally good ideas you can use to go first class on a shoestring budget.

If you don't have the creative touch, then borrow it. The best advice is to pick up ideas from others. Observe. Walk through businesses and keep your eyes open. What cost-saving treatments can you borrow for your ceiling? What inexpensive lighting suggestions do you see? How do walls come alive? What's happening under your feet? What are the small touches that can work for your operation? You too will learn how paint, mirrors, and accessories create optical illusions and attractive businesses at a paltry price.

Interior decorators can help. For a modest fee you can save thousands. Why not? They know what works in a home and the same formulas can work in sprucing up a business. I guarantee it's a wise investment and can save you a fortune in the process.

THE BARGAINLAND OF EQUIPMENT DEALS

The biggest bargains of all are to be found when it's time to buy fixtures and equipment. In fact, you can usually pick up what you need with absolutely no cash outlay.

This is another area where you want to underspend. Never pay top dollar to buy the best or the newest. It pays small dividends. Many small business bankruptcies can be traced to a top-heavy investment in capital assets. Needed cash is gobbled up to buy and more cash is gobbled to pay hefty carrying costs. "High rollers who buy new are making a big mistake," says Ralph DiFonzo of Boston's Central Restaurant Equipment & Supply Company. "A restaurant, for example, can easily cost $100,000 to equip at showroom prices, while the same equipment slightly used may be available for $20,000. And you don't sell fewer steaks from a two-year-old broiler than from a new one."

So where do you find the bargains?

1. The auction pages are your best bet. Paul Saperstein, the largest commercial auctioneer in New England, will tell you that he has 20 to 30 businesses lined up for auction at any given time. "Everything from variety stores to manufacturing plants, with good, serviceable equipment going for 10 to 40 percent of their original cost." Auctioneers in your city have the same bargains. Here's added information. Don't wait for the ads in the paper. Many auctioners bid on their own for auction equipment and warehouse it to sell later at a better price. Make a list of what you need and make some phone calls. And don't hesitate to go to auctioneers in other cities. It's well worth $500 in travel and moving costs to save several thousand.

2. Contact chain stores if you want retail fixtures. Here's why. Oftentimes chains remodel and warehouse older fixtures, hoping to sell them piecemeal to start-up firms. In many instances, they'll buy out a store and remodel to their own specifications. I outfitted two of my drugstores just that way, buying gondolas, wall cases, show cases, and just about everything else I needed for about 20 percent of new fixtures cost.

3. Equipment-supply firms are another stopover. The yellow pages list fixture and equipment firms in every type business. There are some tricks of the trade here, too. They may only advertise new fixtures—and they'll certainly push you to buy new because they make a better profit. Stand firm. They'll lead you to their own warehouse jam packed with bargains. And if they don't have it they can get it. The businesses they're selling new equipment to have their used items which may be perfect for you.

4. The classified ads offer some bargains. Every metropolitan newspaper features columns of businesses looking to sell

used equipment. From my experiences, you tend to pay slightly more when buying from a private party than at a distress sale, but it does offer convenience. Place a few of your own ads. Many business people have equipment they want to unload but haven't actively looked for buyers.

5. Trade journals and associations are frequently overlooked. They lead you to the equipment you're likely to need, and advertising costs are low.

By checking out these five valuable sources, you'll have your pick of bargains, and if you play your cards right you may be able to buy without upfront cash and outlay. It only takes leg work.

Charlie Nardozzi, the proud owner of Charlie's Pizza, a bustling shop for the teenage crowd in Boston's North End, used dimes instead of leg work to equip his start-up. New tables and chairs would cost $2500. Two spanking-new Blodgett ovens another $7500, and a new NCR cash register $2100. "Ten thousand dollars was $10,000 too much, I couldn't afford more than $2500 and thought I was forever stuck in my job as a stitcher in a shoe factory," moaned Charlie.

Seven phone calls proved Charlie wrong. The first call was to an auctioneer who led Charlie to two Blodgett ovens only three years old. The price was an unbeatable $2700, financed by the seller who reluctantly agreed to finance with $500 down and the balance over two years at 8 percent interest secured by the ovens. Charlie was learning. Sellers will finance. Three more phone calls hooked Charlie up with a terrific bargain in tables and chairs. A restaurant under renovation had just what Charlie needed and for $500 Charlie carted them away. Two more phone calls and Charlie had a five-year-old cash register for $250, picked up through the classifieds. "All it had to do was ring up a sale and hold the money. When I'm as large as Pizza Hut I'll upgrade to the fancy computerized registers." So for $1250 Charlie was in business. The final phone call? It was to Charlie's foreman at the shoe factory telling him to look for a new stitcher.

You won't read about Charlie in the *Wall Street Journal,* but success can be a tasty pizza topped with trimmings made in a used oven, devoured on a secondhand table, and tallied on a slightly tired cash register.

100 PERCENT TERMS ANYONE CAN GET

Buy low, finance high, and keep your cash intact. It's a winning formula for shrewd start-ups. So how do you finance high—very high—with 100 percent loans?

Banks and finance companies are prime candidates. One reason they'll consider 100 percent financing on bargain-priced equipment is because the collateral value is there. "New equipment only justifies a 50 to 60 percent loan," comments one banker. "If we have a loan against a new $10,000 printing press, for example, we can only recoup $4000 to $5000 if foreclosure is necessary. But if it's worth $5000 at liquidation, why shouldn't we lend $5000 against it?"

Seller financing is another possibility. Sellers typically aren't as interested in immediate cash as they are in disposing of what's no longer needed. One of my clients even managed to buy a six-seat, $150,000 airplane for his growing commuter airline from a larger airline upgrading to larger aircraft. With the plane as collateral, the seller financed the full $150,000 over five years.

Leveraged financing of new equipment is typically the game of manufacturers or dealers selling the equipment at a sizable profit. Many so-called franchise systems are nothing more than a scheme to sell equipment—often at an inflated price. For example, one poorer but wiser franchisee of a $140,000 car wash franchise now realizes that he bought $40,000 worth of equipment and a worthless name for $100,000. Why shouldn't the franchisor happily finance the equipment? Similar stories come from the dry cleaning, printing, and even the soft-serve ice cream industries. There are good and bad actors in every field, but the point is that a small down payment doesn't make a good deal when you're paying an excessive price for the privilege.

Increased competition in the equipment fields makes manufacturer financing almost mandatory to their own survival. Store fixture manufacturers routinely have arrangements with banks that will finance 70 to 80 percent of the purchase price. Since the manufacturer factors the note, the bank has recourse against the manufacturer. Your credit rating is only important to the manufacturer who has considerably more lenient standards. Computers are another good example. You can't find a major computer firm that doesn't offer a generous financing package, and today you can buy a computer with 5 to 10 percent down, reminiscent of automobile financing.

Manufacturer financing has its downside. Even if you do buy at a fair price, the finance charges are usually 2 to 3 percent higher than a bank's, although lower than many finance companies. The upside is the manufacturer or dealer is more inclined to honor its warranties or service contracts while you still owe them money.

The greatest danger with manufacturer financing on new equipment is that it's too easy to get. A start-up entrepreneur will perhaps call in a store fixture firm and buy $40,000 in new fixtures with $6000 down, and six months later strangle on the $34,000 note. With a few phone calls you may find a slightly used version for $10,000 and perhaps win 100 percent financing in the bargain.

THE MAGIC OF LEASING

Since 1960 the number of firms leasing—instead of owning— has tripled. Tax savings are one reason, since you can deduct the entire lease cost, while only deducting the depreciated value of owned equipment. It's not the selling point with shoe-string start-ups with a different set of priorities.

Why should you consider leasing?

1. Needed cash is low: most firms lease equipment upon payment of only the first month's rent and a one- or two-month security deposit. Buying may require several thousand dollars more in up front cash even with leveraged financing.
2. Obsolescence is another factor: in some industries equipment becomes obsolete overnight. Computers again serve as a good example. With leasing you have increased flexi-

bility to upgrade to newer items. Try to negotiate the clause into the agreement giving you the option to trade up to newer models.

3. Maintenance is a key advantage in leasing. Usually a leasing firm will give you the option to include a maintenance or service policy. Sometimes it's overpriced, but many start-ups prefer it because it does fix costs, avoiding large unexpected repair bills on a fragile cash flow.

Is leasing for you? It may be with motor vehicles and high-cost equipment with rapid obsolescence, and even cash registers and store carpeting. It's generally not the way to go with store fixtures or other capital assets expected to last more than five years.

HOW TO MAKE THE MOST OF
MANUFACTURERS' FREE TRIALS

You can get a trial run on many types of equipment needed for your business—particularly office equipment.

Let's say you need several computers, a copy machine, and a fax machine to start a service business. To buy the equipment in advance may drain your small cash, so instead you ask for a 30 to 60 day trial run at which point you will either buy, lease, or return the items. The advantage is obvious: You have the needed equipment to get started without spending a dime, buying once the cash flow is rolling. It's a common practice, and most dealers have demonstrator office equipment and even cash registers for just this purpose.

Don't try to play one dealer against the other with a never-ending cycle of trial runs; word gets around.

A HELPING HAND FROM BIG SUPPLIERS

If you're a manufacturer, your equipment problems may be solved with the helping hand of raw material suppliers. It's not unusual to buy $100,000 a year of chemicals, plastics, pharmaceuticals, or a host of other raw material and feed it through $20,000 worth of equipment to mold the finished product. So the proposition is this. Since your suppliers are making a healthy profit on your purchases, why shouldn't they subsidize the cost of the equipment? Negotiated properly, it has money-saving possibilities.

This one technique virtually capitalized a small baked goods manufacturer. The entrepreneurial baker projected buying over $200,000 a year from his flour supplier. So he drove a hard bargain, demanding the supplier buy the $40,000 in baking equipment for him. The supplier would hold title to the equipment leasing it to the baker for a nominal $2000 a year until the baker purchased $800,000 in flour, at which time the supplier would hand the baker a free bill of sale. It made sense to the supplier, who looked at it as a 5 percent discount, and made even more sense to the baker, who bootstrapped his company with his supplier's money.

SHARING TIME IS SAVING DOLLARS

Idle equipment is idle dollars, and you need your few dollars working 120 percent of the time. When you can't fully utilize equipment, tap into a time-sharing arrangement, borrowing the equipment only when you need it.

I can show you hundreds of examples where time-sharing made a new business possible, or at the least helped it along. A couple will do.

The Round Table Press turns out specialized newsletters for several industries. Rather than subcontract printing, it time-shares a full printing plant on weekends from a commercial printer operating weekdays.

A 50/50 time-share on a car wash? "Why not?" asks Herb Stolte, who originated a novel business picking up and cleaning autos for car dealers and car rental agencies. Within a month Stolte had 25 dealers and agencies signed up and the promise of 200 cars a week to clean. All that was missing was the car wash.

Noticing a car wash in the next town that suffered from low weekday activity, Stolte bargained to rent the weekday mornings for 20 percent of the total operating costs. "That's all I needed," suggests Stolte, "so why spend more?"

Time-sharing can make as much sense for costly equipment as it does in the vacation resort field. Not only does it keep beginning costs down, but it may provide access to even more efficient equipment than you could afford to buy.

Define your equipment needs. Circle equipment you may only need on a part-time basis. Those are the perfect candidates for a time-share arrangement.

PROMISE A PIECE OF THE ACTION

Many of the best partnerships are marriages between businesses with equipment and start-ups with ideas.

"It worked for us," says Jerry Hillman, referring to his joint venture with Mystic Plastics, a high-powered plastic extruding firm capable of churning out Hillman's innovative disposable clinical thermometers. "No sooner did I receive the patent than I discovered it would cost me $750,000 to buy the specialized equipment. Venture capital was a possibility, but I didn't want to give up my controlling interest as the venture capitalists demanded. Another alternative was to subcontract production, but that too would put me at the mercy of the production people." The ideal formula for Hillman was the formation of a new corporation, with Mystic Plastics owning 40 percent while Hillman retained 60 percent ownership. Mystic, in turn, contracted to produce the thermometers for the new corporation at a very low price.

How common are these joint ventures involving companies with equipment and those that need it? Not as common as they could be. Start-up entrepreneurs facing the hurdle of putting together an intensive equipment business usually look for the money to buy the equipment, or following Hillman's path, seek out venture capital funds trading part ownership. Offering a piece of the action to a company that can provide the equipment is a means to the same end. And frequently it's a better alternative, because you can strike a more favorable bargain with a partner who's only making his equipment work a bit harder.

PRODUCING PROFITS WITHOUT PRODUCTION

The most important message in this chapter is perhaps this last message. You may not need a physical plant to put yourself in business. In fact, you may be better off without it by buying or subcontracting what you plan to sell.

Many start-ups look at their business idea as essentially a production activity, overlooking the common reality that it's more of a marketing activity with production better left to someone else. And when you begin to think this way you'll find it easier—and safer—to start.

I learned that lesson in one of my first start-ups. Two acquaintances of mine were fast developing a reputation as store renovation specialists. So we started a fixture and store remodeling firm, complete with a plant turning out customer fixtures built to order, while my partners and a few hired tradesmen began to rack up sales with their creative approach to store renovations. A year later the report card was in, and we found we were making money on renovations but losing our shirt on fixture production. We quickly closed down the factory, subcontracting production to a much larger firm that could turn out the fixtures at half our cost. It was faulty thinking right from the start. We should have realized our strength was in sales and renovations. We didn't need ten people on the payroll turning out fixtures to go along with the remodeling jobs—not even when we could buy cheaper.

If your business involves manufacturing as well as marketing, consider a two-step start-up. Subcontract manufacturing, and concentrate on marketing during the initial stages. It offers several advantages.

1. You can test the market for your product without extensive plant start-up costs.

2. You'll concentrate on sales and marketing—which your business most needs—instead of diluting your efforts on production.
3. You'll save plenty of money. Few start-ups can generate sufficient sales to keep a production facility humming while sales are building.

Do you really need more than an order book to start? Maybe not.

KEY POINTS TO REMEMBER

1. Avoid the most common and costly start-up error—*overspending* on rent and equipment.
2. Your own home may be the best place to start.
3. Don't scrimp on a retail location. Go first-class for first-class sales.
4. Equipment bargains are everywhere—and will help you save 60 to 90 percent of your start-up costs.
5. You can 100 percent finance fixtures and equipment—if you know how.
6. Leasing can make sense. Check it out and save a cash outlay.
7. Renovations are much cheaper when you use creativity instead of hard cash.
8. Let your suppliers help you buy equipment if the equipment will make money for them.
9. Time-share what you need. Don't let idle equipment drain needed capital.
10. A partner can provide equipment instead of money—and equipment can be as valuable.
11. Do you really need to produce what you plan to sell?

BUYING ADVICE
AT A BARGAIN PRICE

To be successful, today's small independent business person must know a little about a lot of things—including when to seek outside help rather than tackle the job alone.

Even the smallest business is complex. Whether you run a small restaurant or a mom-and-pop retail shop, you face such diverse tasks as inventory control, merchandising, credit and collections, hiring and firing, bookkeeping, budgeting, and marketing. On top of it all are the varied problems of keeping up with the rapid changes in your field and staying out of trouble with laws piled atop laws in a towering layer cake of confusion.

So say goodbye to being a rugged individualist and say hello to an army of people who can give you the right answers at bargain-priced costs.

Few entrepreneurs reach out for help with a welcoming hand. The average business person thinks of outside advice only when the business needs a quick fix. Others ignore outside advice even then, while they wrestle with their ego. It's an expensive mistake. Hyperthyroid take-charge loners may build companies, but when they think they have all the answers they can just as easily wreck their company. Shrewd entrepreneurs know they need answers and know where to look for them.

Expert talent is a double must for the shoestring entrepreneur. You not only need the everyday advice of an established business person, but you need more—and need it earlier—because you can't afford a few costly start-up mistakes. The margin for error just isn't there when you're leveraged up to your eyebrows.

What's amazing is how much valuable help—free or for small pay—you can get from the vast world of outside experts. They're everywhere and can guide you with just about any problem. You'll meet many of these people in this chapter. But don't stop there. There are as many sources of low-cost assistance as there are people who know something about your business. And these people mean business.

TAKING ON TOP-GRADE TALENT

In the market for a savvy consultant to check out your business plans or solve a few specific problems? Forget Booz, Allen & Hamilton or Accenture, the masters of managerial wisdom who peddle their services to the Fortune-500 companies. You want *free* help from people who someday soon may work or perhaps have worked for these or other high-powered consulting firms.

With a phone call you can have a bevy of top-notch MBA students anxious to burn the midnight oil guiding your business. More than 300 universities are members of the Small Business Institute, partially funded by the SBA. The SBA contracts with the university to provide free consulting services for small enterprises that want them, under the supervision of a faculty coordinator. And it's not necessary to be an SBA borrower to qualify.

While students get valuable experience by applying classroom knowledge to actual business problems, your business will benefit from the fresh perspectives these ambitious students can provide.

MBA students are high on my list of free advisors. Bogged down by two years of steady theory, they may not know the practical intricacies of your business, but they earn top marks in finance, money management, production, and marketing.

As a young MBA student, I enjoyed working on many "hands-on" projects, especially for small start-up firms. From that viewpoint it was an eye-opener to see how few people understood the economics of their business or had a financial grasp of where the business was heading. Fewer still knew even the rudiments of reaching their market. Invariably it was a turkey shoot of problems, so we had plenty of work. Now that I'm on the other side of the fence, I still have two or three MBA students at my side.

Think what these young but talented students can do for your start-up, when in a year or two they may be charging top fees. Today their price is right. Very right.

The SBA is another excellent source of free consultants. It now offers several hundred management assistance officers who counsel both start-ups and established businesses. In addition, the SBA's SCORE—Service Corps of Retired Executives—has a roster of close to 13,000 retired executives and entrepreneurs on standby to help you with every imaginable start-up question from location analysis to pricing. Like MBA students, they are strong on managerial theory, but you want the candidate who has experience in your type of business.

The best way to find your right sharpshooter is to shop around. Define the areas you think you need help in, but don't be too restrictive. You may think you have a solid marketing plan and need bolstering in the finance area only to find out the reverse is true. So give these people a reasonably free hand to roam around into all areas of operation while targeting them for specific projects. Interview several candidates. Look for talent that has experience in your type of business.

"No business is too small for a helping hand," says Marcia Kavick, now operating a successful interior design firm by the same name. "You think you have all the answers until someone walks through your front door with a few more questions."

Marcia lived the experience. Two MBA students walked through Marcia's front door—a third floor walk-up loft—and helped her build it to a $600,000-a-year money-maker. As Marcia adds, "It doesn't have to cost for it to pay."

BORROW SOME SUCCESS

Who are the success stories in your field? Your objective should be to borrow some of their success by hiring them on as paid consultants to put you on the right track.

Why not? Most people journeying into their own business check out successful competitors by trying to learn whatever they can about their operation. Go a step further. Don't merely try to steal a few of their ideas when you can steal them all. And if you play it right you can buy plenty of profitable strategies at a very low price.

A good example was a friend of mine who planned to open a gourmet restaurant in Vermont's booming ski area. Although my friend had years of experience as an assistant manager of a family-style restaurant, he was the first to admit a gourmet restaurant was more than another kettle of fish. So my young friend borrowed success from an owner of a fashionable New York culinary paradise, trading $1000 for a three-day intensive course in starting and running a profitable gourmet restaurant.

My friend called it the perfect solution to the "everything-you-always-wanted-to-know-but-didn't-know-who-to-ask" problem. And my friend wanted to know plenty—everything from how many shrimp in a shrimp cocktail justify the price to the best sources of veal.

But it's those small details that spell the difference between success and failure. Books can only give you basic theory. No book, seminar, or general consultant can give you the 1001 tricks of your trade. To pick up the fine points, you need the people who proved through their own success that they do have the answers.

Whenever I venture into a new business for the first time, I chase down two or three people to teach me a few lessons. Usually I bring on board a seasoned manager, but he's not enough.

Three heads are better than one. When I started my first greeting card and gift shop, I imported the owner of an unusually successful Chicago store to help me out in everything from layout to seasonal promotion. He showed up with a computer printout listing his best-sellers by product line. For $800 and travel expenses, my consultant from afar infused 20 years experience into my two-week-old business.

Can you borrow success? Of course. Look for operators in your line with a proven track record. Go well beyond your trading area in your search. You can't expect competitors to show you the ropes. Put your relationship on a firm business footing right from the start. Don't try to ferret free information.

Most of the people you approach will be happy to consult with you—and at surprisingly low costs. They don't really consider themselves consultants, and the idea you want to borrow their brains for two or three days can be flattering. And for you it can be the key to a profitable start-up.

SUPPLIERS WHO SUPPLY INFORMATION

"I don't know what the independent pharmacy would do without top-notch assistance from his supplier," comments George Maloof of New England Wholesale Drug Company. "We provide more than drugs at wholesale—we provide one-stop information on how to start and operate a successful drugstore." Whether it's advice on layout, inventory control, promotion, or an automatic order entry system, Maloof's customers consider him to be the umbilical cord to a healthy start.

Vendors in every industry are gold mines of information and start-up assistance. And it's no longer just a sprinkling of information as more and more firms beef up consulting or customer support services to hold a competitive edge.

When considering suppliers, ask about their management assistance programs. There may be a difference among suppliers. Of course, business is business and you want the best deal you can strike, and valuable start-up assistance is very much apart of the deal.

What can your suppliers do for you? Shop around. Sometimes you have to prod a supplier to throw in some start-up help. And sometimes it pays to push a bit harder to get even more. In fact, suppliers will do anything in their power to help you if you look like a profitable customer and push for extra assistance.

I have talked wholesalers into sending crews in to stock shelves with the initial order. Another supplier with computer capabilities may give you velocity reports on what's selling in your business. Another may send in a design firm to work with you on layout. If you think they can do it, then ask for it. They seldom refuse.

Make a supplier a co-conspirator in your success. It may be a friendly afternoon discussing your merchandising plans, pricing, promotion, or whatever he can contribute to. Maybe you'll buy his suggestions or perhaps you won't. But whatever comes of your conversation, you have an ally. He's likely to be more lenient on credit or give you the extra inch when times are tough.

Salespeople are talkers, and when they talk you listen. You'll learn plenty. The advice and favors they throw your way can be more important than help from the top. I don't care how busy I am, I always have time for salespeople. In the time it takes to share a cup of coffee, they'll give you the pulse of your industry. If they hear about new lines, promotional ideas, problems, or what your competitor down the street is doing you'll know about it before you empty your cup. And don't sell them short. An experienced salesperson can know as much about your business as anyone. Some of my best merchandising strategies were offered by salespeople. And when they're on your side, they can work wonders as troubleshooters between you and their company.

Discuss your proposed plans with potential suppliers. Don't wait until you open your doors. By then it's too late for suppliers to give you the start-up guidance you need.

TEN THOUSAND HEADS ARE BETTER THAN ONE

Every industry has its local, regional, and national associations. While some are glorified political clubs, many others are warehouses of information and can be extremely useful to a start-up.

The larger associations gather specialized technical or marketing data to save you research time. One of the associations I belong to publishes average operating data for comparable businesses in my field. Another offers low-cost training programs to employees and management seminars to owners. One of the most useful pieces of information I pick up from the association is monthly profiles on the fastest moving lines in the discount industry and retail prices charged by minor chains.

You can also save money on the associations' group buying. Health and accident insurance may be at a fraction of the individual subscriber rate and aggressive associations will offer group member discounts on everything from equipment to supplies and credit reporting. One local association in my area offers discounts on rent-a-cars and even a security service to check internal pilferage.

The biggest benefit of membership is the ability to chat with other people in your field. You make contacts, swap problems and solutions, and learn what's going on. You can't operate in a vacuum and expect to make the grade. Ten thousand heads are better than one.

Too many business people ignore the trade journals. They should be high on your reading list. Once a week I set aside two hours to pore through every journal in my field to pick out a few tips I can put into practice. Many associations publish their own magazines, and you may be able to subscribe without membership.

Don't stop with your own trade associations. If you can, join your customers' associations. Learn about the problems they're having and the opportunities it offers you. It's not a bad way to meet some good customers either.

Nathan Goldberg, executive director of the Boston Association of Retail Druggists, is one association exec who agrees that new entries into the field miss the boat by ignoring associations. "Only 20 to 30 percent of the new entrepreneurs in our field take the time to join. It's surprising, considering the wide range of services we can provide a start-up and most of the services are absolutely free."

FREE PRODUCT IDEAS

The federal bureaucracy is itching to help you turn new products into success. They'll even help you find and develop new products, then bolster them with tons of marketing information.

Interested in new inventions ripe for development? There are two places to shop. The U.S. Patent Office will send you descriptive lists of new inventions, many available for licensing or outright sale. The SBA also publishes a monthly "Products List Circular," while a similar list of fertile new product ideas, grouped by industry, is available from the office of technical assistance.

Many of the products and inventions on these lists can be exploited by your business at a nominal royalty charge. You'll also find some developed by the government available to you absolutely free on a nonexclusive basis.

A small army of government researchers are ready to hit the books to come up with answers to just about any question involving a product, process, or invention. How do you put these federal employees to work as your market research department? Write the Science and Technology Division of the Congressional Library, Washington, DC. State your problem or what you want researched, and in a week or two you'll have a fully researched written report either for free (if it's a small research job), or for a few dollars if it takes some legwork.

Other agencies compete for the privilege of doing your market research for a pittance. Do you have a new energy-saving device? The U.S. Department of Energy are the people to call. They'll not only test and evaluate your product, but help you develop and improve it. And when your product is ready to go they may even guarantee a bank loan to help you start.

Consider all the sources of free or low-cost government assistance to move your product along. Washington is loaded with bright technically oriented engineers and scientists on the public payroll and they have one job—to be your product development specialist.

EXPORT EXPERTS FOR HIRE

Do you have a product that can be sold abroad? Uncle Sam hopes so. He's hoping to balance the growing onslaught of imports by showing the rest of the world the good old U.S.A. can still turn out a few good products. And he's working harder than ever to prove it. If you think you can tap a foreign market, you'll have plenty of friends in Washington.

First stop is the Export-Import Bank in Washington, DC. [phone: (202) 565-3946; web site: www.exim.gov.]. Eximbank, as it's known, offers every conceivable export service and can be your bloodhound leading you to all the right markets abroad. It can even arrange credit insurance to protect you from credit losses in dealing with foreign customers. Write the bank for details.

Another agency hard at work assisting exporters is the Commerce Department Bureau of International Commerce. It offers a long list of foreign buyers, agents, and distributors to work with you. If you are looking to market someone else's product, then ask the Commerce Department for the American International Traders' Index. The index lists over 25,000 manufacturers who want to sell abroad, and your name can be added upon request.

An added feature in working with the Commerce Department is its new product information service. The agency will promote your product free of charge and test foreign interest. They'll even arrange to have your product displayed at U.S. Trade Centers abroad.

States have their own export services to offer, particularly the larger industrialized states of California, New York, Ohio, Pennsylvania, and Massachusetts. Check your state and you'll probably find a helpful hand within a specific agency set up to assist its resident firms in going after foreign sales. Most states limit themselves to answering specific questions on exporting, but they can put you in touch with all the right people to produce a successful export program. Massachusetts helped one of my clients become a millionaire. As a manufacturer of artificial bricks made by a patented process, he wanted to expand into Europe and Japan. Freight costs prevented shipping the brick, so a representative from the state's Commerce Department coor-

dinated a meeting with several foreign firms who were interested in licensing the process. Today the artificial bricks are also
manufactured in Florence, Italy and Kyoto, Japan, and negotiations are underway to license the process in England. Income
from foreign sales has tripled the company's profits. And all it
took to get the ball rolling was a phone call.

Travel to Los Angeles and visit its World Trade Center. It
doesn't cost much to participate, but when you do you'll have
access to an "export hot line" and ready answers to your every
export question.

When you talk about "exporting," people jump at the chance
to help you. They have to. Their job is to make sure your product
finds a new home abroad and puts more money in your pocket.

TO MARKET, TO MARKET

"Build a better mousetrap and the world will beat a path to your
door." That's the saying, but it's wrong. The only people about
to beat down your door are the people who want a mousetrap
and know you have a better one to sell. So the name of the game
is marketing. To win the game you'll need plenty of marketing
information to identify and reach your potential customers.
And marketing information can cost you an arm and a leg unless you know a few cost-cutting maneuvers.

Now let's suppose you do develop a better mousetrap. How can
you develop first-class market intelligence at third-class rates?

1. Government agencies are likely to have plenty of answers.
    The Pesticide Division of the Department of Agriculture,
    for example, has a rundown on the rodent population by
    city and state. "Big Brother" knows everything. That's
    why the government needs so many buildings to store its
    files. And the right agency will have the right answers to
    your questions—if you know the right questions.
2. The Commerce Department and Treasury Department have
    established a database profiling every imaginable industry.
    They have all the statistics to show sales, market concen-

trations, and number of firms in the field. For a few dollars you'll have a full report on the mousetrap industry.

3. Your trade association has plenty of information. Did you know there are five associations catering to mousetrap manufacturers?

4. Call the U.S. Census Department. Every industry has its demographics—the breakdown of its market by consumer classification. Once you know who your customers are likely to be, the Census Bureau will tell you where they are—and for free.

5. Public libraries are another good source. But you don't have to do the work yourself. Metropolitan libraries have researchers on their staff who pluck answers to specific questions as part of community service. In a few days they can provide information and more sources than would take you a month to find.

6. If your competitors are publicly owned corporations, ask for their 10-K reports filed with the SEC. They will tell you everything you want to know about your competitors for the price of a postage stamp.

7. Professional information-gathering services will do your market research at a per diem rate of about $400. The typical firm can land all the data it needs to make "thinking cap" decisions for less than $1600.

8. Dun & Bradstreet can give you business data on your competitors if you are or know a subscriber. It's one way of finding out how your smaller (nonpublicly traded) competitors are making out.

9. The National Science Foundation will do all your market research for free—if you have a big project that can benefit the community, such as ecology, education, new drugs, or help for the handicapped. In other cases, they'll give you a grant to hire a professional marketing staff.

Any start-up company can have a complete database of information to make intelligent marketing decisions. And it's not expensive to do once you know the information you're looking for and where to find it. Most entrepreneurs, however, are weak on marketing. Their wisest investment is $200 to $300 to hire an MBA student or a few more dollars to retain a professional firm.

FOUR WAYS TO FREE EMPLOYEE TRAINING

Another area where Uncle Sam is spending huge dollars is in employee training. Uncle Sam wants people off the welfare and unemployment rosters and on your payroll. And he'll train them for you—or pay you to train them—as your part of the bargain.

Many women, members of minorities, and handicapped persons need a chance at "entry level jobs." And many will become excellent workers once they've been properly trained. Here are three programs to investigate:

1. Project transition is a brainstorm of the armed forces. The Defense Department will help you train servicemen about to be released from the armed services. If you are interested in hiring veterans, and want some assistance from Uncle Sam, then contact the Defense Department.
2. Physically or emotionally handicapped workers can be trained through a wide range of government-sponsored vocational rehabilitation programs. Some offer wage subsidies while all provide training grants or payments. Check it out. The handicapped have high scores for reliability and loyalty.
3. Write to the Labor Department's Bureau of Apprenticeship and Training if you want to set up an apprenticeship program. They'll provide plenty of free assistance.

These programs are excellent, especially for start-ups in the manufacturing and service industries. A small electronics firm in our area started in 1983 with 60 assembly workers provided by two state-sponsored vocational programs. The government paid $180,000 for its share of the training and had four instructors in the plant for one month to turn these willing workers into top-notch producers. Management estimates it would have cost the firm over $300,000 to hire and train on its own. Do you need help finding and training employees?

LAWYERS: A NECESSARY EVIL

Lawyers are a necessary evil. You can't do business—or start a business—without one. While the lawyer is necessary, his legal fee is evil. And legal fees are becoming more outrageous every day. It's not antilawyer talk because I'm a practicing attorney myself, but I will tell you that unless you know how to find and feed your lawyer, you can spend a bundle. So while your lawyer is hard at work incorporating your business, negotiating your lease, posturing with your partners, and reviewing the financing agreement, his time clock is happily ticking away. A month later you have your corner store and a $3500 legal bill. Wouldn't you be happier with a $1000 bill? Let me show you how to slash your legal fees without sacrificing quality representation. And you can do it if you follow these fee-saving tips:

1. Shop for the right attorney. What you want is someone with broad-based business experience to handle you while you grow, yet hungry enough to be flexible on fees because he wants your future business. You can't stereotype, but the largest firms are usually a mismatch for the small start-up. You never mean quite as much to them as to the smaller firm. Besides, large firms typically have fixed fee schedules and rigid payment policies. The sole practitioner, on the other hand, is unable to handle a wide range of problems or churn out work quickly if you need it. Chances are you should look for the mid-sized, three- to ten-lawyer firm.

2. Look for the business specialist within the firm. Today's lawyer is a specialist. You may have been referred to someone who primarily practices divorce, criminal, or negligence law. And they may agree to represent you. It's a bad choice. You want the lawyer who spends the day representing businesses—and preferably the smaller firm

whose problems may be somewhat different from the large corporation's. The right attorney can help you mastermind a start-up. Don't forget, yours is not the first business he helped create.

3. Involve your lawyer early in the game. Don't run to him after you've signed an agreement, lease, or bank note. You want advice and not a report card on your own legal brilliance. I see it all the time. Two partners will strike a cock-eyed deal so the lawyers spend triple the time reworking it, or financing what was improperly structured so it's back to the bank.

4. Discuss fees *before* you retain counsel. This is the most important point. Be candid. If you have very limited capital, let your counsel know about it. Work out a budget for legal costs so your counsel knows what he has to work with and you know what your bill will be. Be fee-conscious. If your lawyer has to quote fees before you retain him he may quote on the low side to land you as a client.

5. Don't shop fees on the basis of an hourly charge. It doesn't mean a thing. A $300-per-hour attorney may be twice as fast as a $150 lawyer. Negotiate an estimated total fee based on stated services he *must* provide for you. But remember, it can only be a "ball park" estimate. Extra work may be required, as unanticipated problems can crop up. If extra work is needed ask your attorney to clear it with you but don't tie his hands. When you hold your counsel to a firm $2000-fee quote he has little incentive to spend the added few dollars to do the best job.

6. Lawyers will defer their billing. Ask them in advance so you both know the ground rules. Many of our clients ask us if they can pay their bill over several months, and we always agree. In fact, we consider it a sign of a credit-worthy client. Deadbeats never ask if they can pay it out, since they never expect to pay.

7. All a lawyer has to sell is his time and advice. Keep your phone calls to a minimum and keep office visits to the

point. Every lawyer has horror stories of clients who eat up costly hours on trivia. One way or another you pay for it.

The very best way to cut legal fees is to use alternative services. Incorporating your business is one place you save a small fortune. Commercial firms set up corporations for a fraction of the price. They will set up a corporation in any state and in a matter of a few days. If your attorney will match the price then it may be more convenient for him to do it.

Federal and state agencies live in a world of forms. You'll need forms for everything from obtaining a tax number to registering your business name. You don't need your lawyer to obtain and fill out these simple forms. Your accountant can handle it at less cost.

Common sense is the key to the effective use of an attorney. Don't be your own lawyer on complicated or potentially costly transactions. It's false economy. Just save where you safely can. The dollars can add up.

FINDING AN ACCOUNTANT TO NAVIGATE

A good accountant is the most important single outside advisor a small business has. Navigating by the numbers is even more important for the highly leveraged start-up.

The first rule is never to scrimp a few dollars on accounting services. Many small business people limit their accountants to the preparation of quarterly and year-end tax returns. They don't have financial navigators, they only have tax preparers. It's not the way to navigate your business.

What you do need is tight financial control. That means budgets, cash flow statements, expense analysis, product costing, and numbers, numbers, and more numbers to tell you where you've been, where you're going, and how you're getting there. And if you can't put these numbers together for yourself, you'll need some financial types who can. They're not hard to find.

Most start-ups look for CPAs. As with any other professional group, some do excellent work and others are a waste of money. A small business generally doesn't need a CPA because certified statements aren't necessary. Only the larger firms with heavy bank loans or publicly traded corporations require certified statements, so you may end up paying for a title you won't use.

The best way to get the most service for the least money is to divide the accounting function. Long-range financial planning and tax counseling should be left to the CPAs. They're still the best qualified for the important decisions. The operational accounting should be delegated to someone else. An accountant can help you with budgeting, forecasting, and cash flows, and sets your business up with a precise but easy-to-use daily bookkeeping system. For this sort of service—just what you need to navigate—compare several franchised systems in your area.

A larger firm in the $300,000 to $800,000 sales range may need a part-time comptroller. Some comptrollers do freelance on a part-time basis, serving several clients. Local universities with accounting programs have many students and recent graduates who qualify. Your own CPA firm may have a junior associate available. But don't have his services billed through the firm. You want him or her on a moonlighting basis without the firm's override. Your local newspaper will also list bookkeepers and accountants looking for per diem work.

Unquestionably, the most important factor in selecting an accountant is his willingness to stand up to you and fight for financial decisions he believes are right. You can't afford a "yes" man. One of my earlier accountants would listen to whatever plans I had, shake his head in agreement while thinking he was scoring points. He wasn't. I fired him. My present accountant is the type of pro you need. He'll listen to my plans and fight me tooth and nail if he thinks I'm steering in the wrong direction. It doesn't matter who's right. I may be the captain of the ship, but he's still the navigator. And as long as he is, it's his job to keep the business off the shoals. Don't look for titles. Look for the accountant who'll grab the wheel from you.

BUY THE AGENT, NOT THE INSURANCE

Lawyers and accountants aren't the only professionals you need on your side. Your insurance agent is the third leg in your professional tripod. Unfortunately few people realize it, thinking all agents, like all insurances, are the same.

It's not so. Insurance is too complex today. You'll need your insurance agent for more than casualty and liability coverage. You'll need him to guide you in the rapidly expanding areas of pension plans, Keogh and IRA accounts, and a host of other tax-inspired insurance-related investments. And even the simpler forms of insurance are no longer quite so simple. How many different types of insurance do you need? You have about 50 different choices when buying liability insurance alone. You can buy wisely or buy foolishly. Only your insurance agent can tell the difference.

So you don't buy insurance. You do buy the insurance agent. And what you need is the agent who'll work to get you just the right coverage at the right price. But he has to work for you and not the insurance company. That's the key.

I don't recommend the agent representing only one insurance underwriter. He can't shop around for the best buy and his allegiances are too strong. Look for the agent handling multiple lines. He can play one company against the other until he puts together the best possible package.

Call in several multiple-line agents and compare their proposals. But look beyond their proposals. Look to see if they're trying to sell you insurance or trying to sell you savings.

Insurance, even for the small start-up, can be $8000 to $10,000 a year. It's a major expenditure and you can save 35 to 40 percent with the right agent. Like most laypeople, I don't know a good plan from a bad one and I never quite trust the agent no matter how trustworthy he may be. So I use a retired insurance broker as my personal consultant. For $100 a year he reviews my insurance and tells me whether my agent is doing his job. It's a great investment. Several years ago he pointed out areas of duplicate coverage, saving me $4000. When you have a pro working only for you, you know what you're buying.

Some business people prefer to buy insurance from one of the several underwriters who sell on a direct basis. It's true that you can save 15 to 25 percent but I don't recommend it for two reasons. First, you don't have the expert advice of an agent. You're likely to end up with a poorly designed program. An even more important reason is that you don't have an agent to fight for you when a claim arises. That's when you'll know whose side the agent is on.

MORE PEOPLE FROM MORE PEOPLE

How many sources are there for free or low-cost assistance to make your business a success? Entire books have been written on it. But you can take a page from the stories of other entrepreneurs who know how to put people to work without putting them on the payroll.

John Richards had an entire class of MBA students game-plan his idea for starting a foundry to manufacture wood-burning stoves. The students used it as a case study, and within a week Richards had 42 feasibility studies, complete with marketing and financial projections. Thirty-eight students decided it wouldn't work. But it did work. Today the Hyde Park Home Energy Center grosses $4 million annually. "I still learned plenty about the business," says Richards, "even if I had to prove these budding executives wrong." Wouldn't your business idea be a welcome change for "B" school students using stuffy old textbook cases? Sure it would. Talk to a professor about it.

Do you realize that your electric bill can be sliced dramatically with a few simple techniques? Hub Foods did. It found an electrical engineer whose specialty was rewiring businesses, charging 50 percent of the first year's savings. But saving money is what a start-up needs. You can find firms who will show you how to also save on heat, air conditioning, and telephone costs—all on a percentage of actual savings. Your utility companies will tell you who they are.

Interested in profitable reading? The Government Printing Office has a library of over 35,000 fact-filled books on every type of business. If you'd like an overview of the pamphlets and books available to you, write the Superintendent of Documents, Government Printing Office, Washington, DC, 20402. It has been called the best business library around.

This chapter only scratches the surface of all the people who can help you. Its real mission is to let you know the help is there if you look for it. You're not the only one who wants your business to succeed.

KEY POINTS TO REMEMBER

1. You can't do it all yourself. You'll need help—and the right help.
2. Your best consultants are free or low-pay consultants. They mean business.
3. Suppliers are ready to provide you with a wide range of assistance—if you ask for it.
4. Don't overlook associations. Their only purpose is to help you succeed. Tap their information-rich resources.
5. Uncle Sam can help you develop and market new products at home and abroad. He shares in your profits, so make him work to produce your profits.
6. Small firms can pack a powerful promotional punch, once you have the right people showing you how.
7. Expensive talent—your professional team—is never quite so expensive with a few cost-cutting steps.
8. The difference between failure and success may be one more answer to one more question.

12

FULL SHELVES
FROM EMPTY POCKETS

When Peter Hassan had to borrow quarters from the Coke machine to buy lunch a few years ago, he had his doubts about the American dream.

Now he talks as though he invented it. And anybody who can start a company in 1977 with less than $6500 and turn it into a $6 million-a-year enterprise by 1989 has the right to talk.

Hassan, 46, owns the Henrick Interior Studio, selling fashionable tables, lamps, wall decorations, and giftware for the home. "It was an interesting beginning," says Hassan. "I had the carpet down, lights up, fixtures in place, and sign over the front door. What I didn't have was inventory—or the money or credit to buy it. I thought I could instead sell from catalogs, but that didn't work. Customers wanted to see and feel the merchandise. The business was almost closed before it started."

Wisely, Hassan didn't close up shop. What he did do was lace up his hunting boots and scout out merchandise from any source he could. "I discovered there were 2300 manufacturers whose products I could sell, and another 1700 wholesalers and distributors selling the same and other lines I could move. That gave me 4000 chances to succeed. By pounding the beat I could sell myself. Gradually a patchwork of goods were shipped on a patchwork of negotiated credit terms. Two months later we had close to $100,000 worth of inventory on display, and with it we showed a profit in our second month. The rest is history."

Peter Hassan calls it history. But it is more. It is a success story. And there are thousands of shoestring merchants who start each year facing bare shelves, but with the know-how to get those shelves filled with profitable inventory—the lifeblood of their business. They too succeed. Others don't. With near-empty shelves they watch their business die on the installment plan.

If you're planning a retail or merchandise-oriented business, read this chapter several times. You've met Peter Hassan, and you'll meet several other interesting people who started just the way you'll start—with no money and no credit, but plenty of profitable inventory on their shelves. They'll show you how it's done.

YOU CAN'T DO BUSINESS FROM AN EMPTY WAGON

The secret of a successful merchandising start-up is never to look like you started on a shoestring. It's more than imagery. It's economics. You can't do business from an empty wagon. On opening day you not only need the merchandise to sell—but you need *enough* inventory to start at a profitable level.

Common *sense*? Of course. However, many retail start-ups overlook the importance of starting with the right inventory levels or size operation, believing that somehow the business will build inventory and as a result build sales and profits.

That's what makes retail start-ups so very different from non-merchandising start-ups. While you can start a service or manufacturing operation from zero and gradually build it, this method doesn't work with the retail venture. The retail business must be financially viable from the first day. You can't start too small and expect something better to evolve.

It's a common mistake. Retail business attracts the majority of shoestring operations. Of course, retail businesses statistically dominate the business scene, but what makes them particularly attractive to the novice is the belief you can rent a tiny storefront, throw a few pieces of merchandise on the shelf, and anticipate success. Three months later you walk by and all you see is a boarded-up storefront, or perhaps another cockeyed optimist about to learn the same lesson.

Let's define our terms. What do I mean by too small? Too small is a beginning operation that doesn't have sufficient merchandise to generate profitable sales. The actual store size has little to do with it, except when it restricts merchandising to an unprofitable level.

Harriet Blackman understands the point. Harriet scraped together $8000 in 1979 to open a designer jean shop in the Massachusetts Berkshires, the home of eight leading colleges and thousands of student derrières advertising the latest names in blue jean fashions. Of that total, $3500 went for fixtures and other start-up costs. Inventory? "That was my mistake," admits Harriet. "My opening order was $6000, and since I didn't have established credit I paid 50 percent upon order with the balance due in 30 days. All it gave me was 300 pair of jeans and a store that still looked like an empty airplane hangar. The kids would walk by, look in and keep walking. Those that strolled in usually walked out without buying. Whatever they wanted I didn't have. The business needed $600 a day in sales to make it, and on its best day sales were only $260. Before I knew it, I had worked the stock down to nothing to cover rent and my own salary and the business was gone."

Harriet's story didn't end there. When her store was auctioned, the assets were picked up by two enterprising students from one of the local colleges ambitious enough to send it on its second launch. Within a month they had it stocked with over $32,000 in jeans, blouses, belts, and related casual wear apparel. Spare space at the front of the store was concessioned to another student who set up showcases with handcrafted belt buckles, jade jewelry, and Indian artifacts. It looked like a business and *was* a solid business, ringing up over $1000 a day. The interesting point is that the young partners found the inventory to create their viable business without spending upfront money.

Dr. Barry Bleidt, a professor of retailing management at Northeastern University, claims that most retail start-ups fail for the very reason Harriet Blackman stumbled. "Entrepreneurs merchandise the business based on what they have to spend, rather than on what the business needs to succeed," counsels Professor Bleidt. "Usually there's a considerable difference between the two."

A walk down any Main Street confirms his message. We recently helped a young chap set up a liquor store in a 2400-sq.-ft. downtown location. The accountant ran the numbers and calculated the business needed sales in the $500,000 range to break even. To support the sales, the business needed a $50,000 opening inventory. That's not how our young client saw it, and defying the odds, tried to bootstrap it with a $12,000 merchandise level. The store collapsed two months later from poor sales.

It's far safer to *over*-merchandise a start-up than to *under*-merchandise it. You'll start out with considerable trade debt, but it's counterbalanced by a business launched on its strongest foot. If the sales are there, the business will eventually work down the debt to a manageable level. Conversely, if it's *under*-merchandised it won't have the profitable beginning, and without profits you can't logically build.

How much inventory do you need for a successful start? It's all in the numbers, so pull out your calculator.

1. Define your break-even point. Your accountant can quickly recap your expenses and margins to figure the magical point at which you begin to make money.
2. Aim for a higher figure considering that you'll need *profitable* sales to work down beginning trade credit.
3. Calculate the inventory needed to generate the required sales. Every business has average inventory turnover figures. Follow industry guidelines. Don't delude yourself by thinking you can turn inventory faster than industry standards. It seldom happens.
4. How do you find out what the average turnover is for your type of business? There are plenty of available sources. The Bank of America in San Francisco, California, has operating data available for every type business and you can obtain a copy of the data by writing Bank of America. But here's a word of added advice. If you don't know the

turnover ratios for your business, you probably don't know enough about the business to give it the shoestring try.

Let's pull it all together. When I started my first Discount City Store, I aimed for a $120,000 starting inventory. It wasn't by accident but by design. Operating expenses for the store amounted to $140,000, and we figured we'd be working on a 25 percent gross margin. Therefore, we would need about $560,000 in sales just to break even. But we had to do better than break even to stay in business. Virtually all our inventory and most of our fixtures and start-up costs were financed for a grand total of $200,000. Figuring that we would have to repay at least $60,000 a year to keep the creditors pacified, the business would actually have to generate that much in profits. So with our numbers honed fine, Discount City would have to do about $900,000 to cover expenses and pay back debt. Since cost-of-goods on $900,000 in sales would be about $675,000 (for a 25 percent gross profit), and since we correctly anticipated turning our inventory 5.5 times a year, our calculations pointed to $120,000 in needed merchandise. It's all in the numbers.

Play with your own numbers. We might have been able to set our sights lower and shoot for sales in the $400,000 range, but it wouldn't have made sense in our 4000-sq.-ft. store with its fixed overhead. With a smaller store—and smaller overhead—the lower sales and inventory may have been a start-up alternative, but in our case we deliberately set our sights higher.

Carl Shumrak, owner of Possessions, Inc., a successful greeting card and gift shop in a Boston suburb, followed the same technique but on a considerably smaller scale. As Carl would say, "At my stage of life I don't want to get rich, I just want a business that can give me a comfortable income without killing myself." Carl's answer was a 1800-sq.-ft. location in a high-traffic strip center. Poring over the numbers, Carl found that operating expenses (including his own salary) would be about $85,000. Since his type of business operates on a "keystone margin" (50 percent gross profit), Possessions needed $170,000 in sales to break even. "My target was $220,000 to $240,000 to give me a comfortable edge and the cash flow to pay financing costs. And to generate $240,000 in sales, I knew I needed $45,000 to $50,000 in inventory. A smaller inventory would mean smaller sales and the numbers wouldn't work.

"But for us the numbers did work. We borrowed $10,000 to buy some giftware lines that would only sell COD, and captured $38,000 in merchandise from other suppliers willing to go on extended credit. With a few sharp promotions we hit $262,000 in our first year, and within two years we were out of the woods and didn't owe a dime. You can't do business from an empty wagon—or a half-empty wagon for that matter. When you open the doors it must look like they're open to stay."

A CLOSED CHECKBOOK NEEDS AN OPEN MIND

No matter how much inventory you need for a successful start, you never get it. Not if you're starting with a closed checkbook and no credit rating as the typical shoestring merchant. That brings us to what I call "concentric merchandising." Don't look it up in a business dictionary, for I coined the term myself. What it amounts to is merchandising based on what you can *get* rather than what you *want*. Eventually, and with some profitable sales behind you, you'll be able to mold your inventory to what you wanted in the first place. But for now let's see if you can master the art of concentric merchandising.

A classic example is Highland Jewelry, a now-thriving Long Island jewelry store. But when it started three decades ago, its sign read "Highland Jewelry and Giftware." "The giftware tag was out of necessity not desire," says Evelyn Morton, who operates the store with her son Bob. "We conceived the business as a high-quality jewelry operation and never wanted the giftware lines. However, we only had $12,000 to invest and the banks wouldn't touch us. Jewelry suppliers wouldn't touch us either with a ten-foot pole. We called Seiko, Longines, Rolex, Benrus, and a dozen Providence and New York jewelry firms but they were reluctant to even open us on COD, and virtually laughed us out of their offices when we asked for credit. We discovered that when you talk jewelry, it's either cash or an impeccable credit history going back to the Civil War. So we invested $6000 to bring in a few select lines, but it was hardly enough to start a healthy business. We needed other lines—lines compatible with jewelry—that could be obtained on credit. Giftware was the answer and we even tacked on a luggage department. Giftware and luggage inventory was easier to come by on credit, and it didn't take long to locate $20,000 from gift and luggage suppliers anxious to do business with us. The merchandise mix was enough for a start. For the first year or two we did most of our business with giftware, but gradually we built up our jewelry line while working down giftwares. Within five years we were out of the giftware business (except for some high-priced lines) and concentrating on jewelry. Sometimes you have to use a 'backdoor' approach to build the business you want."

And it can take many forms. While Highland Jewelry did it by dabbling with trade credit in the easier giftware and luggage lines, R. L. Stearns Company, another bangles and beads purveyor, got its foot into the jewelry field by starting with the credit-easy low-priced lines, upgrading as it went. "We only had a 400-sq.-ft-mall store so we were limited for space, forcing us to stay with jewelry alone," says Henry Kominski, 38, its bushy-haired president. "Without cash or credit we couldn't go for the top lines so we started somewhere halfway down the scale where there are hundreds of suppliers and manufacturers looking for retail accounts. They're never as fussy, and we were able to hustle together a $19,000 inventory on workable terms." Concentric merchandising is knowing how to *go for the easier credit lines within your field.*

"Synergistic diversification" is a fancy name for what Helen Cryten calls her "mish-mush" merchandising emporium hiding under the name Helen's Leisure Time, located in a Detroit shopping center. "The business started out as a bookstore and ended up a collection of whatever I could get on credit. The only other criterion was that the goods had to relate in some way to leisure time," Helen confesses. "The twelve top book publishers turned me down cold for an opening order on credit, so I bought their best-sellers for cash, cutting the book department down to 25 percent of the store space, then I went after paperbacks, greeting cards, adult toys and games, party goods, and anything that looked, tasted, or smelled like leisure—including a gourmet cookware department. What I ended up with was nine minidepartments connected only by the common thread of leisure and the ability to get it on credit." Helen smiles when she calls it her "mish-mush," but it's a profitable "mish-mush," generating $290,000 a year in sales. Concentric merchandising is knowing how to *branch out into related lines.*

Unusual stories? Hardly. It's only the science of merchandising born out of necessity. The stories continue:

Helen Olgar's Slacks, a five-store New England chain, was startled when lingerie suppliers said "no" to Jerome Kelm's request for opening credit. "I wanted to compete with 'Frederick's of Hollywood,' but it didn't take long to find out lingerie manufacturers are as stingy on credit as they are on G-string lace," laughs Jerry. "Two days later I was introduced to a New York ladies' slacks manufacturer looking to break into the New England market—and willing to back me with a $25,000 credit line for the privilege. A phone call to my sign painter and he replaced the still wet paint announcing 'Jerry's Naughty Nightime Shop' to Helen Olgar's, which sounded like a safe enough name. I'm not sure I'm having as much fun selling slacks, but it's a damn profitable line. Profitable enough to grow to four more stores. My next store, however," adds Jerry, "will be Jerry's Naughty Nightime Shop. Now I can afford it." Concentric merchandising is knowing how to *start with different lines.*

If concentric merchandising is born of necessity, it sometimes leads to an even more successful business than originally planned. The "add-on" or "substitute" lines oftentimes prove more profitable than the intended line. And in many instances it leads you to a winning format for your business.

That's what happened to me and Discount City. As an entrepreneurial pup, I planned a typical discount department store—a miniaturized version of Kmart with orderly, logical departments and the usual neat array of products within each department. The only problem was that to bring the necessary products together would require credit from 236 different suppliers. I tried and 197 turned me down. My inventory would have more holes than a slice of Swiss cheese. So I switched gears and changed the format to a "close-out" store, in reality closer to a Turkish bazaar or a rubbish dump with neon lights. Now any merchandise was fair game provided I could get it cheap, sell it cheap, and of course not pay my supplier until long after I sold it. So in came the $3.98 garbage cans, and the 49-cent six-fingered back scratchers from Taiwan, and $120,000 in assorted bargains from around the world. But I was no longer "locked in" to specific needs and every possible supplier I could find became my happy hunting ground. Taking the theory of concentric merchandising to its outermost limits, I discovered a more successful merchandising plan. Perhaps you won't have to bend your initial plans quite as much, but you too will find an open mind is needed when you have a closed checkbook.

Plan ahead with this step-by-step guide:

1. Define the merchandise you expect to carry—and its sources of supply. Now expand on it concentrically.
2. What related or "tie-in" lines can you *add?*
3. What similar lines with easier credit can you *substitute?*
4. What alternate sources are *available?*

Use your imagination. For every line—or supplier—you add, you increase your own chances for finding start-up inventory by one.

CREDIT MANAGERS CAN SAY "YES"

That doesn't mean they will. In fact, it's usually in the credit manager's best interest to say "no." After all, credit managers are programmed to avoid losses, not bend over backwards to create risky sales. So your job is to re-program the credit manager and get his nod with a few convincing reasons why you deserve credit.

It's never an easy sell. The woods are full of "bust-out artists," bankruptcy frauds, deadbeats, and ne'er-do-wells who are trying to pry their own share of merchandise from under the cynical eye of the ever-watchful credit manager. Now you come along with a company that is little more than a name on a piece of paper, a few bucks in your checking account, and a business that Dun and Bradstreet never heard of. It's hardly enough to inspire confidence. So how do you get around credit managers who dislike would-be businesses with no sales, profits, credit history, or cash register?

The place to start is by realizing that credit terms, although uniformly stated, are never universally applied. The credit terms you can wrangle from a given supplier will depend on a combination of factors, including demand for the line, competition, the profit potential of your account, the risk-assessment, and even the chemistry between you and the credit manager. Some suppliers are notoriously rigid and live by an unbendable credit policy—usually tied to a Dun and Bradstreet rating. Others have their own policy, but will still listen.

There are proven strategies to get around both types.

1. Build a credit rating before you go credit hunting. Call in Dun and Bradstreet as soon as your corporation is organized. Tell them about your plans, your personal background, and anything else that's favorable. Somewhere along the way the D & B representative will ask you how the business is capitalized. What a nosy question. Just tell him you're still interviewing prospective partners and several bankers. Because you're a new start-up, D & B won't assign you a credit rating, but will publish what you tell them. Even that much of a listing is enough for some suppliers.

2. Line up a few credit references. Make it legitimate. Don't trump up phonies. But chances are that you do have three or four people you've already done business with—perhaps they're equipment suppliers—who'll vouch for you. Check with them first before giving their name as a reference.

3.   Work through salespeople. If it's a large order, try to work directly with the sales manager. Go as high up the ladder as you can. Salespeople, unlike credit managers, are sales oriented. They want to sell you, and if you're halfway credible, will try to sell you to the credit manager. On orders under $1000 it may not be practical. Oftentimes these small orders are automatically cleared without any credit check. But on larger orders a credit check will be done. That's when you want the sales department walking your order through.

4.   How you submit an order counts. Print up purchase orders with your name engraved. It gives you the appearance of an established business instead of a "fly-by-night" operation. Use your own purchase order even when a supplier's order form is available. It's a good idea to enclose a sheet listing your references.

5.   Don't forget your bank as a credit reference. And here's a strategy to put you a few points ahead. Maintain at least a $1000 balance in the business acount. Banks never disclose your exact balance but will report an average "three digit" ($100–999), "four digit" ($1000–9999), or "five digit" ($10,000–99,999) balance. With a "four digit" $1000 balance, you have the same bank rating as a customer with $9999 on account. If you can swing a $10,000 balance during the credit-hunting period, so much the better. It puts you in the big leagues. Check with your banker to make certain he's reporting it out the way you want.

6.   Watch your timing. You'll have the best chance to push an order through during peak selling seasons. September through November are the best months, for example, if you're going after merchandise that can move for Christmas, while March and April are hectic for summer seasonal goods. Credit departments are too busy to be as thorough as they might be. Also be on the lookout for new lines, hot promotional campaigns, or heavy competition from new competitors. That's when suppliers dramatically relax credit in favor of sales.

Play the odds. You may need merchandise from 20 to 30 small secondary suppliers, placing a $300 to $2000 order with each. Don't expect to win credit from them all. It won't happen. What will happen is that perhaps 40 to 60 percent will extend credit (usually automatically) and ship. Another 20 percent will outright refuse and invite you to buy COD or cash-in-advance. The remainder may try a "split-approach" by either asking COD for part of the order, with the balance on credit, or suggest you cut your order size. The point is that you may need "backup" or alternate suppliers when credit is declined. Have their orders ready for submission so you don't lose time when a primary source declines.

It may seem elementary, but even experienced business people often overlook the common sense approaches to credit success.

BUY NOW—PAY LATER

Buying inventory on credit terms is the easy part. Any schemer with a pen and a pile of purchase orders can load up a warehouse with inventory if he wants to work hard enough at it. Thirty days after the goods arrive, it's another story. That's when it's time to pay the piper.

Everything I said so far in this chapter presupposes normal trade credit. What you buy today is due and payable 30 days hence. The harsh economic reality, however, tells you that what you buy today can't be paid for in 30 days because as an initial stocking order, most of it is still on your shelf when the bill falls due.

Now if you're in the game to play it crooked, load up, sell out, and skip to Guatemala, there's no problem—unless you someday wish to return to the United States and the waiting arms of the Federal Marshal. But that's not what you or this book is about. You want to build a solid respectable business, and between that reality and the reality that you won't be able to pay for your opening inventory timely lies our problem. So how do you handle it? The options are few.

One approach is the buy now—pay later (much later) strategy. Essentially, what you do is buy on 30-day credit terms, and then dribble your suppliers as much as you can afford—and as little as they'll patiently wait for—until your bill is paid. Without initially realizing it, your suppliers provided you with long-term inventory financing. That's precisely how most shoestring start-ups go about it. Generally, replacement orders are paid COD; as long as the initial order is being systematically—albeit slowly—reduced, creditors usually do wait for their money. The morality of it all aside—shoestring entrepreneurs accurately say that if they requested a two- or three-year payout on the initial order they'd never obtain credit clearance. When you're talking about secondary suppliers and a $1000 to $2000 order, they're usually right. Small suppliers aren't inclined to grant generous credit terms, and they certainly don't see themselves financing your bootstrap operation.

The problem with this rob-Peter-to-pay-Paul approach is its impact on credit rating. You have to build your business for the long haul, and that means building supplier confidence right from the start. In short, suppliers can understand bootstrap financing and will even live with it, but you have to bring an evenhanded honesty to the situation.

Here's a tempered approach that does work.

1. Try to negotiate extended credit terms for the initial order. Don't ask for two years. As I stated before, you won't get it. However, many secondary suppliers will give you three to six months "dating" if you push for it. They understand why you need it, and when they grant it, they're acknowledging their willingness to help you get started. When you can't pay on time, there's no surprise or resentment. The supplier has been programmed to think in extended terms, and it's not difficult to extend the terms a bit more.

2. Always communicate with your supplier when the bill falls due. This is the key point. Don't let them come chasing you. In my first Discount City venture I had $96,000 in payables fall due one month after I opened. What money I had I needed for operating expenses and to replenish what was sold during that first month. But I did have about $6000 I could pay on my opening stock, and it was even

more money than I expected to have available. Spending three days on the phone, I contacted each of the 47 creditors owed the $96,000, proposing future orders be on COD and so much per month on the back bill. Some blustered, some threatened, but most went along with it. Surprisingly, of the 47 creditors, 38 gave me no trouble at all. The big reason was that I was now buying COD. I may have owed a given supplier $3000 on the opening order, but in the course of a year I may buy—and pay for—another $15,000 in replacement goods. The monies due on the initial order suddenly become a small part of the total equation.

I've discovered another strategy that can work for you. Don't break the bad news all at once. Work it in gently. For example, a supplier owed $3000 would be told that I'd pay $100 for each of the next three months and by then I hoped to bank finance (I knew it was futile). To the creditor it began to look like a three-month problem, although I knew it would a two- or three-year "problem." But in the intervening three months, I faithfully bought and faithfully paid. When I called again three months later to say bank financing was bleak, but why not continue for another six months, it was all anticlimactic. The resistance was gone.

3. I mentioned bank financing to replace short-term trade debt, and it is an excellent idea. Some people will look for bank financing to buy inventory and be turned down for lack of collateral. It's a "Catch-22." You don't have the money so you can't buy the collateral (inventory). But once you have the inventory for collateral, some banks will be interested. In any event, you do owe it to your suppliers—and your credit reputation and cash flow—to try.

4. Return goods help pacify creditors. Your opening inventory may consist of thousands of dollars in slow movers that aren't working for you. Send it back for credit, but when you do it, simultaneously push for extended terms on any balance owed. You're in a better bargaining position before you return the goods than after. Creditors al-

ways look at return goods as a sign of good faith. Once you do it your creditor realizes it's only a cash flow "workout" rather than dealing with a crook or con artist with larceny in his heart.

What will it take to make it through the first year or two while you do a juggling act with your creditors? Everyone seems to have an answer based on personal experiences. Elliot Galahow, an accountant and consultant to leveraged start-up firms, says, "Realistic cash flow projections are the most important item. If the business starts on a profitable level, and continues to turn over its payables, suppliers will wait it out through the survival stage. All the suppliers want is the light at the end of the tunnel." Jeff Kosberg, an attorney involved in small business bankruptcies, claims the decisive factor is communication and developing a supplier relationship. "A retailer, for example, will start with too much short-term debt and panic. Rather than work up a payment plan and sell it to his suppliers he hides while the creditors gang up on him and push him out of business. The smartest thing a businessman in this position can do is hire a bookkeeper or comptroller for a few hours a week to deal with the suppliers," adds Kosberg.

It's good advice. However, success goes beyond tactics. When it's your suppliers' money on the shelf, you can't afford a false start. Show your suppliers a winning business and they'll work and build with you.

TACKLING THE ONE BIG SUPPLIER

Most businesses rely on one principal supplier to bankroll anywhere from 40 to 80 percent of the opening inventory. It's as common as corn in Kansas. Drug wholesalers provide about 70 percent of the merchandise for fledgling pharmacies. Hardware wholesalers do about the same for hardware stores. Liquor wholesalers score higher, oftentimes providing 80 percent of the stock for their retail liquor customers, and small food stores frequently buy all their merchandise from one wholesale source.

Even clothing stores, noted for their diverse lines, may end up buying the bulk of their inventory from one supplier. Chances are your business will lean on one principal supplier for most of the beginning inventory. That's the supplier who requires very special handling. Unlike your small secondary suppliers, your primary supplier is a breed apart and will take a much harder look at your business.

Can you convince a primary supplier to gamble and ship an opening inventory on credit? Absolutely. But let me qualify it. You'll need a proposition that makes sense and a proposition that makes sense is one with a big benefit and a small risk.

"Wholesalers are in business to sell goods," says Sam Roseman, 63, a newborn entrepreneur with his seven-year-old convenience store in a Nashua, New Hampshire, suburb. "If they won't work with you on an opening inventory there has to be a good reason." Sam knows what he's talking about. In fact, he had three wholesalers bidding for the privilege to stock his store.

Sam's story unfolded when he was laid off for the third time in five years from his position as a cost analyst for an engineering firm. He selected food retailing because it was a business he knew something about, enjoyed, and could get his family involved in. "Besides," adds Sam, "a food store is one of the easier and safer businesses to enter." At first Sam considered several franchised food stores including "7-Eleven" and some offered by local supermarket chains. Although the franchises offered financing, Sam decided he didn't want to put up with franchisor control.

"Money was my problem," Sam recalls. "I had $10,000 and it was only enough to buy used fixtures and refrigerated units, with a few thousand left for rent and other start-up costs. But what I did have was a lease for an excellent location and the drive to make it work. Turning to several food wholesalers, I found they were interested in stocking the store on 100 percent credit. I finally negotiated a deal with a Rhode Island wholesaler who makes weekly deliveries to New Hampshire. He agreed to stock me with an opening $35,000 inventory, financed over four years at 16%, secured by a mortgage on the inventory and my personal guarantee. The only other proviso is that I buy at least 70 percent of my products from him and pay current. But that's no problem. My only other vendors are paperback books, newspapers, a tobacco jobber, and my milk supplier. It was a great deal for me because it put me in business. It was not a bad one for my wholesaler either. He's selling me $300,000 a year in merchandise and can't really lose on his $35,000 investment."

I have seen hundreds of businesses in virtually every merchandising line sponsored by a principal supplier anxious to "buy" a new customer. Many of my own businesses depended on one or two suppliers for their start. And as Sam Roseman found out, there is always the right way to put their goods on your shelf. Try these tips:

1. Negotiate with every major wholesaler who could qualify as your primary supplier. Don't limit yourself. You never know which one will give you the best deal until you knock on all their doors. It's no different than shopping for a new car. Shop!

2. The best time to shop is *after* you have the location lined up. Don't sign the lease until your merchandise is committed, but the location still comes first. Reason? Suppliers base credit largely on their assessment of the location and the sales and profits it can produce.

3. Put your proposal together *before* you shop for merchandise. Your business plan should be as detailed as what an investor or banker would expect. Your supplier's investment is no smaller, so why should you tell him less? Your plan should include a proposed layout, description of operations (hours, staffing, pricing, promotion), and financial projections and budget for two years. This is an important step. It not only shows what your business is about, but shows what you know about the business. The reason goes deeper. Your supplier also knows something about the business. He can offer plenty of ideas and criticisms. Pick his brain and make him your free consultant.

4. Meet with the top man. An opening inventory of $30,000 to $50,000 is not an everyday credit decision, and credit managers may not have the clout to make the decision or want the risk of the decision. Some-

times they lack the initiative to check with someone who can decide. It only takes a phone call to briefly explain why you're calling and to invite the president of the firm to dinner. A word of caution. If you know the sales manager or credit manager, try to work through him or her. Protocol is important.

5. Define what you need in opening inventory. Reduce it to dollar amounts and a description of the lines or type merchandise you need. Be prepared to defend the quantity as it's also a test of your managerial know-how. The lines are important because the profit margins vary from line to line. A supplier doesn't want you to "sharpshoot" by using him only for the low-profit lines while you shop the "gravy" items elsewhere.

6. Start selling the benefit—and the benefit is your future buying. For example, if you project $400,000 in sales, a supplier may translate that into $200,000 a year in purchases. While he's enjoying his steak Diane, he's focusing on the $200,000-a-year account you represent. That's the carrot. Now back it up. Commit yourself to future buying. Reduce it to a committed percentage of what you would buy from a wholesaler. For example, if you know that you'll buy 70 percent of your stock from a wholesaler, you may agree to give him all your wholesale purchases except for 10 percent which may go to backup suppliers. How does your wholesaler know you'll live up to it? He doesn't. And your wholesaler can't force you to buy from him once you have his opening inventory. What you can do is put it in writing. If you default on your buying agreement, he can immediately call for full payment on the opening inventory. It's an important point. Your wholesaler isn't in the finance business. He's giving you credit for your opening stock to "buy" your future business. Convince him he'll get it.

7. Don't be a "captive" customer. You'll agree to buy most of your product from the supplier, but you expect the same prices, allowances, advertising rebates, and pro-

motional concessions as any other "cash" customer buying in comparable quantity. Some suppliers will "lock you in" and take away discounts, and so on. It's not only unfair, but you can't afford it. Make sure you're buying right.

8. The payback period is a negotiable item. Two to four years is the average, but the economics of your business and its cash flow is the determining factor. Have your accountant decide this item and work it out with the supplier.

9. Interest? Most suppliers charge 18 percent on overdue accounts. Although this too is a negotiable item, you should be charged a lower rate because it's a financed inventory rather than an overdue account. Most suppliers borrow at prime rate, considering their size, and a fair compromise is to pay 2 to 3 percent above what your supplier pays to borrow.

10. Security. This is the key to reduced risk. Your supplier should be offered a mortgage on all inventory. If you default, he has first claim on the inventory to recoup what's owed. His central concern will be a depleted inventory if foreclosure is necessary. An effective safeguard is to suggest a written provision that you'll maintain a defined minimum inventory. A shrewd supplier may enhance the value of the collateral by taking an assignment of lease besides. Upon foreclosure, he not only gets the inventory but the location as well. It's not unreasonable, but as with all legal documents, have your counsel check it out. Should you guarantee the account? If it's your first business venture, you probably will have to. After you have a track record, it's a bargaining point.

Study these points. How can the supplier lose? George Maloof of New England Wholesale Drug Company admits that it's difficult to say "no" to such a proposal. "Many times a young pharmacist will come to us to stock him for a new drugstore. We evaluate it in terms of our own profits from the account. If we see him buying $200,000 a year from us, we may make $20,000 to $25,000 a year profit. We'll almost always grant an opening inventory of $30,000 to $40,000 on the strength of its profit potential if it does make it, and the strength of our security if it doesn't. Sure, the business may fail a year or two later but we invariably recoup what's owed. If we don't, it's a small loss compared to the potential it initially offered."

That's what they all say once you show them how to look at your winning idea.

CONSIGNMENTS ARE AS GOOD AS CASH

Many businesses don't start by buying goods. What they do is look for merchandise they can sell on consignment. It's a natural for a shoestring start-up and works well in a large number of businesses. It particularly flourishes in the clothing, shoe, furniture, housewares, appliance, and stereo industries and can work in any field with high unit sales and is competitive at the manufacturers' level.

What makes consignment sales so attractive is the fact that the supplier takes no risk. As you sell the goods, you take your percentage and remit the difference to the supplier. Until the goods are sold, the seller retains title. If you fail or close up shop, the supplier only has to step in and remove his goods. And it's that lack of risk that induces a supplier to provide goods to any logical retailer who can move the goods, bypassing the nasty concerns of credit or cash.

Lancaster Dress used consignment merchandise for its start, and now that it can afford to buy, it still adheres to its successful consignment merchandising program. Started in 1979, Lancaster could hardly buy the inexpensive racks for its first Phoenix, Arizona, location. Inventory was a bigger problem. Without cash or credit, the New York houses would only ship token orders. It wasn't enough for a successful start. That's when Lancaster's owners, Scott and Mary Hempstead, grabbed a plane to New York and spotted a dress manufacturer with a bulging warehouse. "We convinced the manufacturer the dresses had a better chance of selling in our store than in his dusty warehouse," says Scott Hempstead, "and the manufacturer agreed. We didn't want to buy the dresses outright, as we didn't know how well they'd sell. It equally suited the manufacturer who didn't want a long-term financing arrangement. So he shipped $40,000 worth of dresses on a strict consignment basis. We discount the dresses by 20 percent and once a week remit the cost on what we sell together with an accounting. This year our sales are up to $2,400,000 and we now buy on consignment from 20 manufacturers in the ladies apparel lines. It's a great feeling to know you can built a multimillion dollar business without investing a dime of your own money or credit on merchandise."

The only way to find consignment merchandise is with an active search. Invariably it will lead you to the doors of manufacturers with excess inventory that for a variety of reasons can't be quickly sold for cash through normal channels. You have to put them in the consignment business by showing the benefits—and how it will turn their excess inventory into cash. Frequently a supplier will ask you to take a smaller markup, considering you aren't buying the merchandise outright, but a slightly higher price shouldn't stop you. You're still working on 100 percent of his money.

Art galleries are masters at consignment deals. The typical art gallery may have 60 to 100 percent of the pictures on the walls placed there by hungry artists willing to be paid when the painting is sold. A friend of mine opened a retail store that I can't even describe. It sells Near-Eastern "anything." It started with about $2000 in Mediterranean-style clothes and since expanded to feature oriental rugs, brass accessories, jewelry, and even art works depicting the Middle East. Some came from suppliers and some from artists or individuals cleaning out their attic. But it's all there—$60,000 worth—and it's all there on consignment.

A burgeoning retail industry is the "consignment shop" itself, where people bring used clothing, toys, or "what-have-you" for whatever it will fetch. It's the entrepreneurs' way of moving the garage sale out of the garage and into their own store.

Big or small, hard goods or soft goods, if it can be sold it can be sold on consignment. It's high on the list for every shoestring merchant.

HOW TO FIND MERCHANDISE AT
ROCK-BOTTOM PRICES

I love auctions. Where else can you pick up good salable inventory for as little as a dime on the dollar? It's the next best thing to stealing it.

How many start-up ventures actually start when an entrepreneur with a few dollars in his pocket shows up at somebody else's broken dream and walks away with a truckload of inventory to nourish his own dream? Plenty.

That's how I got into my first greeting card and gift shop business. Spotting the bankruptcy ad in the newspaper, I showed up on a snowy winter day more out of curiosity than interest. My interest peaked when I realized that I'd be the high bidder for $40,000 in good merchandise for $6300. So I bought, negotiated a new lease, sold a half interest to a working partner for $15,000, and considered it one of my best investments.

It's particularly smart to look for auction merchandise as your "merchandise core." You may find $10,000 to $15,000 in good merchandise as your foundation and build from there with trade credit. And it will help you get trade credit because you have a healthy percentage of what you need to begin with.

Here's a useful tip to consider: You don't actually have to attend an auction to buy for a dime on the dollar. Auctions are conducted for bankruptcy trustees, receivers, and foreclosing banks. If you know a business is going up for auction in the near future, you can negotiate to buy the inventory at private sale without an auction, but at the appraised auction value. It will give you first crack at some very good buys once you let auctioneers know what you're interested in.

Want another source of good merchandise at the right price? Try manufacturers' closeouts. New York is the mecca for this type of merchandise and you may need contacts. Allied Buying Service and Affiliated Buying Service are two recommended buying agents who can put you in touch with the right companies.

SOME IMAGINATION PLEASE!

How many ways are there for landing merchandise with little or no cash or credit? Countless ways. This chapter only scratched the surface. The opportunities extend only to the limits of your imagination. And some people have great imaginations, and with them start some very unusual businesses.

Ron Humphrey built a $400,000-a-year toy business with his own stroke of imagination. Hundreds of woodworking hobbyists turn out wooden planes, ships, trains, and assorted delights for the kiddies set following Ron's specifications. Ron buys their output on 90-day terms, assured that the merchandise will sell long before then.

When IBM turned Hank Jensen down for credit to open an office equipment store, the undaunted Jensen opened a used equipment business. Sending out 20,000 flyers to office firms, Hank soon had $160,000 in used office machines to sell on consignment.

My favorite story involves two young chaps who never did quite make it as shoestring merchants. But they're not complaining. The Winslow brothers took over the lease on an abandoned 20,000-sq.-ft. supermarket, spending their last dime in the process. All that came with the lease was an assortment of abandoned fixtures. The business needed $200,000 in merchandise, and that was $200,000 more than what the Winslow boys had to spend. Bypassing the credit approach, the Winslows shrewdly decided to let others do the merchandising while they collected rent. So they concessioned the meat department to a local butcher, the bakery department to a bakery firm, groceries to a grocery wholesaler, and one by one the tenants—and their merchandise—began to fill the place. The Winslows operated the checkout, crediting sales to the various concessionaires while keeping 10 percent to cover rent and advertising costs. The Winslows show a net profit of $70,000 for themselves—and never sell a nickel's worth of their own merchandise.

What I remember most about the Winslows was not what they did, but what Jack Winslow once said. "If someone isn't clever or imaginative enough to get the merchandise, they won't be imaginative enough to sell it."

There's a bit of truth to it.

KEY POINTS TO REMEMBER

1. A healthy start-up needs the merchandise to give it the successful start.
2. Expand your sights to include lines from suppliers who will give you credit, rather than limit yourself to suppliers who may not.
3. The easiest credit sources are your small secondary suppliers, provided you follow some basic rules.
4. Design a winning proposal for your own primary supplier. Sell the big benefit and low risk, and he'll soon sell you your opening inventory.
5. Don't overlook consignment goods. It's one of the most popular ways to give your start-up the products to sell.
6. If you have cash to spend then spend it wisely. Bargain-priced merchandise is everywhere—if you know where to look.
7. Use your imagination. You'll need it to sell what you do buy.

PROMOTING FOR
A PITTANCE

SHOESTRING MARKETING:
THE CRITICAL DIFFERENCE

Of the 19 million small businesses in the United States, fewer than 50 percent rely on advertising. How do the rest get along in a society where it seems that advertising is the key to success? Where larger companies rely on their reputations and small businesses, lawyers, doctors, and consultants rely on personal recommendations, shoestring entrepreneurs count on creativity.

The burden of making your business known is entirely on you. And it's a heavy burden. Customers do not magically show up because you open your doors. You make them show up with shoestring marketing.

But what is shoestring marketing? It is simply everything that makes the public aware of you and your product or service without your spending lots of money to make it happen.

Shoestring marketing is not just a jumble of low-budget techniques. It's a way of looking at the world that allows you to recognize or create every low-cost or no-cost opportunity to make your business known to your potential customers.

Such marketing is an art, not a science. You must evaluate every strategy by its potential to make your business more profitable. Shoestring marketing is the knowledge that everything you say and do impacts on your business either positively or negatively.

Shoestring marketing is the quality of your business card and stationery. Shoestring marketing is the message you send out by the clothes you wear. It is your choice of business location, the price for your goods or services, and your tone of voice on the telephone. It is also the firmness of your handshake, your involvement in community affairs, the cleanliness of your fingernails, and the service you offer after your product is sold. Shoestring marketing is the smile on your face when you greet customers, the way you treat your employees, and the shine on your shoes.

Good marketing instills confidence in your product or service by favorably placing your business before the audience you seek as clients—making those people familiar with your product or service and therefore making them comfortable with it. If you get the word out and deliver and maintain quality that fulfills your claims, sales inevitably follow. Remember, good reputations spread gradually and mean steady growth. Poor reputations spread like wildfire and bring instant failure. Seldom do you get a second chance.

As a shoestring marketeer, you are your business, and your business is you. Your personal appearance says a lot about your business. So does your language and the way you deal with employees, customers, and colleagues in the business community. And that's as true in the smallest town as it is in the largest city. In reality, the business community you operate in is a very small world of suppliers, competitors, and customers. The way you run your business is likely to be quickly observed. If you contract out work, freelancers soon learn whether you pay competitive rates. If you buy services and goods, creditors learn quickly whether you pay your bills on time. Everything you say and do from the time you begin thinking about your business will directly or indirectly have an impact on its future success. Every word and action must be measured and be consistent with the image and reputation you hope to develop.

Your own appearance is a good place to start. Take a good look at yourself. Acquire a core wardrobe that suits your new endeavor and makes you appear successful. That means a good haircut, well-manicured fingernails, and polished shoes. Your clothes should mean business; they should be well cut and well pressed. If you do home repair work, gardening, or carpentry, clean work clothes for sales calls are a must. If you consult, you'll probably need conservative clothes. You may have to spend precious capital on new business suits and accessories, but you may never be taken seriously if you make your first appearance a poor one.

By now you should begin to realize that there is a difference between *advertising* and *marketing.* The more aware of marketing you are, the more attention you will pay to it and the more successful your marketing efforts will be.

The critical difference between the shoestring entrepreneur and a large corporation is the degree of flexibility each possesses. A small entrepreneurial operation can bypass bureaucratic levels of management and an unwieldly sales organization when implementing its marketing plan. A large company, on the other hand, can invest in a full-scale advertising campaign and has the resources to switch to different strategies when initial marketing efforts fail. This luxury is not available to shoestring entrepreneurs who must get it right the first time and must make every penny count.

Many marketing approaches overlap. Shoestring entrepreneurs have to govern operations by a highly effective marketing strategy, by which all their marketing efforts must be weighed. They also need to examine all of the marketing avenues available to them. The critical difference between the marketing styles of large and small companies is the bottom line. Smaller companies must keep a far keener eye on the bottom line than do larger firms. They must spend far less money testing their marketing tactics. And their marketing must produce results at a fraction of the price paid by big companies. Small companies may not necessarily handle their marketing efforts better than do large companies, but they will be more personalized and realistic in their use of marketing strategy.

Large companies think nothing of producing several television commercials to test marketing approaches. Small companies dare not even think the same thought. Large companies employ many levels of management to analyze the effectiveness of their advertising. Small companies must entrust the judging to one individual. Large companies look first to television and national media. Small companies generally look first to small newspaper ads in local papers. Both are interested in sales that generate profits, but each must achieve its goals in a dramatically different way.

Often, large companies aim for leadership of an industry or for domination of a market segment, and they use marketing ploys designed to attain those lofty ambitions. Shoestring entrepreneurs flourish merely by gaining a tiny slice of an industry, a fraction of a market. Different wars require different tactics.

THREE ESSENTIALS TO SUCCESSFUL SHOESTRING MARKETING

If you want your shoestring start-up to become a large, successful business, you must observe three cardinal rules:

1. Be absolutely 100% *committed* to your marketing program.
2. Consider your marketing program as an *investment,* not an expense.
3. Make your marketing program *consistent.*

Without commitment, your marketing program will never work for you. This means more than "testing the waters." You must believe in your program to see it through, and this requires action rather than prolonged planning and testing. Good marketing plans are seldom completely conceived in advance; the best simply evolve from a general strategy. You revise and revise your marketing effort until it becomes a powerful plan, one that works for you!

Don't expect instant gratification. You'll need plenty of patience to reshape your plan until it becomes a winner. That's what commitment is all about. My advice is to design the best marketing plan you can and then stay with it until it proves itself. This may take three to six months or even a year, but you will never know how effective a plan is in only 30 or 60 days.

Second, don't expect your marketing efforts to quickly pay big dividends. Consider them a long-term investment, but a necessary one, when you're a shoestring entrepreneur. When you must allocate scarce dollars, spend as much as you can possibly afford on marketing even if it means spending less on equipment, inventory, overhead, and other start-up costs.

The third major marketing secret is to make your marketing *consistent.* Put the word out constantly, and don't needlessly change the message or the medium. Don't drop marketing for an extended period. Consistency is regularity. Simple, more frequent marketing is preferable to grandiose, less frequent marketing. Consistency works because it creates familiarity, and familiarity produces confidence, which in turn generates sales.

These three essentials—being committed to your marketing program, considering it a worthwhile investment, and promoting it consistently—are difficult rules to adhere to but they are vital to the success of your shoestring venture.

Now, with these ground rules behind us, how can we promote your business for a pittance?

HOW TO CREATE A PRESTIGE IMAGE WITH BUSINESS CARDS AND STATIONERY

Most small businesses need only business cards and stationery to get started in their marketing efforts, and both can be obtained easily and inexpensively. Remember, though, in many cases your initial contact with customers will be by letter, so you want that first impression to be favorable. Potential clients expect quality business cards and letterhead from you.

You don't have to operate a megafirm to have that first-class look. Quick-print shops offer more to businesses today than just an occasional photocopy. They can supply you with high-quality cards, letterhead, and other materials quite inexpensively, and they usually have large sample stock and print catalogs so you can choose different styles of letterhead, typefaces, layouts, and colors to achieve a custom look for mere pennies.

Full-service office supply stores may offer an even wider

choice of paper and printing techniques and may feature even lower prices. Look for shops with experienced salespeople who can show you samples and make suggestions. The service is free, so take full advantage of it.

Also compare prices you can obtain locally with prices from mail-order stationery firms that advertise nationally in business publications and magazines. Many offer fast, reliable service at competitive prices, and most have a toll-free phone number. Unfortunately, their salespeople are not always equipped to advise you about design and quality.

Should you need a logo, special packaging, or a true custom look for your stationery, hire a good graphic designer. Find one through your grapevine of friends or associates, or, better still, find designs that appeal to you that can often be easily modified to serve your needs.

Hiring a designer is not as expensive as it may sound. Rates vary, and admittedly a good firm or freelancer will not come cheap. However, the high fee can be offset by the fact that a designer often has access to sources of material and can obtain prices from suppliers that are not available to you. In addition, a good designer spares you expensive mistakes.

Once you have the image you want to project, a designer can help you choose paper, typeface, and ink color for your letterhead and brochures. It is then relatively simple to buy labels, envelopes, and other standard materials to carry your design. Many designers will gladly do the creative work and will advise you where to look for commercially available materials to complete your image at a bargain price. Your best bet? Try graphic design students at your local college.

DESIGN AN INEXPENSIVE WEB SITE

Big companies spend megabucks to design and maintain their complicated web sites. Does that mean you have to go bankrupt imitating them? Not at all. In fact, the Web is one of the start-up entrepreneur's best, most cost-effective resources, and you don't have to spend a bankroll to use it effectively. You can use templates and other short-cut methods to design a site, and hosting services are often quite affordable. Some Internet Service Providers (ISPs) will even design a site for you at minimal cost.

Since the topic of web sites is complex and important, I've devoted a whole chapter of it in this new edition of *Starting on a Shoestring*. See Chapter 14 for details.

FREE WORD-OF-MOUTH ADVERTISING IS BEST

Movie moguls who enjoy virtually unlimited advertising budgets know that while advertising creates public awareness of a mega-dollar production, it is word-of-mouth advertising that leads to megaprofits. Small, independent filmmakers with tiny advertising budgets find that favorable word of mouth can create the excitement that translates into box-office success. The same is true for your business.

How do you create a strong word-of-mouth campaign? In a world long on hype and short on quality, most people are willing, even eager, to share their discovery of quality. They know that sharing the find makes them stand a little taller in the eyes of their friends and business associates.

Help the process along by simply asking your clients to spread the news. You do this with a parting word as they go out the door, a phrase in your brochure, or a note placed on top of your merchandise, such as the one used by a hardware dealer in San Francisco that opens with a big "Thanks" scrawled across the top and reads: "We hope you feel shopping at Acme Hardware was a pleasant and worthwhile experience. If you agree, please mention us to your friends. We are proud of more than a quarter of a century of success based on 'word-of-mouth' among our valued customers!"

If possible, offer clients a direct benefit for recommending your business. A discount or rebate on their next purchase or free use of your services for every new client they bring you can work wonders.

Friends are often an overlooked source of referrals. They can be enthusiastic supporters, eager to spread the word about your business. Don't mistakenly assume, however, that friends understand what your business is. This is especially true if yours is a new type of product or service. In an economy where new services and products spring up fast, it is vital to take the time to explain precisely what you do. Show friends your office, let them leaf through your sample book or portfolio, demonstrate your computer program, or do whatever else will better help them understand your operation so they can recommend you to potential customers.

HOW TO OBTAIN FREE MEDIA PUBLICITY

One page of free publicity can pull in more customers than ten pages of paid advertising. Local neighborhood and daily newspapers; alumni, professional, and national magazines; trade publications; newsletters; radio; and national, local, and cable television all have enormous media space or airtime to fill with newsworthy items. Public relations experts estimate that as much as 90 percent of all news is planted by PR specialists. This figure may be an overstatement, but it is true that much of what we read and watch is prompted by public relations firms and individual business people who know how to capture the attention of the media.

The good news is that you don't have to pay exorbitant fees to PR firms to get the free publicity your business needs. You can easily create your own PR campaign by knowing the basic rules.

As with most things, the best way to capture free publicity for your business is to use the simplest and most direct method: Write a straightforward letter to your local newspaper stating what your business offers, how it is unique or different, and why the public would benefit from knowing about your service or product. Send a good photograph that helps tell your story, along with a descriptive caption. Enclose other promotional materials also.

Newspapers want news concerning local residents and businesses. If you have worked in the community or are new to the area, your paper may be interested in you. A business might also attract attention because its owner has an unusual background for the business or because it is simply a new business to the area.

Before rushing your letter off to your newspaper, radio, or TV station, carefully study the contents of programs and articles. This will give you a better idea of what subject they will be interested in promoting. Make your press announcement lively and quotable. Most of all, give the media a news "hook" on which to hang your story. What is it that you think is most interesting or unusual about your business? A catchy name or slogan might be enough. Nathan Cohen's many wind-up toy stores, called "The Last Wound Up," have attracted international press attention as much for their whimsical name as for their unusual merchandise.

Starting a business itself is often worth a few lines in the local paper, an alumni magazine, or the trade press. The same is true when opening a new branch or appointing a new company officer. Your first birthday sale or special seasonal rates might equally merit an article or a mention. Even your age can be of interest to readers. Going into business after fifty is still a relatively new phenomenon, and magazines such as *50 Plus* and AARP's publications *Maturity* and *My Generation* are interested in such entrepreneurs. Business monthlies such as *Inc., Entrepreneur,* and *Fortune,* and even the business sections of *Newsweek* and *Time,* are constantly in search of new businesses with a new wrinkle.

Press coverage is perceived by the public as an endorsement of your business. Laminate or frame any article about you and place it in your shop window or office, or make photocopies for every mailing. Don't rely on this one article alone. A three-year-old review in a store window will likely make customers wonder why reviewers have not been back since. Notice how very successful restaurant owners, who are savvy in public relations, feature all their recent press credits and reviews next to the front door.

Here are a few words of caution about media coverage: Broad exposure can produce an onslaught of inquiries and business. This may not sound like a problem, but you must be prepared to handle the sudden rush of interest without compromising quality or service. Hiring more help, ordering extra merchandise, or working longer hours is not always as easy as it seems.

Work out in advance all the logistics for increased service or product demands. One fancy dessert maker plunged into the mail-order delivery of its luxury pies and cakes before it had solved basic packaging and shipping problems for its highly perishable cheesecakes. While enthusiastic food columnists promoted the business, the company spent a small fortune scrambling to make good on merchandise that arrived spoiled.

The media won't always run a release on your business based on information you provide. Reporters often find you on their own. In either case, be prepared to answer additional questions thoughtfully and concisely. Never give out information you don't wish to see in print. Don't talk "off the record." If you should receive unsolicited calls from reporters, provide materials with the exact reference information you want to see published. Always remember that you have no control over, and sometimes no inkling of, what reporters focus on when they actually sit down to write.

MAKE YOUR BROCHURE A PROMOTIONAL TOOL

A brochure is more than a document that expresses who you are and what you do. It should also tell why your business is unique. No word should be wasted, and all illustrations or graphics must reinforce your story. Because no one wants to be the first to try a new business or service, list satisfied clients in your brochure to help build credibility.

Unless you are a whiz with words and graphics, you will probably need the expert advice and services of a writer and a designer. Explain what you hope to accomplish with your brochure and how you intend to use it. Will it be a handout at trade shows, an enclosure for direct mail, or an enclosure with your product? All of these? Collect your competitors' brochures and materials for some ideas.

BECOME ACTIVE IN COMMUNITY SERVICE

As a local business person, your involvement in public or community service is an excellent vehicle for creating visibility and goodwill and for making contacts for your business. It can be the most effective marketing effort you make. To succeed you must be sincere in your desire to give something back to the community that helps you prosper. If you are motivated only by profit, your motives will show sooner than you think, and your business will then suffer rather than benefit from your efforts. Donate your time. It's as important as your money. Why pay for T-shirts for the annual bike race through town when being on the race committee or at the finish line until the last racer comes puffing in can show more goodwill and give you greater visibility?

It's easy to get swept up in the community spirit. Endless opportunities abound to help you build your business and the community at the same time. The difficult part is choosing activities that are appropriate for both the community and your business and finding the time to carry out your good deeds. But you can match what you have to offer with community needs. Pete Kosow, who runs a flight service and pilot training business, contributes discounted flight time to high school and college students interested in learning to fly. His generosity has sparked press interest, and Pete finds that the students come back later to complete their training for their pilot's license. This is the type of marketing shoestring entrepreneurs find most valuable.

HOW TO SLASH ADVERTISING COSTS

Once you start your business you will be besieged to advertise on radio, in directories, and in other media. The high-pressure selling is usually done through telemarketing, and sales tactics can be intense. Advertising media can praise your business to the skies, name-drop (so-and-so is on the editorial advisory committee), or promise you stunning results. Beware!

Too many entrepreneurs respond eagerly and spend precious dollars advertising in publications they have never seen and that don't effectively reach their markets. It is just plain bad business to buy media space until you can judge its value for yourself. Talk to others who advertise in these outlets. What benefits has their investment brought? Be skeptical.

Don't count yourself out of advertising in national publications simply because of the cost. As you see, you can cut down on that cost by establishing an in-house advertising agency, by purchasing remnant space or space in regional editions, and by purchasing small space ads. You can also advertise in the classified sections found in many national magazines, several of which offer attractive discounts to mail-order advertisers. And virtually all magazines offer impressive merchandising materials: easel-back cards, reprints, decals with the name of the magazine (for example, "as advertised in *Time*"), and mailing folders. The magazine's advertising sales representative will gladly tell you about all of the merchandising aids offered. Be sure you take advantage of them. They will be useful at your place of business and in other advertising you do. Your business will be helped if you simply say, "You've probably seen our ad in *Ladies Home Journal.*" And these materials can be used as enclosures in direct mailings or personal letters; as signs on bulletin boards; as counter cards; as display pieces at trade shows, exhibits, or fairs; and as part of a brochure or circular. The cost of these aids is ridiculously low, and they're sometimes even free, so use them to the fullest extent. Magazines can help you immediately, and well into the years ahead. It's the years-ahead part that's going to result in profitable business for you.

MORE SECRETS OF SAVING MARKETING MONEY

There's no end to the number of ways you can advertise or promote your business. Conventional media advertising (magazines, newspapers, radio) is what initially comes to mind, but you will also want to consider:

- Billboards
- Cable TV
- Direct response
- Flyers
- Web advertising

These, of course, only scratch the surface of the many possible ways to reach your market. Which will work best for you depends largely on the nature of your business. No matter how you advertise, however, there are countless ways to save big money once you explore less conventional approaches to marketing.

For example, you can save considerable sums of money if you realize that magazine, radio, and television rate cards can be likened to Aesop's fables. In short, they are fiction and not to be taken seriously. If anything is negotiable, it is the cost of media, radio, and TV time. Of course, prime airtime or media space is hard to buy and therefore hard to negotiate. But understand that if media time or space is unsold, it is wasted forever. Therefore, the media will usually accept prices far below what's on their rate cards.

To entice new advertisers, the media will ordinarily offer even more attractive prices. Just knowing this will save you money. Large advertisers know that rate cards are works of fiction, but small advertisers often believe what they read. Don't you believe it. Remember that you can save media money by making an offer you can afford. You'll be surprised at how many will accept your offer, even at 50 percent off scheduled rates.

While discussing the cost of advertising, consider one of the most efficient money-saving strategies: creating an in-house advertising agency. Advertising agencies receive a 15 percent discount from publications and broadcast stations where they place advertising. If an ad or commercial costs an advertiser $2000, that same ad space or commercial time costs an advertising agency only $1700, that's big savings!

It's easy to establish your own in-house advertising agency. You usually need do no more than tell the media that that's what you are. In some cases the medium may require that you have a checking account in your agency's name and agency stationery.

With this money-saving strategy, you can save 15 percent on almost all the advertising you place for yourself, except for newspaper and classified advertising, where you pay only the retail rate, which is low. Yes, it's easy to set up an in-house agency, and pocket those 15 percent commission checks for yourself.

Don't overlook remnant space. Many national magazines publish regional editions, in which they sell advertising space to regional advertisers. Magazines often have unsold space when publication date is right around the corner. What do they do with that extra remnant space? They sell it at an astounding discount to a shrewd local advertiser! If you want to be that local advertiser, just contact the publication well in advance of the date you wish your ad to appear. Better yet, get in touch with Media Networks, Inc., a national company devoted to selling remnant space to local advertisers, with headquarters at 530 Fifth Avenue, New York, New York, 10036 (212-536-7800). This company may be able to put your ad in the regional issues of most national magazines, at a far lower cost than you would believe possible.

Another strategy to save big money is to barter your goods or services. Perhaps your local TV or radio station or newspaper doesn't want what you're selling. But usually, you'll be able to find someone to trade with items the advertiser wants. You'll then get your ads for a fraction of their usual cost, since you'll be paying indirectly with your own services or goods swapped at their full price.

Many barter houses specialize in organizing such trades. Look in the yellow pages, listed under "Barter Companies" or "Barter Services." Also bear in mind that at least 800 magazines now trade ad space. But policies vary at these publications, so trades must be individually negotiated. Just remember that every media needs something. By learning what your selected media need, you might negotiate a money-saving trade.

If you operate a retail business, you can also save big money with cooperative advertising funds. Large advertisers frequently pay cash rebates to small advertisers who promote these large advertisers in their ads. For example, a small furniture store features a large mattress company in their ads and receives ad rebates from that company. Their ads also mention the name of other large manufacturer that offers these co-op ad funds. It not only helps save money but also adds credibility by associating with the name of a nationally known company. Both large companies and smart entrepreneurs interested in saving marketing money feature only companies offering co-op ad allowances, thereby saving sometimes 50 percent or more of the ad cost. If you're interested in saving money, ask your suppliers directly.

With a little effort you can also set up a P.I. or P.O. arrangement with an advertising medium. P.I. stands for "per inquiry" and P.O. means "per order." Both are rather common methods entrepreneurs use to save advertising money. Basically, the medium gives you ad space or time in return for a set sum of money per inquiry or per order. These deals work particularly well for mail-order and direct-response firms since they have no ad money at risk.

Here's how it works. Imagine you want to sell books for $10 each by mail. You arrange a deal with a magazine whereby the magazine gives you free ad space and you give the magazine $4 per every order that comes in as a direct result of the ad. Notice that no money has changed hands up front. The magazine might ordinarily charge $100 to run such an ad. Then the ad runs, producing fifty orders for the book. That means the magazine receives $200 but you also receive $300 and risk no advertising costs. Should you make similar arrangements with 100 magazines, you can win enormous profits without risking a dime.

It's not difficult to find P.I. and P.O. arrangements. They are available with many magazines, radio stations, and television stations, but few newspapers offer these deals. But send a letter to selected media outlining the arrangement you're proposing. If they believe they can make money on your offer and have available space, they'll accept. In this way, you can undertake high-level promotion with virtually no up-front costs other than production costs. Of course, the media might put your commercial in an undesirable slot—one that couldn't be sold to another advertiser. But remember the media wants to make money also, and it will go all out to make money for both of you.

These few ideas are just the tip of the iceberg when it comes to saving big money on your marketing and advertising programs. The opportunities to gain enormous exposure at very little cost are enormous when you employ all the tricks available. Let me recommend three of the best books on the subject. Pick up my friend Jeffrey Davidson's excellent *Marketing on a Shoestring: Low-Cost Tips for Marketing Your Products* (John Wiley & Sons, 1994) for starters. Jeff knows all the pennypinching tricks. Also, pore through *Guerilla Marketing* by Jay Levinson (Houghton Mifflin, 1993). I highly recommend it.

Once you read these and other fine publications on marketing, you'll soon realize that good shoestring marketing is nothing more than exercising the art of creativity. In short, this means that you must defy convention and do things differently. You find ways to stand out from the crowd and find ways to save money while your competitors spend theirs.

Look around. Who are the leaders in your industries? What are their more unique marketing strategies? How can you improve upon them? What "spin-off" ideas can you formulate?

What shrewd marketing ideas can you gain by observing leaders in other industries? Scan some of the more progressive business magazines such as *Entrepreneur* and you'll find plenty of clever people successfully promoting their business for a pittance.

KEY POINTS TO REMEMBER

1. Small shoestring ventures succeed with marketing strategies that defy conventional techniques.
2. The image you and your company project is all part of marketing. Make appearances count.
3. A good marketing program requires commitment, investment, and consistency.
4. A good reputation is the most effective—and least costly—form of advertising.
5. You and your business are newsworthy! Find the angle and cash in on free publicity.
6. Countless money-saving advertising techniques exist. Use creativity, not cash, to promote your business.

14

USING THE
WORLD WIDE WEB

During the heady days of the late-90s dot-com boom, thousands of entrepreneurs set up World Wide Web-based businesses and assumed they'd quickly rake in the greenbacks. Whether these start-ups made much money was debatable even at the time; many companies never reaped what they sowed. However, this much is certain: That boom is over. At the time of my writing this new edition of *Starting on a Shoestring*, the United States is at war, and the formerly robust U.S. economy is climbing out of a recession. No doubt the outlook will improve by the time this book reaches the bookstores, but the notion of simply throwing a catchy e-business concept online and making a quick profit now seems almost quaint, even laughable. Few start-up firms can count on easy profits from the Web alone.

That being said, it's not possible for an U.S. business *not* to have a web site. Unless you're an Amish cabinetmaker selling only to the brethren, you need to have a web site. (There are, in fact, hundreds of sites that sell Amish furniture.) You need a site for the same reasons that you need a telephone, a fax line, a business card, and stationery: These are simply the basic tools of the trade. The issue isn't whether to have a site but, rather, what kind of site you need.

Actually, there's another issue as well: How best to make your web site into a powerful business start-up tool. If you plan cor-rectly, you can make a well-designed, well-maintained web site into an asset that will not only launch your business, but also speed you on your way to success. The key is to think through each step, move carefully, and avoid deluding yourself with il-lusions left over from the high-rolling '90s.

Don't get me wrong. The Web is one of the greatest boons ever to arrive in the business world. Here's what Alan Canton of the Adams-Blake Company (www.adams-blake.com) has to say about his Web-based books-and-software firm: "Someone hears about our software. They go to our site. They download the pro-gram. They install the demo and try it. They like it. They go back to our site. They enter their credit card. The transaction takes place online in real-time. They get an e-mail saying where to link to download the unlocked version. They do this. They install it. They are now set. We get our money in 24 hours. We have not done a thing, have not touched a key, have not had to make a call, send a salesman, or mail a letter. Explain to me how things could get any better or easier."

Is this a revolution, or what?

Precisely because the Web is so flexible, you can put it to al-most any use that suits your purposes. Your emphasis can be marketing, direct sales, client education, or whatever. The pos-sibilities for the form and content that you present to the world are almost infinite. For this reason, your first step is to deter-mine exactly what those purposes are.

SETTING YOUR GOALS FOR WEB USE

Ed Myers is a writer in the New York City area. Specializing in children's books, Ed has published many successful adventure stories for school-age kids. Yet he felt frustrated by his publish-ers' lackluster efforts in promoting his books, so he decided to take matters into his own hands. Ed founded a small company called Montemayor Press that would publish his and other au-thors' works. Starting on a shoestring, Ed got his press up and running for less than $1,000 in investment and, within the first few months, he'd published several books by using digital publishing technology. Costs would stay low, Ed decided, because he could use the Web to sell books online. Ed's web site (www.monte mayorpress.com) would be his virtual store. So far, so good.

The catch: It's hard to sell books this way unless you happen to own Amazon.com. (And even Amazon has yet to turn a profit.) Ed discovered that, despite a handsome web site, he wasn't getting as many orders as he'd expected. So was Montemayor Press a failure? Not at all. As it turned out, Montemayor Press didn't bring in abundant book orders, but it prompted a lot of interest in Ed's other business, which is giving presentations about creative writing to school kids. Ed created a second web site (www.edwardmyers.com) that provides information about his work as an author and author-in-the-schools. By creating links between the two sites, Ed saw a big increase in demand for his school-related activities. He now has a thriving business as a visiting author.

What's the moral of the story? Simply this: The goal you initially set for your web site may not be what ultimately best serves your purposes. You may not be grasping what the Web has to offer you. You may be too grandiose in your expectations. You may miscalculate how many people are willing to do business with you over the Web. You may miscalculate regarding the *kind* of people wanting to do business with you. You may make decisions that prevent you from putting your best foot forward. In short, you may misgauge what you're doing online.

Actually, there are *two* morals to this story.

1. Think through what you're doing as fully and as clearly as possible *before* you take the first step toward establishing an online presence. Save yourself the time, effort, expense, and aggravation of setting up a site that just doesn't fly.
2. Be ready to retool your site—or your expectations about your site—as you proceed. This process of retooling is crucial anyway. (Few web sites should stay the same for

more than a few weeks—a subject I'll address later in this chapter.) You need to assess your site constantly, add new material, change the format, and make it new on an ongoing basis. My main point is simply that you may need to change your *perception* of your site from a business standpoint.

Combined, these two aspects of the situation mean that you'll need to do good planning both before and during your Web-based business activities. That's what Ed Myers did in setting up the site for Montemayor Press. His concept for his company wasn't fundamentally flawed; he just wanted to create a niche publishing company and distribute his books to a specialty audience. That concept wasn't a problem in its own right. But he ran into trouble believing that a web site would solve his marketing problems. It didn't. If he'd stuck with his initial concept for the site, he would have gotten nowhere. Cracking into the complex world of book distribution wouldn't have been easy by these limited means. Instead, he retooled the concept and moved on. Myers realized that his real audience wasn't the retail book business but, rather, the network of librarians and teachers who buy books for their schools and who hire writers to visit their students.

To set goals for your web site, here are some of the questions you need to ask yourself. There are no right or wrong answers, but you should clarify each of these issues to help you decide what purposes the Web can serve for you, and how you attend to accomplish them.

- What are your main goals for setting up a web site? (Typical goals are marketing, promotion, direct sales, and client education.)
- Will your site be the primary means for presenting your business to the world, or will it be simply the online equivalent? (For example, L.L. Bean maintains retail stores as well as llbean.com.)
- How much money are you willing to spend to set up the site?

- Will your site be freestanding, or will you link it to an e-business network of some sort (i.e., a digital mall)?
- Will your site accept credit card orders?
- Do you understand the legal and tax issues that apply to on-line sales?
- Are you able to respond to the demands of 24/7 customer service?
- Will you accept banners and other forms of advertising on your site?
- Are you ready to deal with issues of Internet security, including credit card fraud?

Deb Venman and Bill Venerson own and manage Beau Ties Limited (www.beautiesltd.com), which sells hand-crafted bow ties, pocket squares, cummerbunds, ascots, cravats, and other specialty items. Describing their own process of sizing up Web issues, Deb Venman says, "Our original goals when we started our web site in the spring of 1998 were primarily to increase our catalog customer base. But we quickly recognized that if we were willing to spend the time, the site could act as another selling arm for our company and potentially begin to generate a significant portion of our sales." She goes on to state that "As we acquired more Web-based customers, it became clear that we needed to upgrade our site and spend more resources, both time and money, to keep it fresh and up-to-date."

SETTING UP YOUR WEB SITE

Depending on your goals, setting up a web site is both ridiculously simple and infinitely complex. The big question is simply how big and how elaborate you want the site to be. Some small businesses achieve success through little more than a few well-designed pages; others maintain huge, complex, interactive sites. If possible, start with a relatively small site that's attractive and user-friendly. You can always increase the complexity and interactivity as you go. If your site is too grandiose, you risk alienating customers and stunting your business before it ever gets under way.

The following sections cover the basic steps I recommend for setting up a small-business web site. (For more detailed information, see any of the many Web-design guides.)

Decide on Using Your Own Server or a Web-Hosting Service

The first decision you have to make is whether to set up an on-site server or have a Web-hosting service host your site. Predictably, there are advantages and disadvantages to both.

The chief advantage of an on-site server is autonomy. If you take this route, you can:

- Select the precise combination of hardware and software that suits your purposes
- Control access and maintain security according to your own exact preferences
- Adjust the site's content to your changing needs and specifications
- Control interactions between the site and other systems within your company (order entry, billing, and so forth)

Depending on your technical know-how and willingness to tackle the whole process, these advantages can be significant. The main downside of going it alone, however, is just that: You'll be the chief problem solver when emergencies arise. (Don't kid yourself. We're talking about computers here; emergencies *will* arise.) You can, of course, delegate server maintenance duties to someone else within your company, but you'll still be more involved than if you outsourced these tasks.

Using a Web-hosting service also has pros and cons. The advantages are:

- You can wash your hands of hardware and network problems.
- You won't have to learn as much about hardware and software, which frees you to concentrate on content and other business issues.

- You may be able to participate in virtual-mall arrangements, which have the potential for increasing traffic to your site.
- The hosting service probably has on-site staff members who are more knowledgeable about Web issues than you are, so you can learn from them about site design, copywriting, and other content and format issues.

What are the disadvantages of the Web-hosting approach? Most of them are a side effect of having your Web server off-site. You won't be able to integrate your site with other software systems in your company (though this shouldn't be a big issue in a small, start-up business). You may be limited in the range of server scripts you can install, which can limit functional issues, such as the size of the online shopping cart, the way orders are processed, and the kinds of interactivity you can offer. And you'll have to administer the site remotely, with transfer tools such as File Transfer Protocol (FTP) as the means to transfer files back and forth between your computer and the hosting service.

My own bias favors using a Web-hosting service. Running your own site in-house may be a good option for a large company, but it's a huge and perhaps counterproductive task for a start-up business. If you have the knowledge and time to run your own site, by all means do so. Personally, I feel that most businesses—especially most shoestring start-ups—should outsource these Web-oriented tasks. You have more crucial things to do than attend to the complexities of hardware and software issues. (You probably don't do your own automotive maintenance, either, right?) More to the point, you can find high-quality, customer-oriented service through many hosting services. Working with these companies will save you much time and money, as well as lots of headaches.

Select a Web-Hosting Service

There are hundreds of hosting services to choose from, so your biggest task will be narrowing down the options and selecting one that suits your purposes and is cost-effective. To get an overview of what's available, use any of the standard search engines (google.com, altavista.com, lycos.com, and so forth) and search for "hosting services."

Once you narrow down the search for the companies that appeal to you, here are some of the main questions you should ask:

- What kind of Internet connection do they have?
- Do they have at least one leased T1 line with peak saturation below 50 percent?
- How saturated (filled up) does it become at times of peak usage?
- Will they allow you to have a dedicated server for your own use, and how much control will you have over that server's administration?
- Will your site have its own top-level URL and distinct welcome page (if the hosting service offers several virtual sites on a single server)? That is, will your Web address be www.yourbusiness.com or www.hostingservice.com/~your-business.html?
- Can you reconfigure the server and install server scripts?
- Will the hosting service present you with surcharges if your site experiences a spike in Web surfers' usage?
- Will the hosting service let you upgrade the server software, if necessary?

In addition, you should determine what sorts of business-related features the various hosting services provide. Here's a partial sampling of what these services may offer:

- **Site design.** Some hosting services will design your entire site for you, based on your specifications, which saves you the trouble of performing this task yourself or outsourcing to a third party.
- **Domain registration.** Make sure that your company can use its own domain name rather than have a name that's a sub-directory of the hosting service's name.

- **Wizards and templates.** These features allow you to assemble a virtual store without writing the HTML code yourself.
- **Promotion.** Your ISP may post your site on various search engines or provide other promotional services.
- **Online credit card processing.** This service allows you to accept credit card payments for customers' purchases.
- **Security.** Especially crucial, this service allows you to protect customers' online use of credit card numbers.
- **Site management reporting.** Because you want to track access to your site, management reporting will let you gather data about how many Web users have visited, how long they're staying, what resources they're using, and so forth. (This is important information if you're spending a lot of time and money building your site.)
- **Storage space.** Each hosting services will allow you a certain amount of space for your site's files.
- **Shipping options.** Some hosting services offer interactivity with shipping services that can calculate shipping costs at the time of a customer's purchase.
- **Customer support.** No matter how responsive and efficient your hosting service is, you may encounter difficulties now and then. If so, what kinds of customer support does the provider offer you, and with what sort of response time?
- **Accounting.** Ideally, you should have use of accounting services, which will help you not only keep track of inventory, but also trigger inventory adjustments as necessary.

The bottom line: As in so many other aspects of life, it pays to shop around. Take the time you need to gather good information. Don't hesitate to ask lots of questions. Because so many hosting services exist, you should be able to find the right mix of features you'll need to help make your site successful, so don't be shy about demanding what you need.

Determine Your Domain Name

One of the most crucial decisions you'd make will be determining the best domain name for your site. Like your company name itself, the domain name will be the sign you hang up for the world to see, so it needs to present you as effectively as possible. However, this situation isn't as clear-cut as it seems, and it involves more than a few pitfalls.

You may wish to use the company name—no more, no less—and this is a good choice if your company's name is short, catchy, and capable of accurately reflecting your products or services. Beautiesltd.com is a prime example of this approach. So is maineholidaywreaths.com. On the other hand, long, complex, or ambiguous company names may prove counterproductive when used for a domain name. For instance, a company name such as greatamericancheddarcheesecompany.com isn't difficult to remember, but it's so long that many customers may find it annoying. A consulting firm called Braxton Braithlewaite Higginbotham Axelrod would do well to consider alternatives to this URL.

There's a convention among trendier companies to use clever, obscure, or ironic names for their sites. Peachpit.com, justducky.com, piginablanket.com, and toodleoo.com are characteristic of this sort. Clever? Of course. Effective? Well, that's hard to say. If you can't guess really what these companies have to offer, is their cleverness helpful? Maybe not. On the other hand, successful companies such as Google, Yahoo!, and Amazon. com have all thrived despite—or because of—their peculiar names.

What's the best bet? I suggest that you brainstorm the possibilities, try out an initial list on friends, acquaintances, and total strangers, narrow your options, and create a short list. Then you'll have to do a search through Network Solutions to determine if your choice conflicts with someone else's domain name. If you're home free, register the name to secure use of it. My recommendation regarding Web suffixes is that you stick with .com or .net if you're a for-profit business; use .org if you're not-for-profit. Other suffixes (.info, .tv, .cc, .biz, .bz, and so forth) may serve good purposes down the line, but the tried-and-true standbys are better if you can secure them.

Write Your Site's Web Pages

If you have good design sense and working knowledge of HTML, you can probably create a basic web site on your own. Any of the dozens of books about web site design can provide ideas and techniques to incorporate into your design. In addition, executable server scripts and applets can enhance what your site has to offer. Typical additions include:

- Keyword searches to help users find products or documents on your site
- Database access for customers looking for information
- Graphics, spreadsheet files, and calculators
- Feedback forms that allow users to send you comments or data
- Charts created by scripts and applets

On the other hand, you can arrange for someone else to perform any or all of these design services. Too expensive for a shoestring start-up? Maybe so. There's no question that Web-design services can be pricey. However, don't rule out hiring someone to tackle these specific and often highly technical tasks. As Deb Venman of Beau Ties Limited says, "We originally worked with the wife of a customer of ours who was essentially teaching herself Web design. She put up a great site for us at a truly minimal cost that worked well in the short run. Now we work with a local company that provides us with ongoing site improvements and performs the portion of the maintenance that we lack the expertise to do in-house."

One route that many small businesses take is to find fledgling computer consultants among college students, who are often savvy and imaginative in dealing with these tasks. Call your local college or technical school, check with people at the computer sciences department, and inquire about students' availability to perform these design services. The costs involved will be much lower than what you'd encounter at a corporate venue.

Allocate Duties for Running the Site

The same holds true for running your site; you can probably find someone in your area to perform maintenance duties on a routine basis. Doing so frees you to focus on running the business itself. If you prefer to maintain the site yourself, though, here are the basic roles involved:

- **Web author.** Your site isn't a static entity; it needs to change as your business grows and changes. For this reason, you need someone to upgrade the site on an ongoing basis—adding catalogue entries, graphics, information about the company, support documents, news, and so forth.
- **Web script developer.** This person is a programmer who develops customized programs that extend what your site can do. Ideally, the Web script developer either works in collaboration with the Web author or is the same person.
- **Web administrator.** This person has responsibility for operating the server software, monitoring the site's usage statistics and logs, adjusting settings, backing up the system, and handling security issues.
- **Webmaster.** Just as a postmaster interacts with the public at a post office, the webmaster is the primary interface between the public and your site. This person's main responsibilities are to answer questions about the site, respond to complaints, and help users obtain the information they need.

Publicize Your Site

Setting up a web site is ridiculously easy. Getting your site noticed, however, is the hard part. Several million web sites are in existence, and the number grows by many hundreds every day. How will customers find you?

As always, I feel that the best way to succeed in business is to create a good product or service—something that people will want, buy, and tell others about. However, there's no question that many wonderful products and services go unnoticed for lack of successful marketing and promotion. This reality holds true in the Digital Age as it did in times past. How, then, can you get noticed? Word-of-mouth is one way, and you should never underestimate its power. But you need more than that—you need successful ways to spread the word.

Get your site listed on such general-interest search engines as Yahoo.com, Altavista.com, Lycos.com, Webcrawler.com, and Google.com. By providing data about your site (which you can provide online), your site appears on these search engines' listings. (Look for a link that says, "Add a URL.")

Alternatively—or additionally—you can approach a listing service, which will register your site with dozens of search-engine sites simultaneously. You may have to pay for these service at some sites, but others are free.

Keep Your Site Current

Getting your site online is just the beginning. If you plan to offer online shopping, you'll have to keep your Web pages current on a day-to-day basis; nothing will alienate your customers faster than out-of-date product lists or inaccurate descriptions of services. Even if your site primarily provides information, you'll have to make sure there's new material at frequent intervals. Web surfers are notoriously impatient. Bore them at your own risk.

For instance, Deb Venman has her designers add content to the beautiesltd.com site frequently. David Morgan, whose davidmorgan.com site sells hats, Celtic jewelry, and other specialty items, adds content on a daily basis. J. Paul Lanza of Cottage Furniture Ltd. (seachests.com) adds content on an as-needed basis. Alan Canton at adams-blake.com says that he adds "a new page every week."

PROMOTING YOUR BUSINESS ON THE WEB

The Internet revolution has made it easier than ever for even the smallest companies to take their products and services to the farthest reaches of the world. The bad news: Your company is a needle in the haystack. So, once you have your site up and running, your business tasks have just begun.

Basically, what you have to do is make yourself known by both traditional and innovative means. The traditional means are the old standbys in the advertising world, both in print and electronic media. The innovative means are those that generally involve the Internet. The issues of promoting e-commerce are numerous and complex, but here's a quick overview of venues you should explore.

Traditional Advertising

Just because you're now running an e-business doesn't mean you won't rely on traditional forms of advertising. Your company will probably need to make use of certain kinds of standard advertising. Now that you're doing business at least partly through the Web, though, you have a new task: raising customer awareness of your site. You'll never attain brand-name recognition on the level of Amazon.com, but that doesn't mean you shouldn't help the public understand who you are and what you have to offer.

A further complication, however: Traditional forms of advertising are often staggeringly expensive for a shoestring entrepreneur. Forget about national magazines, let alone national television. Even cable TV may be prohibitive. My recommendation: Start by making yourself known through newspapers, special-interest magazines, radio, and targeted direct-mail campaigns. Select your venues carefully. Craft your message thoughtfully. If you emphasize the advantages of e-commerce—and, ideally, your own product's special features—this kind of targeted advertising will boost your site's name recognition.

Online Advertising

The more innovative, electronic equivalent: banner ads. These are a mixed blessing. On the one hand, they are a relatively cheap way of getting your message out there. An added advantage is that, in general, you don't pay for banner ads up front; rather, you pay an agreed-upon fee according to the number of visitors that click on the banner. On the downside, it's easy to misjudge where your ads should appear, and lots of Web users regard banners as a nuisance worth avoiding. One option: Try banners on an experimental basis and size up where the payoff occurs, and to what degree. Another possibility is to pursue banner-swapping arrangements: In exchange for putting other companies' banners on your site, they'll put your banner on theirs.

Search Engines

A more productive idea is heavily listing your site on search engines. This method probably achieves the most bang per buck. Web users rely on search engines more than any other method for zeroing in on sites that interest them, and getting listed has a high cost-to-benefit ratio.

To get noticed, however, you have to register your site. You can accomplish this task manually: Go to a particular search engine site, such as Yahoo.com, Google.com, and so on; click on the "Add a URL" or "Register a URL" icon; and proceed from there. This process is free. However, keep in mind that since there are hundreds of search engines, registering manually may not be practical or effective. The answer to this dilemma: registration services. These are web sites that register your site for a fee using automated means. It's worth the cost, though, for registration services can list your site on literally hundreds of search engines simultaneously. To see what's involved at the most frequently used registration service, see www.submitit.com.

As for the major search engine sites, here's a short list:

- Altavista.com
- Dogpile.com
- Excite.com
- Google.com

- HotBot.com
- InfoSeek.com
- Lycos.com
- WebCrawler.com
- Yahoo.com

Ed Myers, the author mentioned earlier, had his two sites—edwardmyers.com and montemayorpress.com—listed on hundreds of search engines through a listing service. "The cost was minimal," Ed says, "and the Web design service did all the work for me."

E-mail Promotions

As you spread the word about your web site, a definite good news/bad news joke takes shape regarding e-mail promotion. The good news? It's cheap, and it's especially cheap as you attain an economy of scale. The bad news? It puts you in the realm of spam, and lots of people are going to hate you for cluttering their mailboxes. Yes, you can barrage the world with lots of messages. Yes, you'll get a few folks interested in doing business with you. My advice is to skip it. Many ISPs will filter out your messages along with all the other junk mail flying through the ether, and most people will delete your mail unread. There are better ways to spend your time and money.

Online Newsletters

A better idea: your own online newsletter. Mind you, this isn't an advertisement as such. Rather, it's a useful, informative e-publication on a topic you understand. You distribute it electronically to past, present, and prospective customers and, avoiding hard-sell techniques, you simply let them decide whether they wish to do business with you. The goal is to share some sort of data or recommendations that people may find worth reading; doing so establishes trust and promotes your authority. Doing so assumes that you won't toot your horn too loudly. Instead, you'll simply let your expertise speak for itself. The downside: Publishing a good, substantive online newsletter can be time-consuming if you tackle the whole task yourself, and it's expensive if you hire a professional writer.

RISKS

As the old saying goes, there's no free lunch—and sometimes even a lunch you pay for has hidden costs. This certainly holds true for the Web. E-commerce may seem easy, efficient, and cost-effective, but it's not without some expenses you have to consider in advance and factor into your start-up plans. Some of these expenses are monetary; others have more to do with risks and hassles that can take up your precious time and energy. The following are the main issues you have to think about.

Taxes

Sorry, but doing business over the Web won't simplify your life as you deal with the various taxing authorities. On the other hand, you'll face most of the same issues whether you're doing e-business or business by conventional means. The only sensible course of action is to get your house in order from the start, then keep it that way. This chapter can no do more than suggest the basics; I urge you to find a good accountant, then follow his or her recommendations carefully.

Fraud

The Web has been a boon to scam artists. Credit card fraud, especially, is easy to perpetrate and hard to catch. Common frauds include payment with invalid cards, payment with stolen cards, payment with stolen data (e.g., name, card number, pin number, etc.), and identity theft, in which the perpetrator has acquired credit cards using someone else's identity.

How do you protect yourself from these risks? Here are a few ways that help you identify potentially fraudulent transactions from legitimate ones.

- **Leave-at-door instructions.** Although some customers may instruct you to have packages delivered without notifying the occupant of the residence, some scam artists use this ploy to avoid giving their own address.
- **Fake billing/delivery addresses.** Since someone who steals a credit card may not know where the owner lives, he may order products for delivery at a fake address. Merchant banks' address verification services (AVS) can help screen out fraud of this sort. AVS isn't foolproof, but it's helpful. Note, however, that AVS is an optional, fee-based service, and that it works only for domestic addresses.
- **Ship-to addresses in certain countries.** Fraud is common for online orders send to Belarus, Colombia, Egypt, Indonesia, Lithuania, Macedonia, Malasia, Nigeria, Pakistan, Romania, and Russia.
- **Discrepancies between shipping and billing addresses.** Again, many legitimate customers may bill their purchases to one address and request delivery at another. Be on guard, though, and zero in on such customers for further verification.

How can you respond if you're suspicious about an order? Press for further verification. Call the customer; ask for further information. Legitimate customers will appreciate your caution; perpetrators of fraud will be evasive or uncooperative. If you have lingering doubt, ask for payment in advance or cancel the order.

Delivery Problems

If your company is already involved in shipping merchandise, you have some prior experience with the ups and downs of filling orders. E-business simplifies some aspects of this situation, but complicates others. Among other things, you'll have to comply with Federal Trade Commission (FTC) rules on orders placed by telephone, fax, or the Web. Here are the main implications:

- If you claim that a product can be shipped within the time you state, you must have a reasonable basis for believing that you can meet that deadline.
- If you don't state the shipping period, the default time is thirty days, and you must have a reasonable basis for believing that you can comply with that deadline.
- If you can't ship within the stated delivery time, or within thirty days, you have to alert your customer to the delay, provide a new ship-by date, and alert the customer to his or her rights to cancel the order and obtain a prompt, full refund.
- If your alert your customer of a delay of greater than thirty days, you must obtain the customer's explicit consent.
- If you alert your customer of a delay of up to thirty days, and the customer doesn't respond, you can regard that silence as a consent to the delay.
- If your customer doesn't consent to these arrangements, you must refund his or her payment, whether with or without a request for this refund.

Is this unreasonably complicated? Maybe so. However, don't push your luck. If you attempt to simplify the situation and make claims you can't meet, you run the risk of false advertising.

Advertising Problems

Perhaps you faced the boons and banes of advertising even before you took your business online. In some ways, advertising on the Web presents similar pitfalls to more traditional forms of advertising. There are risks of spending more on ads than their payoff justifies. There are risks of believing that ads will solve problems you've created by other means. There are risks, too, of making claims that exceed what your business can fulfill.

I find this last issue especially worrisome for shoestring start-ups. Web technology makes it easy and tempting to overstate what your business has to offer. Put up a glitzy web site, promise your customers the moon, sun, and stars, and pretty soon you'll believe that's what you're selling. My advice: watch your step. Don't let the smoke-and-mirrors aspects of the Web deceive you. Make sure that what you're claiming is really what you can deliver to your customers. Otherwise, you'll find the FTC knocking at your door.

Here are the main legal/ethical issues you have to keep monitoring:

- All disclaimers and disclosures have to be clear and conspicuous.
- Disclaimers and disclosures won't relieve you of the responsibility for truthfulness in advertising.
- Your advertising has to be truthful. What you say can't be deceptive either by commission or omission, and you must be able to substantiate any claims you make.
- If you offer refunds to customers, you must follow through to dissatisfied customers.
- Any demonstrations you make or refer to must involve products that are performing under normal conditions.

What happens if you violate the FTC regulations on advertising? You don't want to know. A hint: up to $11,000 in fines per violation, plus injunctions and court orders to boot. You'd also risk civil law suits.

Issues Regarding Children

If you think the Federal Trade Commission is picky about advertising, wait until you try selling products to children. The FTC maintains a set of regulations—the CARU rules—designed to protect children from exploitation. Some of these rules are fairly general; others are incredibly specific about what you can and can't do. Here's a partial overview of the *general* rules:

- You must use only factual, age-appropriate language when advertising to children.
- You can't use advertising to mislead kids about your products' features, benefits, or performance.
- You must be capable of substantiating any product claims.
- When advertising food, you must show people eating only in a healthy manner.
- You must offer only demonstrations that are realistic and safe, showing age-appropriate protective equipment and adult supervision.
- You must target kids only in an age-appropriate manner.
- You can't use frightening material.
- You can't use peer pressure—including promises of social success or threats of social rejection—to entice kids into purchasing your products.
- You can't use the words *only* or *just* in conjunction with prices.
- You must use only endorsements that represent the endorser's actual experiences.
- You must present clear, age-appropriate disclosures about required notices, the need for assembly, batteries, or auxiliary materials that require separate purchase.
- You must clearly distinguish premiums from products.
- You must distinguish club memberships from purchases.
- You must clarify (in age-appropriate language) the odds involved in any contests.
- You can't have cartoon characters pitching products adjacent to entertainment involving those characters.
- You can't urge kids to ask an adult to buy a product.
- You can't advertise medications, drugs, or supplemental vitamins to children.

Think that following these rules will get you out of the woods? Sorry—you're not there yet. In addition to these general rules, there are more specific rules governing online business with kids, too. Here's a quick overview:

- You must clearly and prominently state in any on-screen ordering instructions that kids must have a parent's permission to order.
- You must always tell children when you're targeting them for a sale.
- You must label any web sites sponsored by advertisers.
- You must label any ad pitches as advertising that use cartoon characters as part of the pitch.
- You must provide a clear means for children or parents to cancel any on-screen order.
- You must also follow complex guidelines (mandated by the U.S. Children's Online Privacy Protection Act) that regulate how you're allowed to collect and use personal information from children younger than age thirteen. Among other things, these regulations govern:
  - Data disclosure to parents on demand
  - Parental notification
  - Exceptions to the parental-consent rules
  - On-site disclosure notices
  - Situations that require new consent
  - Parents' right to revoke consent and delete data

THE GOOD NEWS

After hearing all these caveats, you may be eager to call it a day and fold your digital tent. Don't go rushing off. Despite all the hassles and regulations I've described, putting up and maintaining a web site offers more benefits than liabilities. The good news far outweighs the bad. The Web makes it possible for even the smallest businesses to have a shot at national—even international—sales. Maybe the Web won't level the whole playing field. Maybe the Web won't let you play David to the Goliaths in your industry, but having a good web site can allow you the possibility of success in a niche and maybe, just maybe, a shot at wider business success. The World Wide Web truly offers revolutionary advantages for shoestring start-ups.

More to the point, there's really no alternative. The question isn't whether to have a site, but rather *what kind of site* and *for what purpose.* These are complex questions that you should think through as carefully as possible. If you're imaginative and energetic, though, you can make the Web into an affordable, flexible way of taking a start-up business far beyond what entrepreneurs would have thought possible in the past.

SMALL-BUSINESS OWNERS' TIPS

Here are some small-business owners' suggestions on web site issues:

- "A well-run web site can reach a worldwide audience twenty-four hours a day, seven days a week, providing a form of contact and sales for great numbers of people during hours when small businesses can't justify manning telephones or staffing storefronts."

  —Deb Venman, beautiesltd.com

- "People who put up a poor site or do not maintain it well would do better not to have a site."

  —David Morgan, davidmorgan.com

- "People who know nothing about designing or maintaining a web site should hire a pro to do it. It's just that simple."

  —Alan Canton, adams-blake.com

- "The biggest pitfall is probably the bottomless-pit aspects of web site design and maintenance, to say nothing of Web page optimization and pay-for-placement options to enhance search engine positioning and directory results."

  —Deb Venman, beautiesltd.com

- "Design the site to meet the customer's needs, maintain it fully at all times, and back it up with complete honesty and integrity."

    —David Morgan, davidmorgan.com

- "Get competent professional help in designing and maintaining your site."

    —J. Paul Lanza, seachests.com and toy-chests.com

- "It is not enough to build a web site; unless you're willing to invest some dollars to maintain and promote it, it may not be a cost-effective means of attracting customers."

    —Deb Venman, beautiesltd.com

- "Too many people design their site and put all sorts of flashing, dancing graphics on it because they think it looks cool. They pop on huge graphics that take forever for the site to load. Then they wonder why no one stays on the site long enough to buy anything."

    —Alan Canton, adams-blake.com

- "Don't assume that having a glitzy web site will make up for a poor product or lapses in your business judgment. The Web certainly has some goods worth buying, but it's also the greatest source of hucksterism since P. T. Barnum."

    —Ed Myers, edwardmyers.com and montemayorpress.com

KEY POINTS TO REMEMBER

1. What you first imagine for your business site may not be what the Web really has to offer you. Be flexible—and imaginative.
2. Clarify and set your goals for Web use as early as possible in the process.
3. Unless you have a lot of time and digital know-how, find a good contractor to set up the web site for you.

4. Don't assume that "if you build it, they will come." Millions of web sites exist out in cyberspace, so you'll have to work hard to distinguish yours from all the rest.
5. Keep your site current. Hell hath no fury like a bored Web surfer.
6. Watch your digital p's and q's. Pay close attention to the tax and FTC regulations that govern e-commerce.
7. Don't expect miracles. At the same time, be ready for unexpected payoffs and breakthroughs.
8. The Web offers lots of sizzle, but don't neglect to sell your customers a first-rate steak.

15

A BLUEPRINT
FOR BUYING A BUSINESS

Name your business. Whether it's an accounting service or a zipper factory, you have the inevitable decision to make. You can start from scratch as you may be planning—or take a short cut and buy an existing business. And many bootstrap entrepreneurs are discovering the fastest, easiest path to becoming their own boss is through acquisition instead of the tortured route of building from the ground up.

Flirting with the idea of a buyout isn't switching gears or chilling your creative spirits. You have one objective—to get into your own business with as little cash as possible. Buying a business can be a strategic alternative to starting, and as Barry Levine, an acquisition consultant, counsels: "Buying may be even wiser than creating when you consider the dozens of businesses available in every field begging for a fast takeover. It's indeed a bootstrap entrepreneur's playground."

BUY OR CREATE?

The debate continues. Which is better—to buy or create a business? There's no one right answer as the decision rests on the facts of a given situation. I have started nine businesses and purchased ten. I now know that I should have bought some of the former and started some of the latter.

However, you should expect an acquisition to offer these advantages:

1. *Less Risk:* This may be the most important reason why so many people prefer to buy. The established business has a track record. You know its sales and profits and you can reasonably predict what the business will do for you. A start-up is guesswork at best, and you never know how it will perform until after it's in operation. The statistics prove the point. Businesses in operation for five years fail at the rate of 20 percent within the following five years, while new companies face an 80 percent failure rate.

   Many entrepreneurs take a split approach, buying their first venture and expanding through start-ups. With an established business behind them they have the base to support a start-up gamble. And as so many report, it's safer to learn the ropes with a going concern that can absorb managerial error. Consider the possibilities.

2. *Faster Cash:* The going concern has its sales base and cash flow working for you from the first day. Even if the business is operating at a loss, you do have a sales threshold to build from. In contrast, the start-up may have sizable losses until sales do reach the break-even point. This can be a key consideration in many lines of businesses with a predictably slow sales curve. As you've seen in Chapter 3, the most common start-up error is inability to gauge the losses until profitable sales can be reached, with the resultant inability to fund the losses. "Everyone's an optimist," says Ray Johnson, who in 1981 opened his Strathmore Press, a small printing plant serving the large printing plants for short-run subcontract work. "We needed $20,000 a month to break even and thought we'd hit it within two months. We were wrong. Nine months later we folded with our best month at $8000." Ray adds this pointer, "Don't start unless you can realistically assess how long it will take to reach profitability and can keep the business afloat until you do. If you're shaky on

the projections you're smarter to buy a business and pay the premium for the privilege of solid sales."

3. *Easier Entry:* It takes a very special breed of entrepreneur to put together a start-up venture. Whipping together a physical plant, employees, suppliers, and customers may look easy, but many entrepreneurs go through several false starts before realizing their best approach is to take over a going concern. "You have to understand your creative level," recounts Bob Kuzara, who started several firms. "While some people enjoy the challenge of piecing together an enterprise, many others consider it too burdensome an obstacle, and will only venture into business if they're handed the keys."

    In a very real sense, the decision to buy or create is not based on the numbers but on the personality of the individual. For every entrepreneur who enjoys the innovation, planning, and maneuvering to put together a business, there are three others who lack the self-confidence and momentum. Perhaps only one person in ten is equally comfortable with either approach.

4. *Lower Cost:* You may be able to buy an existing business for even less than it would cost to duplicate the tangible assets under a start-up. One reason so many people avoid considering an acquisition is that they erroneously believe buying is more expensive. In many cases it's true, as sellers of a profitable company will want a premium for goodwill. But there are the exceptions, particularly with the troubled firm with turnaround potential that can oftentimes be picked up for a fraction of the value of the tangible assets. One of my best buys was a large discount store with a $150,000 inventory and $30,000 worth of fixtures picked up for the bargain price of $120,000. It would have cost me substantially more to buy these assets on the open market. You can save money with the *right* acquisition.

5. *Better Financing:* You can win better financing with an existing business. Banks and other lenders have more confidence lending to the established business and you

have many more sources of "built-in" financing available with an acquisition. I consider financing one of the most favorable advantages of buying, and later in this chapter you'll see how and why you can bootstrap yourself into an existing business with little or no cash of your own.

When should you discard the idea of buying a business in favor of starting from scratch? When you have a very unique or different business format in mind and can't find a matching business for sale. Traditional businesses are always a candidate for a takeover, and even if you plan operational changes, it usually doesn't take much to alter the format of the business to match what you want the business to be. And the advantages that came with buying can still make it your best move.

Years ago I faced the "buy or create" dilemma for my first pharmacy. If I had wanted a traditional drugstore I probably would have preferred to buy, but what I had in mind was anything but traditional. My plan was to set up a prescription shop without the typical front store merchandise and sell prescriptions at wholesale cost plus a $1.00 dispensing fee. I had the plan down to a science and even had the name "Cost-Plus Pharmacies" trademarked. Buying an existing pharmacy and converting it to what I wanted would have been a waste of money since we'd have to tear out fixtures, discard most of the inventory, and renovate to our own specifications. Obviously, it made more sense to start with a clean slate.

Essentially the buy or create decision is a competitive process as you weigh the benefits of each against the realities of what the marketplace has to offer. It's not unusual to find entrepreneurs intending to create only to come across an attractive acquisition, just as it's not unusual to find a corresponding number who consider themselves buyers until they see the price tags sellers place on their business.

I will, however, offer this advice. Don't make the decision to start from scratch until you have thoroughly checked out available businesses. It's the only way you can compare the tradeoffs and decide your right path.

PROFITABLE BUSINESS FOR SALE: NO CASH DOWN

Ask 100 shoestring entrepreneurs why they decided to create rather than buy a business and 95 will tell you, "I couldn't afford the down payment to buy. The only way I could get into business was to set up shop from scratch." Would you give the same answer? If so, this may be your most important chapter because the buy or create decision can only be intelligently made when you have all the facts. And the facts are:

1. You *can* buy any size or type of business with absolutely no cash of your own.
2. You *will* find it considerably easier to buy without cash than to *start* without cash.

Admittedly it's difficult to sell that message to people who have been conditioned to think it takes more money to buy than to create from scratch. And why shouldn't people be conditioned to think that way? Have you ever seen a business advertised for sale on no cash down terms? Ever hear of such a deal from a business broker? Of course not. But ask yourself one more question. How many business acquisitions are you familiar with?

I can tell you from firsthand experience of at least 240 no cash down transactions and thousands more where very little money exchanged hands. I've acquired ten of my own businesses, and my largest personal investment was $1000. And several of my acquisitions had price tags in excess of $100,000. How many others share my experience? I estimate that 50 percent of all small businesses could be rapidly sold with absolutely no cash investment from the buyer and still satisfy all the seller's objectives.

It's too common a story. A seller will put his business on the market for $50,000 and ask for a $25,000 down payment. He doesn't ask the important question: "Will buyers with $25,000 be interested in my business? Can a qualified buyer with little or no cash satisfy my objectives and help me sell quicker?"

For their part, buyers who listen to such demands reason that they can't qualify for the business with only $5000 in available cash and never ask: "Could I both satisfy the seller and buy the business with only $5000? Do I really need $25,000?"

And so it goes, sellers want to sell and buyers want to buy but few know how to swing the no cash down deal.

YOU CAN BUY ON 100 PERCENT TERMS

How many ways are there to achieve 100 percent leverage in a business acquisition? I can tell you at least 200 proven techniques you can use to close the gap between price and your meager bank account. Used in combination, the possibilities of a cashless takeover are endless. In my own book, *How to Buy a Great Business for No Cash Down* (John Wiley & Sons, 1991), I uncover the strategies in detail and show how others bought their profitable business with little or no cash down. I'll highlight a few of the more common methods in this chapter to give you the broad picture, but if you do have a strong interest in buying a business as an alternative to starting one, then *How to Buy* should be on your reading list.

I advise readers that it is far easier to buy on short cash than create a new business. I offer two reasons: (1) The existing business typically provides its own built-in financing for 70 percent to 100 percent of the purchase price; (2) You have many more sources and alternatives than you do with a new venture when you do have to scout the few final dollars to complete the financing package.

Jim Corcoran can show you the anatomy of a cashless takeover. Jim is one entrepreneur who didn't back away when he came across a Steak and Ale restaurant selling for $100,000 in Frisco's Bay Area. The seller refused to assist in financing, leaving Jim with a $100,000 problem considering he had no cash of his own to invest. Rolling up his sleeves, Jim designed his own 100 percent financing plan.

"The large dollars come easiest," says Jim, who quickly found a bank sufficiently impressed with the history of the business to lend $60,000 payable over five years. That chipped the balance down to $40,000.

The next strategy was for Jim to inquire about existing liabilities owed by the business. The seller acknowledged that the business owed $20,000 to creditors, which the seller would be obligated to pay at the time of closing. Jim had a better idea. Jim would assume the liabilities and deduct it from the purchase price. Why shouldn't the seller agree? It was only money he'd otherwise have to part with when the business was sold. Now Jim only needed $20,000 to close.

The last dollars to put together a deal are always the hardest, but Jim gradually whittled away at the elusive $20,000 to close the gap. The business broker, due to a $10,000 commission on the deal, helped by lending $5000 from his commission to save the sale.

Knocking on the doors of several suppliers found some additional money. A meat supplier selling over $100,000 a year to the business considered a $5000 cash loan a good investment to maintain goodwill, followed by another $5000 loan from the cigarette vending machine firm anxious to maintain its machines at the profitable location. Now Jim had $95,000 in financing locked up and needed only $5000 to close. The solution was found in some used kitchen equipment that would be Jim's when he purchased the business. With a few phone calls Jim found a buyer to take out the excess equipment at the time of sale in return for $5000. The final scorecard:

$ 60,000	bank financing
20,000	assumed liabilities
5,000	broker loan
10,000	supplier loans
5,000	sale of excess assets
$100,000	

The results?

The seller enjoyed the same net cash he would have received had Jim walked in with $100,000 of his own money.

The broker salvaged his commission.

The creditors don't care who pays them.

The supplier loans guaranteed the suppliers strong profits for many years to come.

These strategies do work, and many of my own leveraged acquisitions come together in much the same way. The important points to review are:

1. Buying a business on no cash down terms does not necessarily mean that the seller ends up with no cash at the closing. As you can see from this case, the seller cashed out with all his money and with seller financing the process of achieving 100 percent leverage can be even easier.
2. With an acquisition you can readily find 60 to 80 percent of the purchase price with a bank, SBA, or seller financing. The focus is always on the remaining 20 to 40 percent—that portion of the acquisition price typically represented by the down payment.
3. There are countless ways to find and use sources of capital other than your own to achieve 100 percent financing.

FINDING THE LARGEST DOLLARS

Your first objective is to cement 60 to 70 percent of the financing with the large dollars that can be routinely financed with bank and/or seller financing.

Earlier in this book, we discussed bank financing in terms of funding a shoestring start-up, and I pointed out that although bank financing is always a possibility with a start-up, it's seldom a priority source because both collateral and a track record are missing.

An existing business will catch a banker's eye and it's particularly so with a business with collateral to offer. A survey of 100 recent acquisitions in our area shows that bank financing represented on average 58 percent of the purchase price, and in several transactions the banks financed over 80 percent for buyers with apparently few assets of their own to pledge as collateral.

Your one best source of financing on an acquisition is the seller himself. In the vast majority of the leveraged takeovers I've been involved in, the seller agrees to finance anywhere from 30 to 80 percent of the purchase price, and I've had several deals where we convinced a seller to go the whole route and provide 100 percent financing. Sellers, of course, usually resist self-financing, preferring to cash out, leaving you to scurry to outside sources for financing. It's always a pipe dream for a seller anxious to unload a business pitted against a buyer wise enough to call his bluff.

Why do you want to negotiate for seller financing?

1. Sellers will finance more of the purchase price. While a bank may stop at 60 percent, you may be able to push a seller for 70 to 80 percent financing.
2. You'll win better terms from a seller. For a small business loan, banks may charge four to six percentage points over the current prime rate, but many sellers will agree to a lower interest rate. Don't forget the seller's motive in financing is to help sell the business and not make money on the interest. The length of the note is another factor. Banks seldom finance for longer than five years, while sellers may agree to seven- to ten-year terms. I know of several cases where a seller accepted a 20-year payout, considering it a form of annuity.
3. You'll need less collateral to back up the loan. Banks typically try to obtain personal collateral to add to the collateral the business can offer. However, sellers are content to accept the business assets as security.

A smart strategy is to pyramid seller financing on top of bank financing. A seller, for example, may say, "I'll sell the business for $100,000 and finance $50,000 of the price." Once the seller holds a first mortgage on the business, you can no longer go to a bank expecting the same security. The tactic then is to counteroffer that you'll obtain $50,000 in bank financing if the seller will instead accept a second mortgage on the business for $20,000 to $30,000. While the seller will be in a slightly weaker position coming behind the bank in terms of security, the seller may be sold on the advantage of financing less in return for more upfront cash for himself. But you can see the benefit for yourself in terms of having 70 to 80 percent of the financing through the combination of both bank and seller financing. And when you do have 80 percent of the money can the other 20 percent be far behind?

LOOK FOR THE LIABILITIES

The one valuable financing block that both sellers and buyers overlook is the debts of the business. In most cases, a seller will quote a required down payment sufficient to pay down existing liabilities, and in many cases the lion's share of the down payment is earmarked for creditors. Oftentimes you can substantially slash a down payment by assuming the liabilities and turning the money owed to creditors into a source of built-in financing. It's a very common and workable technique. Several of my own deals have been substantially self-financed by taking over the seller's liabilities.

The near-bankrupt business offers its own interesting possibilities. In your travels, you'll come across businesses that owe so much money that you can walk in without investing a dime. In fact, companies in trouble can present fabulous opportunities for no cash takeovers. Some of the very best deals involve companies just one short step from the auctioneer's hammer. Sellers are usually willing to let you take over the business just to rid themselves of what they see as a problem business or perhaps in exchange for a token payment or even a job.

I'm always on the lookout for troubled companies with turnaround potential and quickly channel them to shoestring entrepreneurs with the skills to straighten them out. And the right owner in the right business can do wonders. One recent example was a client who picked up a grocery superette grossing $400,000 a year, floundering under $120,000 in trade debt. So without a dime to his name, he acquired the shares of stock in the near-defunct corporation and threw the business into a Chapter 11 Bankruptcy reorganization, settling the debts for $40,000 paid over three years. He now tells me he can sell the same business for over $100,000 and pocket $60,000 in equity. That's not bad when you consider he walked into the deal with neither cash nor personal risk. And it's done every day.

Shoestring entrepreneurs are natural candidates for the troubled business because the management skills needed to handle the insolvent firm are very much the same as those needed to walk the financial tightrope of a shoestring start-up. Ken Barron, who has leveraged his way into both start-ups and acquisitions, reasons, "If you're the type who can start from zero and accumulate $100,000 in assets and $100,000 in liabilities to build a business and make it work, then you're the same type to inherit the same shaky business from someone who can't make it work."

Ken's not the only one who knows how to turn a seller's nightmare into a personal fortune. Lurking in every area and line of business are other shrewd entrepreneurs waiting to grab the floundering business they can mold into a money-making machine with no personal investment. It may also be your smart alternative to a shoestring start-up.

A creative buyer and willing seller can always manipulate debt levels to cover a buyer's cash short position. In one of our recent cases, a business was selling for $90,000. The seller agreed to finance $60,000 and allow the buyer to assume $15,000 in existing liabilities owed to trade suppliers. However, the seller insisted on $15,000 in "walk-away" cash, which was $15,000 more than the buyer had. The solution? The seller agreed to increase the debts by an additional $15,000, taking the money out of the business instead of paying creditors, while the creditors became the unwitting financiers for the cashless buyer.

The technique of using existing liabilities must be looked at from the perspective of the buyer, the seller, and the creditors. The buyer's objective is to use liabilities in place of his own cash. The buyer's corresponding concern is how much short-term debt can the business safely handle?

The seller is primarily concerned with protection from creditor recourse, should the liabilities remain unpaid. The creditors for their part must be willing to both allow the buyer to assume the debts and provide the time for the paydown of anything beyond normal trade debt levels.

While the respective interests can usually be protected by legal agreements and indemnifications, it's the buyer who must take the initiative and ask, "Why not allow the existing business debts to take the place of my own money?"

SQUEEZE CASH FROM CASH FLOW

There are hundreds of ways to squeeze the cash flow of an existing business to take the place of a clown payment.

You've seen how increasing liabilities can free up cash for a seller. You can accomplish the same objective by reducing inventories. For example, a business may be selling for $100,000 based on an inventory of $60,000. If the inventory at the time of sale is only $50,000, the price is reduced to $90,000. But couldn't the $10,000 reduction be deducted from the down payment portion of the price? Of course. The strategy then is to negotiate your deal so that the seller intentionally liquidates part of the inventory in advance of the sale using the generated cash to replace all or part of your down payment.

Another example. Accounts receivable may be included as part of the price. Whenever I come across a deal involving receivables, I negotiate for the seller to retain the receivables and deduct its value from the down payment of its reduced price.

Cash flow can help you in other ways. I can tell you about a buyer who could only raise $260,000 toward a $300,000 price on a supermarket. The buyer candidly told the seller he was short $40,000 and offered to issue four $10,000 post-dated checks, dated one week apart. Until the checks cleared, the seller could hold the closing documents in escrow. It was no magic trick to cover the checks from a business grossing $60,000 a week. Many sellers will allow you to tap cash flow *after* you take over the business to squeeze the last few dollars needed to push the sale through.

One advantage of the going business is that it can be shaped in so many ways to create cash for a seller without the need for buyers digging into their own pockets.

To show you just how these techniques can come together to satisfy both a seller and buyer, I have only to tell you about one of my best acquisitions—a large cosmetic shop in the western suburbs of Connecticut. The seller was asking $120,000 for the business, free of liabilities and with $60,000 down. In addition, the seller guaranteed an inventory at closing of $80,000. With conventional haggling, we negotiated the price down to $110,000 and then began to negotiate the deal that would provide 100 percent financing. Here's how we put our financing blocks together.

1. The seller originally agreed to finance $60,000 for three years at 15 percent interest. It was a start, although we managed to negotiate the term to five years at 12 percent.
2. The business had $15,000 in liabilities and the seller agreed to our assuming the debt; however, we asked him to increase it to $25,000 and take out $10,000 from the business that would otherwise go to maintain liabilities at their current level. With his consent we now had $85,000 in financing.
3. We didn't need a $80,000 inventory to profitably operate the business. We estimated the inventory to be overstated by $20,000, so we bargained for the seller to reduce inventory by the $20,000 and cut the price—and our down payment—by the same amount. So now we had $85,000 toward a reduced price of $90,000.
4. The final $5000 was the easiest part. As part of the deal we would be acquiring the prepaid utility deposits and insurance premiums, which amounted to $7000. Since the business had established credit with the electric and telephone companies, they agreed to return the $5200 in deposits which we turned over to the seller to complete the $90,000 financing.

There was a postscript to the story. Included in the sale was a $20,000 Buick sedan. At the closing the seller asked if he could buy the car from the business, which we happily agreed to. We actually walked out of the closing with not only a business grossing $420,000 a year—without spending a dime of our own—but pocketed $20,000 in cash besides.

It may all appear a bit too breezy and pie-in-the-sky for you, but believe me, deals such as this do exist, and smart buyers know the right buttons to press to shape a business into a no cash down situation.

HIDDEN ASSETS MEAN HIDDEN MONEY

We've only scratched the surface. One of the best ways to find your down payment is to uncover hidden assets within the business that can be turned into instant cash.

It's a four-step strategy:

1. Locate any business asset you can sell, borrow against, exploit, or turn into instant cash.
2. Arrange the sale, lease, or money raising transaction in *advance* of the sale, but make it conditional upon the sale.
3. Coordinate the transaction to closing the sale so you can use the money to fund your acquisition.
4. Make certain it's an asset you will have the legal right to sell, rather than assets mortgaged under the financing plan.

Now with the basic strategy behind us, let's see what assets are the best money-raising candidates. Here's a checklist to consider:

1. Excess equipment.
2. Customer lists.
3. Patent rights.
4. Trademarks or copyrights.
5. Excess motor vehicles.
6. Cash surrender business life insurance.
7. Pension funds.
8. Sublet or concessional space.
9. Advertising space.
10. Credits due from suppliers.

In *How to Buy a Great Business for No Cash Down,* I listed these top ten cash generating assets; several months after the book was published, I received a letter from a chap in Illinois who told me he successfully used his own list of 93 potential assets to cannibalize for a down payment. In his letter, he tells how he once managed to take over a tire and muffler shop for absolutely no cash of his own by preselling 20,000 discarded used tires cluttering the rear yard. The seller wanted $50,000 for the business and to the seller the tires were an eyesore and a liability. Not to this buyer. He heard that electric power plants use rubber as fuel and negotiated the sale of the tires at $1 apiece to come up with the $10,000 down payment. "It was remarkably easy," says this imaginative entrepreneur. "I obtained the contract to sell the tires to become effective upon the closing. In turn I assigned the $10,000 receivable to a bank who loaned me the $10,000. A week after I acquired the business, the electric company picked up the tires and paid the bank, while I had my business and an empty rear lot to begin collecting more tires and a down payment on maybe another business."

The stories continue:

A buyer of a tile manufacturing plant prearranged the licensing of its secret process to a Mexican manufacturer for $25,000.

A buyer for a car dealership arranged to lease billboard space on top of its building bordering a high-traffic highway for a $12,000 advance rental.

A buyer for a plastic extrusion plant had a clever accountant who negotiated the purchase of the seller's ownership interest by borrowing against the employees' pension plan funds.

Bill Finneran, a creative buyer with several no cash down acquisitions to his credit, approaches a target business with this philosophy, "I look for assets that can quickly produce cash. And once you start looking, you'd be surprised at what can be sold, rented, licensed, or borrowed against. When you have it down to a science, you can usually free up more than a down payment." Finneran is quick to add, "One of these days you'll even find me taking the penny out of the fuse box."

Study your target business before you buy. What assets can you turn into cash to make that sale happen?

YOUR TWO BEST MONEY SOURCES

In most cases you can find ways to uncover your down payment from sources within the business. Occasionally you need a helping hand from external sources and your two best bets are:

1. Business Brokers.
2. Existing Suppliers.

Never overlook the importance of a broker as a source of cash. Seventy percent of all businesses are sold through a broker, so there's an excellent chance a broker will be involved in your deal. Now here's another interesting statistic to consider. The average conventionally financed small business acquisition requires only a 20 percent down payment. Conversely, the typical brokers fee is 10 percent of the sales price. This translates into the inescapable fact that 50 percent of your down payment is earmarked to pay the brokers fee.

The obvious but cash-saving point I'm leading to is that a commission deferred is a down payment saved. The strategy is to convince the broker to loan you a portion of his commission for the privilege of saving the sale and his total commission.

For example, on a $100,000 deal, the broker stands to earn a $10,000 commission. While brokers earn their living from commissions and not lending money, any broker will tell you the two inevitably must co-exist. So you ask the broker to loan you perhaps $5000 from the commission, secured by the business, and payable over one or two years with reasonable interest.

Will the broker go for it? Absolutely. There are only two exceptions to the rule. Several of the large firms won't lend or compromise on commissions as a matter of policy and precedent. These same firms also lose plenty of sales. However, all brokers will resist if they believe you're bluffing and can raise money from other sources. And that's when they should refuse. Your job is to convince the broker. The only way you can buy the business is with his help. When they think their commission is at risk, they seldom refuse.

Suppliers are your second best source. Suppliers are discussed elsewhere in this book as the primary source of credit for a start-up; however, few people think of suppliers as a source of cash for a down payment. I never did see a difference between asking a supplier for $10,000 in credit to merchandise a new business as opposed to $10,000 in cash to buy a business. Money is money, and in either case the selling point is the value of your future business to the supplier.

Earlier in this chapter you read about Jim Corcoran, who is now comfortably established in his Frisco restaurant partially financed by a $5000 loan from his meat supplier. Why wouldn't it make sense for the supplier to lend a paltry $5000 for an account that would create $100,000 a year in sales?

Supplier loans would happen quite often if more buyers simply asked. Suppliers seldom turn down a reasonable request. Don't call it charity. An advance loan is only another form of credit.

One leading hardware wholesale firm president says, "A new customer is not shy in asking for $10,000 to $15,000 in credit *after* they buy the business, but few will ask for the few dollars *before* to make the takeover possible. Many buyers bypassed opportunities because they don't think of their suppliers in terms of writing out a check. Not long ago a young couple asked us for a $10,000 loan to help with a $30,000 down payment for a health and beauty aid store. We were already selling the business over $200,000 a year and a turndown would only mean a lost account. So we'd be foolish to say 'no.' We charged high interest on the loan, but more importantly, we saved a $200,000 a year profit generator for our own business."

Buying power is borrowing power and it underscores all negotiations with suppliers. Existing suppliers will lend for fear of losing an account. Prospective suppliers will lend to *win* an account. Both are prime candidates.

Confine your search to the major suppliers. You don't have enough to offer small secondary suppliers. Project the sales of your business and tie the loan into a commitment to buy in the future. A two- to four-year payback on a cash advance loan is reasonable, and so is 10 percent interest plus a personal guarantee and/or a business mortgage to secure the loan.

Taverns, restaurants, and other businesses with concessioned jukeboxes, cigarettes, and other vending machines are always prime candidates for loans from the vending machine companies. Typically the vending company and the owner split profits 50/50. Two or three high-volume machines can generate $15,000 to $20,000 in annual profits for the owner. Since the competition for good location is fierce, vending companies routinely will pay anywhere from one-half to a full year's profit as an advance for a concession lease. I once came across a young couple who, trading on this advice, purchased a bowling alley with no cash of their own. The bowling alley was selling for $180,000 and with bank, seller, and other financing blocks in place, the enterprising buyers were still $20,000 short. Along the rear wall of the bowling alley stood a row of soft drink, cigarette, and candy machines grossing $100,000 a year. The owner's share of the profits from these machines exceeded $20,000 a year and three vending companies engaged in a bidding war to win the choice location. The high bidder agreed to an advance against commissions of $20,000 and an outright cash bonus of $5000 besides.

As the buyer of an existing business you should be able to negotiate anywhere from 10 to 20 percent of the total purchase price from suppliers (it may be sufficient to cover a down payment), without being overly clever in other areas. Unlike the start-up venture, you can prove what money your suppliers stand to make from you. It's as good as money in the bank.

PLAYING BY THE RULES

Leveraged takeovers have their own set of rules which go contrary to traditional financing strategies. You've seen the financing blocks that can take the place of your down payment, but now let's put it together as a strategy:

Rule 1. *Ignore Down Payment Requirements.* Pretend the words *down payment* don't exist. Whenever a seller tells you what you need for a down payment, he's looking at it in one of two ways. First, it may be the *seller's* perception of what is needed to finance the deal, or *his* perception of what he wants to walk away from the closing with. Now you already know you'll find many more financing sources than the seller ever dreamed of, and still be able to hand the seller all the cash he needs.

Rule 2. *Build from the Ground Up.* Building your no cash down financing pyramid requires one careful step at a time. Start at the bottom with the largest financing blocks, gradually climbing to 100 percent leverage by adding your layers of financing. The reason most cash-shy buyers fail is that they are intimidated by the big picture and never face the financing challenge in small manageable steps.

Rule 3. *Maximize the Borrowing Potential.* Don't leave one level of financing to go on to the next until you've exhausted all the possibilities for more cash. Every extra dollar in bank or seller financing means one less dollar to search for higher on the financial pyramid.

Rule 4. *The Deal Dictates the Financing.* No two leveraged takeovers have precisely the same financial structure. While this chapter shows you the most common techniques, your best sources of financing will depend on the deal, what's most readily available, and what provides the greatest economic benefit.

Rule 5. *Bigger Deals Are Only Bigger Numbers.* While most no cash start-ups do begin on a small scale and grow through a build up of profits, the leveraged takeover can be on a grandiose scale. A leveraged takeover allows an entrepreneur to start on the mezzanine level rather than wallow for several years at the bottom with a cash poor start-up.

Rule 6. *You Don't Need Cash.* Lock up your checkbook. If you can't swing a leveraged takeover on totally borrowed money, you have either the wrong deal or wrong approach. If it's the former, then move on. Eventually you'll find the type of business you're after that can be fully financed. If it's the latter, then perfect your technique. While I can only show you the basic strategy, you'll need your own style, persuasiveness, imagination, and perseverance to close your winning deal.

KEY POINTS TO REMEMBER

1. Determine whether you're a business buyer or creator.
2. Buying a business may be a better alternative to starting from scratch.
3. Who needs money? Thousands of businesses are available for little or no cash down.
4. Don't fall victim to a seller's down payment demands. Create your own 100 percent financing plan.
5. A bad business can be a very good buy.
6. There are hundreds of ways a business can generate its own financing. Look to the internal sources first.
7. Brokers and suppliers are your best sources of external financing.
8. A leveraged takeover can put you into a larger business faster and easier than a shoestring start-up.

16

PYRAMIDING
TO THE TOP

You can only wonder whether Ray Kroc, founder of the wildly successful McDonald's fast food chain, envisioned thousands of outlets scattered throughout the world when he opened his first hamburger stand in the 1950s. Did the youthful entrepreneur who toyed with new computer software programs somehow dream that his Microsoft Corporation would make him a multibillionaire? America is the land of Horatio Alger stories. Where else can you start a business without two nickels to rub together, and cash out with more money than any one person can rationally spend in five lifetimes? That's what makes the game of business so fascinating. No matter how small you are at the starting gate, you never quite know how big you'll be at the finish line.

For every Ray Kroc there are 10,000 names you'll never hear of. But entrepreneurs everywhere in every type of business someday reach the point when they have one solid, stable business off and running and sit back and ask, "Where do I go from here?" It's the beginning of the long march to real success. One store becomes two and then four. Before you realize it, you have a small empire of 20 or 30 moneymakers. Then you look back and remember where it all began and still wonder where it will all end. It's indeed a fascinating game.

IT'S EASY TO MULTIPLY A WINNER

A successful operating business can give you incredible leverage for fast expansion. As any fast-track entrepreneur can tell you, starting your second business is considerably easier than your first, and once you have the blueprint perfected, you can easily propel your way to the top by continuously duplicating what you have.

Winners can be magically multiplied from their own momentum. You have cash flow available to you. Trade credit is yours because suppliers are doing business with you and are being paid. Banks and other lenders know that you have more than an idea—you have the ability to operate a winning venture. Prospective partners begin to focus on growth and not risk. Management and manpower seasoned from their embryonic start are ready to tackle an expanding operation. In short, you've marshalled assets, power, and influence. Expansion is trading on what you *have done* and not on what you *might do*.

That's how it always is when you have a winner behind you. Putting together my first Discount City was a nightmare. I had no cash to work with. Suppliers had never heard of me, so why should they sell me on credit? Bankers thought I had leprosy. Who could blame them? Even I had my lingering doubts. It was a different story with the second Discount City. I could tap $30,000 to $40,000 from my first store for working capital. Stacking the shelves was only a matter of a few phone calls. My banker was now anxious to lend me whatever the business needed. Two prospective partners offered $400,000 for a small piece of the business. Suddenly you find people coming to you with money and you're now turning them down. And you can turn them down. You worked to put together your first shoestring deal, and now it's time for your business to work for you as the foundation for more.

BUT WHO NEEDS IT?

That's more than a rhetorical question. Someday your shoestring venture will be flying high and it too will be ready to expand. The chances are you'll be the one holding it back.

About 99 percent of us fall into the "who needs it" category. You work your fingers to the bone to start and build the business until it is successful and you reach a comfortable income. Ambition runs out and the business is stalled in a holding pattern. You've heard the rationalizations: "How many steaks a day can you eat?" Or, "A Chevrolet will take you anywhere a Mercedes can."

I'm not going to preach on how you should live your life. Plenty of people are very content with one small business and don't want a life of "wheeling and dealing," collecting businesses like squirrels collect nuts.

This chapter is for those who do, or perhaps only want to take their business one notch higher on the ladder of success.

You've heard of the Boston Red Sox, Celtics, and Bruins, but I bet you never heard of the Boston B.U.M.S. It's a very exclusive club of Boston's Unemployed Millionaires. Membership is limited to entrepreneurs who started on a shoestring and cashed out with at least one million dollars. They tell some interesting stories on how they launched and built their business. Most say the decisive point was when their business was ready to expand. "It's easy to sit back, rest on your laurels, and let the business take you where it wants to go," says one member who started with a bicycle rental shop in a local resort town, and ended with 15 businesses ranging from a car dealership to a partnership in a large restaurant. "But it doesn't happen that way. You build not for the money, but for the sheer joy of it. Call it ego trip, power, drive, or satisfaction—something makes you go for one more challenge."

Maybe you're the type who needs it even if it is for the sheer joy of it.

BIGGER CAN BE BETTER

There are many good reasons to set your sights on a larger operation and consider expansion. And expansion doesn't have to change your lifestyle or turn you into a workaholic. In fact, you may find running several businesses not only more profitable, but even easier than operating one. Look at the possibilities:

1. *You Have Management Power:* It's the best reason to expand. Growth can allow you the management team to really succeed. Running a small one-man show makes you a generalist in an era of specialists. And it does make your life easier when you have specialists aboard. With my first store I had to do everything but the sales and stock work. When I expanded into the second Discount City, I could afford a buyer-merchandiser for both stores. The combined operation immediately became sharper. We've since added a full-time ad specialist, a comptroller, another buyer, a personnel manager, and best of all, an operations manager to oversee the 12-store chain while I play golf.

   It doesn't take more time to run a larger operation, only more time on the important decisions. With strong subordinates to help manage your business, you will probably find that you can take even more time off and stop being married to your one-man show.

2. *You Have Buying Power:* It's critical for many businesses, especially in the retail lines. Unless you're dealing in an exclusive product line, you're fair game for all the bigger boys who can buy better and sell lower. Many businesses expand because they must expand to compete with the chains and discounters in a very competitive jungle. Independent clothing, liquor, drug, food, hardware, and toy stores—to name only a few—have been clobbered by their lack of buying power. You may find a competition-free location, so perhaps you can survive with one store, but if you expect to grow you'd better expand fast so you can match the competition on their terms. Your customers are watching your prices.

3. *You Have Advertising Power:* It's as important as buying power. The independent business can't afford saturation advertising. What it can afford is feeble at best. A friend of mine now owns a chain of seven jewelry stores, and for the first time he can afford large space ads in the metropolitan newspapers. Since he started his ad campaign sales have increased 30 percent. Can you afford to reach your customers?

4. *You Have Location Power:* In Chapter 10, I explained why retailing is now primarily a real estate game as competitors jockey for high-traffic mall and shopping center locations. If you're a retailer you need the strength of size to put you into the right money-making spots.

5. *You Have Cash Flow Power:* What do I mean by cash flow power? The ability to cover the slumps in one business by the cash reserves of another. Every business has its ups and downs. When an independent goes into a long sales slump, or suffers an unexpected loss, he has no place to turn. The multiple-business operation only has to borrow from a sister business.

6. *You Have Staying Power:* I love staying power because I intend to stay in business for a long, long time. That's why I expanded. "Why put all my eggs in one basket?" I reasoned. When you have one business—even a successful business—1001 things can happen to quickly kill it. A formidable competitor can move in next to you, a landlord can refuse to renew your lease, new technology, or a fatal labor strike, to name a few. So I spread my risk and opportunities by branching out. An owner of a small business has security for as long as he or she is in business, but with thousands of ventures closing every year for one reason or another it isn't that much security. Can you predict how long your shoestring enterprise will last?

Maybe none of these reasons makes much sense for you. Then you may be like Joe Tevald, the only mechanic I know who drives a Rolls-Royce. As Joe explains it, he needs a Rolls to comfortably drive between his 68 gas stations. As Joe says, "The fun is owning them, not working in them."

WHERE DO YOU GO FROM HERE?

Suppose you've dived into the water with a business of your own. The hard part was the cold water of doubt—wondering whether you'd make it. If you haven't drowned, expansion should be easy. Why not? You not only have your feet wet, but you're already swimming. Now all you have to do is add a few strokes to your repertoire.

But before you enter deeper water you have to know where you are, where you want to go, and how you expect to get there. Those are the three essential questions, and on the next few pages you may find some answers. For now, put away your crystal ball. Don't worry about five, ten, or fifteen years from now. Long-range planning is fun and can get the adrenaline pumping, but you can only take it one step at a time. The objective is to make each step the right step.

TEST THE TIMING

When do you expand? As with any other management decision, timing is critical. Some moves come too quickly. The existing operation isn't sufficiently strong to support—or gamble on—another start-up. One of the most common reasons for business failure is an eager beaver entrepreneur who expanded too far too fast, and had the whole operation come down around his ears. On the other extreme are the too conservative types whose caution retards the progress their business could safely make with a more aggressive expansion program. So you try to walk the tightrope.

There are some ground rules you should follow. The first is that you're not ready to expand until your existing operation is running profitably and with a surplus cash flow. Cash flow is an important ingredient. You may have a profitable business and still have a negative cash flow, as so many shoestring start-ups do as they try to work down their initial debt.

In reality, expansion is only the re-deployment of excess cash or available credit where it will do most good—in another leveraged operation. So you can't intelligently expand if your existing business needs those same dollars or available credit to improve its own performance.

Look at it as a competitive process. Your existing business is competing with the prospective unit for the capital or assets needed to expand. Where will that money give you the best return? Measure it carefully. You should only consider expansion when your money will make more money in yet one more business.

The second step is to assess when a new start-up will reach its own break-even point, and whether your existing operation can support it until it does. Some businesses rapidly reach a level of profitability, while others take time to reach it. We once consulted to a small but rapidly expanding chain of donut shops. It's an incredible business. A donut shop in a good location can hit a profitable sales level one week after it opens. Since each addition isn't a cash drain on the existing operation, expansion is limited only by the owner's ability to find locations, hire competent help, and put the shop together.

I play the "what if" game in making an expansion decision. What I ask is: "What if the new operation doesn't work out? What impact will it have on my existing operation?" Assessing risk is part of the expansion formula. If we have to pledge the assets of our existing operation to finance a new start-up we move slowly—very slowly. One failure could destroy the entire business. Conversely, I've expanded into other businesses that did stand on their own financially and legally. Some made it and others didn't, but as independent units none posed a financial threat to any of my other ventures. I think this is the best way to expand at first. When each business is on its own, you have the best of all worlds—opportunity with very little risk.

That brings us to what I call the "push-pull" theory of expansion. Logically you'll "push" toward expansion because you do have a sound base to grow. Sometimes it's equally logical to be "pulled" into expansion to save what you have. The strategy is that the future will somehow bail out the past.

A perfect example of the "push-pull" theory hard at work is one of my best clients who couldn't run one business, but somehow thought he could run three. His stores are losing a bundle and we have only one of two choices—to contract or expand. If we contract to one store, he'll have to contend with a mountain of debts existing from the closed stores which would jeopardize his one remaining store. We decided to expand into a fourth store that would hopefully have high enough sales and profits to stabilize the existing stores. Of course, my client plans to go on an extended vacation while we bring in a real manager to turn the entire operation around, but with a new store ringing up $1 million in sales we have a cash flow to work with.

It's not a unique story. Many chains are losing their shirt, and the more they lose the faster they expand. The chase is on for cash flow to cover up their past managerial sins.

In still other cases, expansion is needed to cover fixed overhead—particularly an owner's salary. For example, I know a small computer store trying to support three partners and each partner needs a $1,000 weekly salary to survive. Simple arithmetic tells you that you can't pay out $150,000 a year in salary when the business only has a $180,000 income. Expansion was the only solution.

THE MANY PATHS TO SUCCESS

Do you have a winner to multiply? Most chains and franchise systems are nothing more than a nucleus of two or three carefully shaped and profitable prototypes duplicated countless times as the pyramiding process propels the owners to enormous wealth.

Many shrewd entrepreneurs start their first business intending to expand as a chain or through franchising. For the first year or two, they carefully tune the business to a profitable pitch and add several more units following precisely the same formula. The theory is that if five prototypes can make it, 5000 can.

Franchising is in its heyday. Farsighted entrepreneurs with an attractive business concept to sell are finding they can cash in fastest and easiest by going the franchise route. Many choose franchising because they don't want the headaches or risk of multiunit management. As franchisors they need only to sell, establish policy, and supervise while avoiding the problems of daily operations. Expansion speed is another factor. Company-owned stores can only expand at a rate consistent with the company's financing and manpower. Even with fast concentric growth, an emerging chain could hardly dominate a local market within ten years, while many franchise systems started less than five years ago have a national network of thousands of units. And don't ignore the economics. Collecting franchise fees and royalties can produce powerful profits, and you *can* start a franchise program on a shoestring.

Manufacturers have their own avenue of cashless expansion. Many owning valuable patents or trademarks are licensing these valuable rights to other firms, preferring royalties to the capital intensive alternative of building more factories or trying to crack important markets.

Not every business is the whopping money-maker that will have lines of prospective franchisees waiting in the wings, or be the first of many in a dynamic chain. Ninety-five percent of all businesses are "me-too" operations generating comfortable profits for their owners in their own nondescript way. Their expansion potential is not in their self-multiplication, but to continue to pump the profits by which other acquisitions can be made.

David Seltzer, an ex-sales representative for a Pittsburgh paper firm, decided on a different path. In 1974, Dave started a printing plant, and with his wife working beside him, sales leaped to $2 million annually. By 1977, Dave was debt-free and with heavy cash on his hands. Expansion was the only way his money could make more money. Another printing plant was out. Why compete with himself, Dave figured. Uncomfortable with businesses he had no experience in, Dave expanded "vertically," opening a business forms distributorship. Now Dave prints the forms through his printing company and sells them through his form company. Dave now has his sights on buying a paper supply firm. When he does he'll control three businesses at different points in the distribution channel.

Imagine starting your day by visiting your appliance stores, journeying into your car dealership for lunch, and checking in at the headquarters of your sporting goods chain in mid-afternoon. Before heading home you check your movie theater to see that everything's shipshape. Now that's an entrepreneur. It's also Ken Volpi, a daredevil type, unafraid to tackle any business provided he can start or buy it on a shoestring, find the right people to operate it, and sit back and have it make money for him. Ken remembers growing up poor and watching his father's garment business get wiped out during the Depression. Ken learned from his father's experience and decided the only security was to

have different businesses working at the same time. "If one industry is down, another is bound to be up," Ken philosophizes.
"Besides, I enjoy the different challenges, problems, and opportunities of a spicy mix of ventures."

You've met several people who traveled their own road to
success. You'll have your own path marked "opportunity."

UNLEASH YOUR GROWTH POWER

What is your present business worth? Surprisingly few business
people carefully analyze their business' net worth, and fewer
still understand how to parlay the net worth into more businesses. And many start-ups—even the highly leveraged shoestring start-up—can quickly build equity and the borrowing
power to launch another business or two.

Periodically I conduct "start-up seminars" at local business
colleges. About 40 percent of the participants are already in
business and are looking for ways to find expansion capital. I always ask this one question, "What can you squeeze from your
existing business?"

A participant in one of these seminars, Selma V., showed up
one week with her financial statements to put me to the test.
"Show me how to get the money out of my fabric shop to open
another," she counterchallenged. Of course I enjoy challenges,
particularly when there's a small fee attached. So with our bargain struck I went to work:

1. An inventory reduction program was the first step. The in-
    ventory was slashed from an excess $80,000 to $50,000 by
    discounting the slow-moving overstocks, generating
    $20,000 in cash.
2. The fabric shop always paid COD for merchandise. Open-
    ing the business up on 30-day credit terms gave us an-
    other $20,000 to add to the pile.
3. Some spare office furniture and equipment was sold
    through a used equipment dealer for another $4000.
4. Noticing that 1000 sq. ft. of space stood empty we found an-
    other tenant to sublet the space for $2000 on advance rent.

That gave us $46,000 to work with and we had hardly started. The big money was yet to come. One trip to Selma's bank and we had a commitment for a $60,000 loan. Now we had $106,000 to work with. But what would it take to open another fabric shop for Selma, our friend and willing student? If you ask Selma, she'll tell you it can't be done for less than $100,000. Selma was wrong again. In a month, her second store was off and running in a suburban shopping center complete with a $50,000 inventory ($40,000 purchased on lenient credit terms), $12,000 in fixtures and equipment (leased for no cash down with an option to buy), and a big red and white sign proclaiming: "Selma's Sewland Fabrics," designed by a sign painter willing to have his $2000 bill paid in 12 convenient installments. So for $12,000 cash, Selma had her second store, and her business had the growth power to finance eight more. It's not high finance, but only common sense and the ability to see the dollars hiding in your business.

Jeff Kosberg, a consultant to many small growth companies, points out, "Expansion-minded entrepreneurs are always looking for capital, while the money is usually under their feet in the form of excess inventory, old receivables, or other pockets of waste. While they continue to look to external sources they should first concentrate on the internal."

Shake the growth dollars loose from your business:

1. *Test your new borrowing power:* Even if your business is heavily mortgaged, it may have plenty of borrowing power. Consider the equity you've built since opening. Assets are up and your loan balance is down. And you have the track record, which is a bankable item. One banker explains that an existing business is the perfect vehicle for "bridge" financing. If a new unit needs $50,000 to start, the combined assets of the two businesses are usually sufficient to justify 100 percent financing. Many businesses decide to expand years after they first opened; as mortgage-free enterprises, their equity would produce a better return invested in a second unit rather than lie idle in the first.

2. *Make your inventory work harder:* Show me a business with excess inventory and I'll show you a business with

its expansion capital sitting on the shelf. Take the case of Heritage Hobby & Crafts. Heritage was operating one store with a $140,000 inventory. All the business needed was $70,000 to support sales. So Heritage divided itself into two stores with double the income. Operating with a lean inventory can free up enormous amounts of cash. Suppliers may accept overstocks for new merchandise to help launch another unit, or you can turn it into cash yourself. But merchandise is money, and when you need money you never overlook your merchandise.

3. *Expand with suppliers' money:* Leverage is the name of the game, and you don't have leverage unless you're using every dime of credit safely available to you. Many times we'll come across a business with very small accounts payable that can safely be pumped up by $20,000 or more, freeing cash for another start-up. This technique of playing with your suppliers' money for as long as possible certainly helped Discount City along. Stretching payments from 30 days to 60 days gave us the equivalent of one month's purchases for expansion capital. And when you're buying $500,000 a month, it's a lot of money to expand with. We lay no claim to inventing the concept. Even Fortune-500 companies are sluggish on payments as they wheel and deal their way to an expanding empire. It has nothing to do with morality, but only with the decision of where the money in your checkbook will do the most good.

4. *Use your credit clout:* In our operation we have a standing rule. If a supplier won't extend us 100 percent credit on an opening stocking order for a new store, it's no longer our supplier. You have that clout once you have one or two businesses in operation and now need inventory for one more. We look at it this way. We may give a supplier $500,000 in business a year. It's a small trade-off to ask for $25,000 in lenient credit to help inventory another store which will give him even more business. Many of the largest chains have been propelled along by suppliers pouring in the needed merchandise and never daring to refuse. Of course, quite a few suppliers have been burnt in

the process of succumbing to the charms of their fast-growth customers, but as one poorer but wiser supplier says, "When your customer is growing, you either help them grow or pull out. There's no middle ground."

5. *Check your pockets of waste:* Don't leave stones unturned when shaking the money loose. When Carl Shumway wanted to expand his northern California wholesale book distributorship to a second San Diego operation, he estimated it would take $160,000 in capital. "I was ready to take in a partner to finance the deal, but instead I did some housecleaning. We did everything from liquidating $60,000 in slow inventory to chasing down slow receivables. We borrowed $48,000 from the company's pension fund and even talked the electric company into returning our $4000 deposit. We had more money than we needed and didn't have to go beyond our four walls to find it. Not only do you find money, but you find inefficiency, and you don't expand from a soft, sloppy base."

PROSPECTING FOR THE BIG DOLLARS

Internally funded growth can take you only so far and so fast. Eventually you'll begin to think in terms of prospecting for equity capital to grow even faster and on a safer footing.

If you return to Chapter 9, you'll see a slight bias against partnerships as a way to finance the initial start-up, and for good reason. It's usually not necessary to go after partnership funds to put together a shoestring deal because so many better sources of capital and credit are available.

The expanding venture, on the other hand, may begin to look at partnership money as one of the best sources of financing. While the advantages and disadvantages of taking on partners remain the same, you can strike a considerably more beneficial bargain with partners during the growth stage compared to the idea stage. So the partnership decision is really a matter of timing.

Benefit from the example of Cy Cunningham, enthusiastic over the idea of opening a medical billing firm in Akron, Ohio. Cy saw the need for a service to handle the complicated third-party billings for the area dentists, physicians, and pharmacies, and with fair accuracy estimated it would take $150,000 to properly capitalize it. His best partnership offer was $75,000 for a 50 percent interest in the business and bank financing for the difference. Cy turned down the deal and instead managed to borrow $100,000 in bank financing and ten of his largest physician accounts agreed to finance another $60,000. It was a heavily leveraged start-up but Cy owned it all. Within three years the business had a $600,000 income, $85,000 profit, and virtually no debt. It was a success story worth repeating, and Cy decided to repeat it by opening offices in Cleveland, Cincinnati, and Toledo. To raise the $800,000 in expansion capital, Cy now went after partners—convincing a large computer firm to invest the $800,000 for a 30 percent interest and the commitment to lend the corporation another $1.5 million for further expansion. Cy knew the right time to strike for partnership funds. Had he started with a 50 percent interest, it would have been diluted to 35 percent when it came time to go for the big dollars.

Hal Lynch, a finance consultant with a long string of growing clients, admits that timing is the critical factor when considering equity capital. "Too many people sell a piece of the business too soon and give up too much in the process. Others wait too long and either fail because of overexpansion or never reach full potential. There is always that perfect moment to pull in a partner or two, but for each of us it's a different moment." Keep your eye on your perfect moment.

SEVEN GROWTH RULES

Before you leap into an expansion program, take a hard look at some of the most common mistakes and the strategies to avoid them. And people who have traveled the road before you offer these words of advice:

Rule 1. *Evaluate Your Own Strengths.* Do you have what it takes to manage multiple operations? This requires the ability to set controls, delegate, and motivate. You're no longer a one-man show, and that means the ability to work through other people.

"I breached the Peter Principle when I opened my second shoe store," smiles Ben Pike, who engineered his way into the shoe business with a $6000 loan from his father-in-law and parlayed it into a $400,000 profit center in Brooklyn's south side. "I could be everywhere and do everything with one business to run, but when my second came along, I had to work through my two store managers. I was no longer in the shoe business—I was in the people business. And it's a very different business."

Rule 2. *Don't Build on Quicksand.* Make certain your existing operations are solid, smooth running, and in good financial health before you expand.

Connie and John Krasnow, like so many people, stumbled on this point. The Krasnows had two nursing homes in southern New Hampshire when they decided to open their third. "We weren't ready and it was as simple as that," admits Connie. "Our existing homes were too deeply in debt and losing money and we had no blueprint to correct the situation. We were probably running away from our two nightmares by thinking a third would somehow solve our problems," adds Connie.

Rule 3. *Protect Yourself.* Set up each business as a separate corporation. If one goes sour, it won't take your good businesses with it.

"Legal organization is important when expanding," say Frank Lainer and Keith McCarthy, who once owned a prosperous greeting card and gift shop in a Chicago mall. "We made the mistake of using our original corporation to open our second store in a suburban mall. This mall turned out to be a dud, and we lost $120,000 which our corporation—even with its one healthy store—couldn't absorb. So we filed bankruptcy, losing everything. If we had the foresight, we would have used a separate corporation for our second store, protecting our first."

Rule 4. *Consider Logistics.* "I thought I was Superman who maybe could don a red cape and fly from Boston to Buffalo to check on the third employment agency we had opened," confesses Blanche Lerner of Lerner Employment Agencies. "At best

I could get to the Buffalo office only once every two or three weeks, and that's too little supervision for my business, even one with a strong manager. So we sold the Buffalo unit at a loss and learned never to locate beyond our reach. Business people think a business can run by itself. Unless you're constantly on top of it, you have problems. And you're never on top of it literally unless you're on top of it physically."

Rule 5.   *Watch Cash Flow.* Every acquisition or addition has to stand on its own two feet without draining cash from existing operations. If you plan to support a start-up, make sure you know what the support payments will be and that you can afford them.

Expanding into a deficit operation can topple an existing company with an insufficient cash surplus to support it. "The best advice I can give is to set limits on the money you'll pour into a new start-up," offers Pat Pellini, who admits to draining his once viable Pellini Bakery of $120,000 to keep his second bakery afloat. "But it floated just long enough to kill both businesses," he adds.

I offer my own postscript on this one. Whenever I set up a new business, I'll set aside a cash reserve from the other businesses. That's it. If it's not enough to see it through the survival stage, it doesn't survive. You have to know when to turn off the spigot.

Rule 6.   *Don't Bite off More than You Can Chew.* Growth is a gradual deliberative process with each step being logical in context to the existing organization. Each addition is one that must be easily assimilated in terms of management, markets, money, and know-how.

Allen Van Kamp, a management consultant with the firm by the same name, claims that the most common growth error is moving into new ventures the existing organization can't handle. "And what a firm may not be able to handle covers a lot of territory," adds Van Kamp. "The most common error is going outside your field. The Bankruptcy Courts are loaded with companies who, for example, may have successfully operated four or five restaurants and suddenly you find them in the hotel business. But what did they know about hotels? Size is another stumbling block. Plenty of people have the management mentality to run a $300,000-a-year business and they think they can now handle a $3-million operation. It takes considerably different skills. Don't bite off more than you can chew. Stay with what you know."

Rule 7. *Don't Forget Your Humble Past.* Growth can dim memories. And when you're growing helter-skelter, you tend to look only to the future and forget the past.

Now take my advice. It was the past that gave you the winning formula. You scrounged for pennies and wrung a dollar from each dime. You fought the odds, gambled on the risks, and did it all your own way.

You've changed just as your business has changed, and you'll go through more change before you reach your finish line. But you do have a heritage and a mighty proud heritage. Not everyone can be a shoestring entrepreneur, but once a shoestring entrepreneur, always a shoestring entrepreneur. You wouldn't want it any other way.

KEY POINTS TO REMEMBER

1. Your first business can be the springboard for many more.
2. Everyone will jump on board to help, once you show them what you *have done* rather than what you *might do*.
3. Bigger can be better. Size is power and it all leads to more profit power.
4. Test the timing. There is always a right—and wrong—time to take your next step.
5. Expansion can take many paths. Choose the one that's right for your business—and you.
6. Your business has growth power. The money to expand can be found internally.
7. The best time to consider partnership funds is during the growth stage.
8. Expand by the rules. Take a lesson from others who can show you the right way to success.

INDEX